BERRY BROS. & RUDD WINE SCHOOL

Exploring & Tasting Wine

A wine course with digressions

With a foreword by Emma Thompson

Photographs by Jason Lowe

PAVILION

Contents

Foreword *Emma Thompson*
The idea of this Course *Rebecca Lamont*
How this book works

FOREWORD

There is no more inspiring place to study or indeed drink wine than at Berry Bros. & Rudd. The very name sounds viniferous.

The trouble is, once you walk in and breathe its own delicious and inspiring bouquet, it becomes difficult to leave. The floors, rendered uneven by the march of countless bibbers (and the shift of London's very foundations, so antique is this building) give the pleasing sensation of having knocked back a glassful rather too quickly.

The Wine School course is the perfect excuse to stay for an evening – a day, a week, a month – learning, under truly expert tuition, why you love wine and where, exactly, it springs from.

The more I learnt about wine, the more I began to understand its essential nature, its DNA, the more I felt able to savour it.

This is not a place for snobs. Do not darken its doors if your aim is to impress your dining companions with the monetary value of your tastes.

Go if you believe that one beautifully, thoughtfully, poetically created mouthful is worth an entire bottle of inferior quality, go if you are fascinated by the variety of flavours and scents, go if you would like to learn a little more about your passion without ever blunting its sweet power to enchant; above all, go, if, like me, you believe that wine is the soul of every meal.

Emma Thompson
Actor, author and screenwriter
Wine School student July 2008

London, March 2015

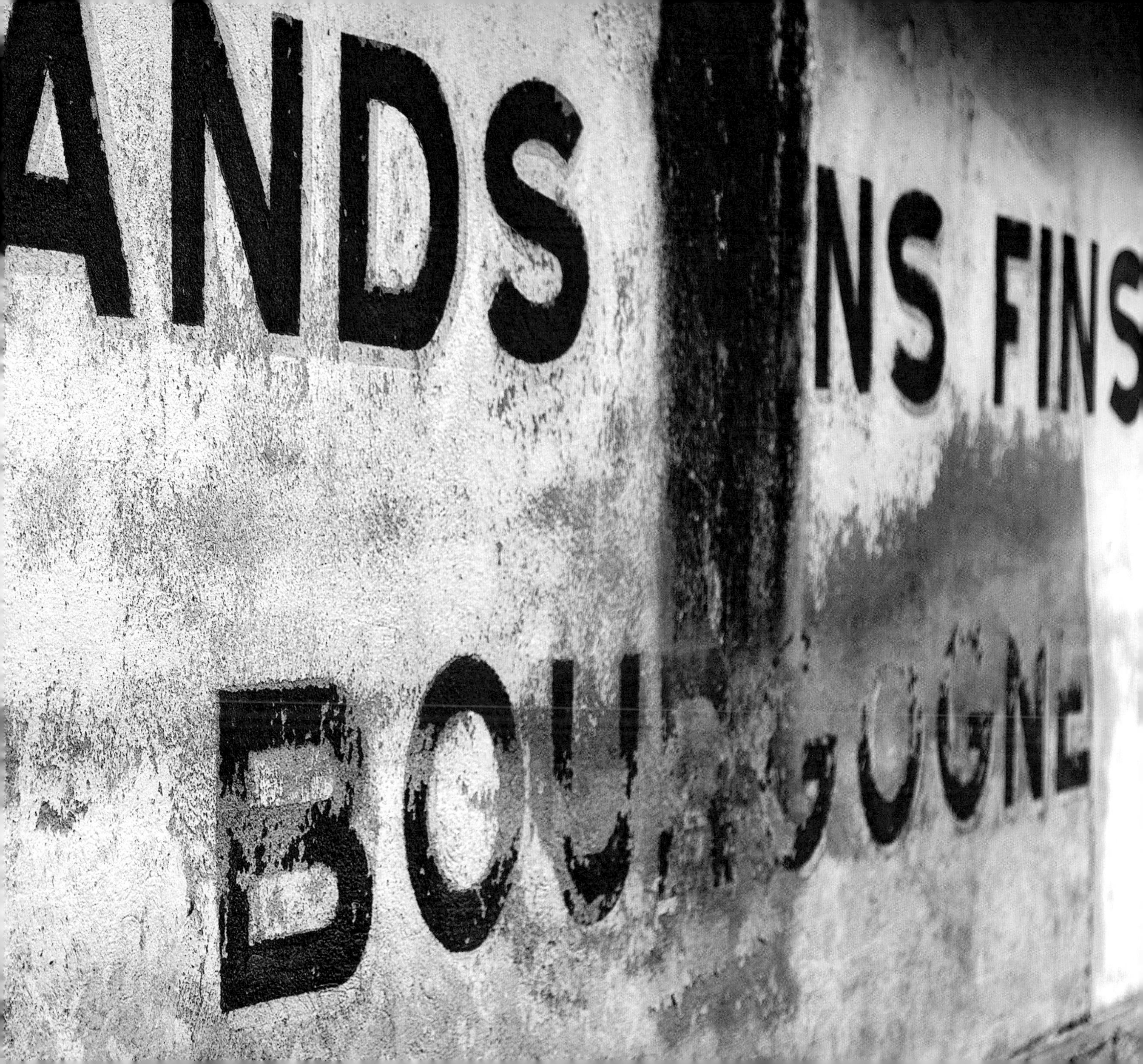
ANDS
NS FINS
BOURGOGNE

THE IDEA OF THIS COURSE

At No. 3 St James's Street, where the firm has been since it began three centuries ago, you can not only buy wine but learn about it. We have been running the Wine School since 2000; but there is only so much time in the year and not every wine-lover is in reach of the heart of London. Hence this book, which brings the Wine School to you.

Perhaps I should begin by explaining who our Course is for. You need only one qualification: you enjoy wine. Whether you have just discovered this (the Course assumes no prior knowledge) or whether you have simply never had time to pull together your knowledge, we can prove to you that anyone can be a good taster.

That is the ethos of this Course, and our approach is to draw out your innate expertise. We are all good tasters, and when you realise this it can be incredibly empowering and exciting, and you can fall in love with wine. You learn to trust your reactions, and to build a framework that will allow you to identify what wine styles you love and why – and thus what other wines you will enjoy.

So at the heart of the book is a tasting course, based around the key grape varieties that produce the world's favourite wines,

both everyday and sublime. We give you the tools to analyse and remember what you think as you are experiencing the aromas, flavours and taste of wine.

Take two wines made from the same grape variety, but from different areas. How do the two differ? Is one wine richer, smoother, softer, more bitter, acidic, sharp (we could go on and on...) than the other? Why? What makes a good, satisfying drink? Where does that wine come from? What food will this one partner? Should I drink this now, or keep it longer?

Want to know more? Alongside each tasting session are background information pages. And in addition, our Masters of Wine and colleagues from other parts of the business have contributed their insights on the key debates and digressions that we discuss on the Course.

The point is that we are all on a voyage of taste discovery together, and the whole aim of it is to have fun using your senses.

Rebecca Lamont
Head of Wine School

wineschoolbook@bbr.com

Left: Pickers wait for lunch at a Loire vineyard after a hot morning in the sun

HOW THIS BOOK WORKS

Exploring and Tasting Wine is planned to be used and enjoyed on whatever level suits you. This book is used by Wine School attendees as a hands-on course-book: the six Sessions follow the six weekly lessons of the Introduction to Wine course.

It can be your course-book for informal lessons at home, where you and perhaps a group of friends can work through the **Practical** pages of the Sessions. (See page 216.)

Or use the book as a friendly but expert guide to the charms and the whys and wherefores of wine — a pulling-together of **Background** information: the facts, the figures, the places. And there are insights into the wine world today through the digressions and **Discussions** from the Berry Bros. & Rudd Masters of Wine and other experts.

Session 1 is about the technique of tasting: the way to approach and enjoy wine — and how to remember what you discover.

Then each Session profiles three or four grape varieties, using their characters, tastes and flavours to gain insights into what makes wines taste way they do.

The **Choosing and Enjoying Wine** section — Appendix I — continues the practical theme: we explain the reasons behind matching food and wine, give you a wine-taster's crib sheet, and much more.

Maps, guides to wine laws and classifications, plus a glossary fill in the details.

THREE KINDS OF PAGES

In the five main Sessions, the kind of information is signalled at the top of each page, starting with:

Practical pages that begin each grape chapter. First comes an introduction, then pages which create a visual portrait of that grape's aroma, flavour and the factors that create balance — the way the wine tastes in the glass.

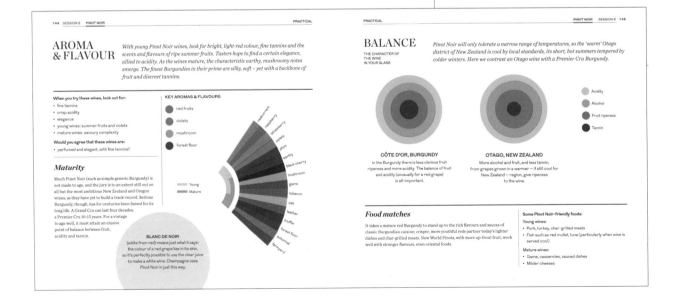

KEY REGION:

The Central Loire

Follow the river west from the Sauvignon Blanc vineyards around Sancerre and Pouilly, and you come to Tours, an ancient city and capital of the main red-wine zone of the Loire (see map page 42). Cabernet Franc is the most important grape here, in and around Saumur in the neighbouring Anjou region.

In Touraine and Anjou, the wines are named after districts rather than villages. **Bourgueil** is generally thought the best, with **St-Nicholas-de-Bourgueil** and **Chinon** in the next rank, followed by the wide zone of **Saumur** and (slightly superior) **Saumur-Champigny**.

Once again, limestone subsoil is important: much of Bourgueil is on tuffeaux, the local name for the deep beds of limestone, though good wine is also made on the river-bed gravels. Cabernet Franc thrives here, because it ripens early and the Touraine vineyards are well to the north – even by autoroute, it is a three-hours-plus drive (335km) south across virtually vine-free country until you reach the Bordeaux winelands, where Cabernet Franc plays a minor but useful part.

KEY REGION:

Bordeaux

Cabernet Franc may ripen early, but in many of the vintages from the 1960s to the 1980s it failed to ripen properly or at all, and the red wines of the Loire faced decline. There has been a turnaround in weather patterns, allied to greater sophistication in winemaking, and the last three decades have seen a far greater proportion of successful years. Indeed, 1990 was a standout vintage that set the tone for the next 25 years.

There are few grand wine estates in the Touraine country: the best wines come from small-scale family concerns – and not all the best are in the most prestigious appellations. Those who come to love this unusual but delicious style of red wine learn to follow the fortunes of vintages (still variable) and growers (some rise, some fall). You will have competition: much wine is sold direct to Parisians.

Of the three grapes that make red Bordeaux, Cabernet Franc has the lowest profile. It is rare for a Bordeaux estate to be driven by Cabernet Franc, but one star château, Cheval Blanc in **St-Émilion**, gives it the prime role in the blend in certain years. Vieux Château Certan in Pomerol has 30 per cent of this variety in its vineyard. Yet without Cabernet Franc, many a Claret would be leaner, less interesting – and in some vintages, in rather shorter supply.

We talk about the way Bordeaux blends its palette of three red grapes overleaf. In most Right Bank districts, Cabernet Franc is blended with the predominant Merlot. Over the river in the **Médoc** and **Graves**, the grape does double-duty: as an insurance against possible poor ripening of Merlot and Cabernet Sauvignon, and as a bringer of bouquet and delicacy. These Left Bank vineyards may have up to 15 per cent Cabernet Franc, though some estates have none at all.

SCIENCE SOUNDBITE: pH AND PURPLE PIGMENTS

Cabernet Franc makes wines which generally have a low pH (i.e. high acidity) – especially so in the Loire Valley. At lower pHs, the blue-purple hues of a wine's colour pigments are preserved, accounting for the vibrant youthful-looking colour of many Loire reds.

Above: Cabernet Franc flourishes high in a valley near Stellenbosch, South Africa.

Cabernet Franc worldwide

Ambitious winemakers who want to market a 'Bordeaux blend' have planted Cabernet Franc, alongside Cabernet Sauvignon and Merlot, in places from **Tuscany** to **Chile** via **California** and **Argentina**. Its presence in blends will only be apparent through a careful look at the back-label, if at all.

As a majority or sole partner, it is grown in northern and central **Italy** (Friuli is one place to look for it), in **Hungary** and in **South Africa**.

Back in France, Cabernet Franc wines can be found from St-Chinian (limestone again...) in **Languedoc-Roussillon**.

Just as in its Loire heartland, Cabernet Franc does well in cool places where most red-wine grapes struggle to ripen. Thus it crops up on wine lists in the **USA's** East Coast, in **Canada** and in **China**.

It shows promise in **New Zealand**, is making rapid strides in **Argentina**, and is quite widespread in **Australia**.

CLARET
The term came originally from the French 'Clairet' – a dark rosé wine still produced today. The English borrowed the word and changed it to Claret, which refers not to rosé but to any red wine made in Bordeaux.

Background pages follow, taking us to where the grapes are grown — the key regions — with side-notes on aspects of winemaking, climate and other factors that shape the character of wine.

'GERMAN? IT MUST BE SWEET – I WON'T LIKE IT....'

Many wine-drinkers make this leap – and miss some stunning wines. Modern German wines range from dry and appetising to gloriously sweet... but which is which? Catriona Felstead MW has the key.

Knowing what's in a tall, elegant Alsace or German bottle used to be easy: Alsace wines were nearly always dry, Germany's predictably sweet. However, this simple rule no longer applies: dry German wines are increasingly common, while some Alsace wines (see page 118) now have high levels of residual sugar. Result: a puzzle when trying to match wines with food. Both have tried to clarify sweetness on the label; whether their efforts have reduced or increased the confusion is somewhat debatable....

The German Wine Law of 1971 categorised (controversially) the quality of a wine by the sugar-ripeness level (**must weight**) of the grapes at harvest. So, in theory, the levels go:

Deutscher Wein and **Deutscher Landwein** are the lowest (driest) categories, followed by **Qualitätswein bestimmter Anbaugebiete** (QbA), the first 'quality wine' level, which often comprises simple, fruity, slightly off-dry wines.

Prädikatswein. If you see any of the terms defined on the facing page on the label, then you are looking at the higher quality level, Prädikatswein. There are six levels, in increasing order of ripeness.

This all sounds like good German logic – however, grape ripeness and wine sweetness do not necessarily correlate. It would be reasonable to expect a Kabinett to be fruity and off-dry, a Spätlese to be a touch riper with greater intensity, and an Auslese (my personal favourite) to have noticeable sweetness and concentration.

However, any wine from Deutscher Wein to Auslese can actually be made in a dry, medium-dry or sweet style, according to the winemaker's preference in that vintage. Beerenauslese (BA), Eiswein and Trockenbeerenauslese (TBA) are always reassuringly sweet.

If you are wanting a dry wine, all is not lost. Look for **trocken** (dry), **halbtrocken** (medium-dry), **Classic** or **Selection** on the label: the wine should taste dry (Classic being of QbA level, and Selection essentially a dry Spätlese).

Feinherb generally means a slightly sweeter style than halbtrocken – but be aware, this is an unofficial term.

Secondly, look for an eagle logo on the bottle's capsule. This winemaker belongs to the **VDP** (Verband Deutscher Prädikatsweingüter), an association of specialist producers who have broken away from the German wine law and categorize quality by terroir, as in Burgundy, not by grape ripeness. They have a much clearer distinction between sweet and dry wines.

VDP **Grosse Lage** is their equivalent of Grand Cru; VDP **Erste Lage** of Premier Cru and VDP **Ortswein** of a Village wine. If any of these are sweet, they will have one of the Prädikatswein terms (see right) on the label. If they are dry they will have 'Qualitätswein Trocken' on the label.

A dry VDP Grosse Lage wine also has its own special designation: VDP **Grosses Gewächs** ('great growth' is a rough translation).

My advice? If you are looking for a specific style, then always ask your wine merchant for an opinion – and then, if you pour a glass which is not to your taste and has no sweetness indication on the label (or on the merchant's website), do not be afraid to take the bottle back and ask for a different style. But please, do not be deterred from trying a bottle; these can be amongst the finest and most rewarding wines in the world.

Opposite: In the Mosel, steep means steep....

GERMAN PRÄDIKATSWEIN TERMS

Kabinett Fresh and fruity in style; often off-dry but can be dry, medium-dry or sweet.

Spätlese From grapes that are picked later, after the rest of the harvest. Can have more richness than QbA or Kabinett wines; often medium-dry but can also be dry, medium-sweet or sweet.

Auslese From selected bunches, these wines can be concentrated and intense. Often medium-sweet but can also be dry, medium-dry or sweet.

Beerenauslese (BA) Meaning 'selected berries', these are produced from overripe grapes, often affected by noble rot, and can produce rich, sweet dessert wines.

Eiswein 'Ice wines' are rare. They are made from grapes of the same minimum sweetness as BA wines – but this sweetness is due to their being picked so late that they have frozen on the vine. They tend not to be affected by noble rot, so the result is a very pure, sweet style that can have delicious freshness.

Trockenbeerenauslese (TBA) 'Selected dry berries' produce the highest sweetness level of Prädikatswein. Grapes affected by noble rot are individually picked so late in the autumn that they have dried and shrivelled on the vine and are almost like raisins; lusciously sweet wines.

See page 118 for Alsace terms

Discussion pages take us further. Some explore debates such as: what oak-ageing does for a wine? does organic wine taste different? These are contributed by the Berry Bros. & Rudd experts and Masters of Wine.

INTRODUCING TASTING

EVERYONE CAN TASTE | BALANCE
WORDS AND MEMORIES: THE FLAVOUR SPECTRUM
AGE AND MATURITY
THE PRACTICALITIES OF TASTING

"Is it good to drink?"

EVERYONE CAN TASTE

The trick is how to remember those scents and flavours

Everyone can taste. You do it yourself every day, when you enjoy food, or check that it is fresh. People may say 'so-and-so has a good palate'. But as the professionals – sommeliers, wine buyers, teachers – will tell you, wine tasting skill can be learned. They did; so can you.

WHAT CAN WE TASTE?

'Full of violets, ripe cherries, with a whiff of old sock...'

What you do **not** need is an arcane vocabulary. The words we all use are our own: they're the tags that help us to remember.

The reason that tasters describe wines in such seemingly flowery – or even pretentious – terms is simple: there is no extensive vocabulary for tastes!

The basic sensations our tongues can detect are:

- Bitter
- Sweet
- Salt
- Acidity
- Umami, or savoury

And that's it. The other sensations are delivered by your sense of smell.

WHAT IS IT LIKE?

So to describe a flavour or scent to others – or, vitally, to fix it in your own memory – you need to think about what it is like: what it reminds you of. This is the key to remembering and recognising a wine. This is where the violets come in.

WHAT CLUES CAN THE WINE GIVE YOU?

To discover what a wine is like, and to fix it in your memory, there is a simple sequence. Use your senses, step by step:

- Sight
- Smell
- Taste
- Memory

COMPARE AND CONTRAST

The best way to learn to taste is to take two wines which create a pair: the same wine, say, but one younger, one older. Or both are from the same grape variety, but different climates; or made in different styles....

This Course will suggest, on the Balance pages and elsewhere, wines to compare and contrast. The Tasting at Home lists – page 216 – offer some ideas.

Seize every chance to appraise a wine – but especially, go for the opportunity to taste in pairs, to compare and contrast.

MOST OF WHAT YOU CAN TASTE IS SMELL...

The fact that your nose is just above your mouth is no accident: their taste receptors are inextricably linked. Although we may not consciously sniff what we eat and drink, most of what we 'taste' is actually what we smell.

Take a good, deep sniff of any glass of wine and you'll double your pleasure.

Try tasting a food or a drink while holding your nose, and see how much you lose by preventing its scent from reaching the sensitive cells in your nostrils.

Here's the tasting sequence: look, sniff, swirl, sniff and 'chew'....

Start with a neutral palate, with no strong tastes lingering....

1. LOOK

There are clues from the colour and clarity of the wine

2. SNIFF

First sniff — as you would with, say, milk — just to check if the wine is faulty

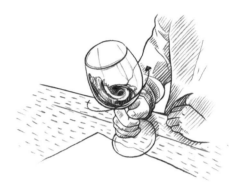

3. SWIRL

Swirl to release its scents

4. SNIFF

Second, deeper, sniff: what does it bring to mind?

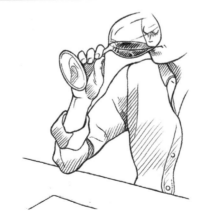

5. TASTE

'Chew' for 3 seconds, then draw a little air into your mouth; spit or swallow

AIM:

To compose a mental 'taste photograph' in your mind that sums up this particular wine, to fix the taste as an image in your mind — and therefore in your memory.

If you are doing this with friends, or in a class, you will find that everyone may have a different impression. This is normal…

Here it is in more detail:

Pour a moderate serving of wine into the glass. Not too much, or the swirl bit gets messy.

1. LOOK

Tilt the glass away from you, looking down at, and through, the wine against a pale background. Look for colour and clarity. Later on, we'll discuss the many hues that both red and white wines can display, and tell you what they indicate. For now, make a mental note of what it looks like. If a red, is it pink, deep red, even brown? For a white, is it lemon, or straw, or gold?

Next, clarity: is the wine clear or opaque? This will be a clue to what the wine is: some wines are denser than others. But if it's muddy, or hazy, this may signal a faulty wine.

2. SNIFF

Your first sniff should be a brisk, fast appraisal: does it smell of anything (some wines don't smell of very much at all....)? Or does it even smell bad?

'Corked': The most dramatic fault is the musty odour wine-tasters call 'corked'. If you smell an unpleasant fungal, mushroomy aroma, the wine is tainted by mould that has formed in the cork. Such wines are generally undrinkable: the smell can get worse as the wine meets the air. Note: 'corked' does not mean bits of cork are floating in the wine: that's a sign of a poor cork or corkscrew.

'Bottle-stink': Give a wine a few minutes if there is a strange smell, however – it may be a passing phase. Remove the cork from an older wine, and the first smell and taste may be flat and tired; there may even be a slight smell of rot. With air, this can clear.

3. SWIRL

Pick up the glass and gently swirl the wine around, so that it covers more of the glass surface. This will help release the scents by getting air into the wine.

4. SNIFF AGAIN...

This time, inhale deeply. There should be more to smell this time. What does the scent remind you of?

5. TASTE

Take a mouthful of wine. 'Chew' it, moving it around your mouth and tongue for three seconds. Suck in a little air: you'll notice this boosts both flavours and aromas. Swallow (spitting comes later). Are there any clear signals: the tartness of acidity, sweetness, bitterness, the mouth-puckering sensation of tannin? Again, what does the taste remind you of? How long does the taste linger in your mouth?

Does it taste good?

'LEGS'

Swirl the wine: can you spot a clear liquid clinging to the sides of the glass and making its way down like tears, or 'legs'? Usually it's a clue to fairly high alcohol, but you can also spot it in lower-alcohol, sweet, viscous wines.

BLIND TASTING

Frequently, wine-lovers and professionals taste wines 'blind'– without knowing what the wine is.

Why is it best to do so?

Simply because it avoids being influenced by the price or status or origin of the wine.

Cunning tasters can spot clues to the wine's identity in the shape or even weight of the bottle, or the colour of the capsule.... So savvy tasting organisers decant the wines into clean, anonymous bottles.

See Appendix for a checklist of clues to wines' identities (this will be useful once you have worked through the Sessions which follow).

HOW LONG IS A WINE?

This is not a trick question.... The **length** of a wine refers to the time those delicious flavours linger in your mouth.

Spare a moment to dwell on this.

The better the wine, the longer its taste will linger. Tasters talk about **length** or **finish**.

It's been argued that a fine wine is better value than an ordinary wine because its finish lasts so much longer....

TEMPERATURE

When we taste, the temperature of the wine causes subtle but vital differences in our perception and enjoyment. Warmth makes alcohol more pronounced: the wine will taste sweeter and flabbier, so no wine should be served warm.

Red wines are served less cool than whites because tannins taste softer when the wine is warmer, so a young red wine, yet to reach maturity, will taste less harsh at room temperature. Though please note that 'room temperature' is a hangover from less centrally-heated days.

Likewise, no wine (even white) should be served too cool, because this prevents the aroma compounds from volatilising, and means that we cannot enjoy the scent – the bouquet.

The practicalities and temperature advice for serving wine are on page 208. For now, when tasting, the best rule is: **too cool is better than too warm**. A cool wine will quickly warm up in the glass: a cupped hand round the bowl will help.

Note that in very hot weather (or an overheated bar or restaurant) an everyday red that has got too warm can be rescued by treating it like a white and putting it on ice.

'Would you like to taste the wine?'

The full tasting sequence is not what you need to do in a restaurant. Here – when you're asked to approve the wine – the waiter or sommelier is asking you:

- is this the right wine?
- is this bottle OK?

The waiter will show you the label for you to see if it is the wine – and the year – that you ordered. Then the waiter opens the bottle in front of you and pours you a sample.

The next step is to give it a bit of a swirl and a sniff, so that you can immediately detect if the wine is faulty (see opposite) – or if all is well.

Often, you will find, this is all you need to do. A quick taste to double-check, and the wine can be served.

Don't forget to check subsequent bottles, if you have more than one of the same wine. Any bottle can be faulty: say so immediately.

Don't be embarrassed to ask for an ice-bucket, if needed, to chill either whites or too-warm reds.

For tips on choosing wine in a restaurant, see Appendix

BALANCE

What makes a good, satisfying glass of wine?

The answer is the **balance** between all the factors that contribute to the taste and character:

ACIDITY
FRUIT RIPENESS
ALCOHOL
TANNIN (in red wines)
OAK — or its absence
COMPLEXITY
 also **AGE & MATURITY**

Acidity, ripeness and alcohol all tie in together with sweetness to produce the character of a wine. Oak, tannin and age can add nuances.

Over the page, we look at these factors one by one. For now, consider the concept of balance.

A wine can be out of balance: is one of these components too dominant for the wine to be to your liking?

BALANCE IS PERSONAL

Your palate has a unique reaction: every taster is different. Some wine-lovers will prefer more acidity, or more fruit, or an oaked wine, right across the spectrum. So they may like New Zealand Sauvignon Blanc, which means (when they choose a red) that they are likely to prefer the fruit and freshness of a young Bordeaux over the depth and complexity of a mature one; the brisk acidity of a Loire Cabernet Franc over the lushness of a Syrah.

This concept of balance helps you to realise **why** you prefer one wine over another.

When we talk later in the Course about specific wines and grapes, we use graphic means – 'Targets' – to show balance factors.

They show how the various factors are **perceived** by your palate, one wine compared to another.

In each Target, these are the three or four factors you are looking for.

Thus for a young white wine, the factors may be acidity, fruit and alcohol. You will rarely find tannin in a white, and oak is less common. A young red might offer balance between fruit, alcohol, tannin and oak.

The maturity of a wine, red or white, may add further levels of complexity to the mix.

BALANCE, GRAPES AND STYLE

As you explore the five chapters that follow, you will find balance 'Targets' for thirty wines. Most of the pages on the important grape varieties – Cabernet Sauvignon, Chardonnay and so on – have a pair of Targets. They compare the balance factors for different styles of wine from the same grape: for instance, the Gamay pages contrast a simple young Beaujolais and a mature Cru Beaujolais; the Sauvignon Blanc pages look at a Loire wine (Old World) and a New Zealand one (New World).

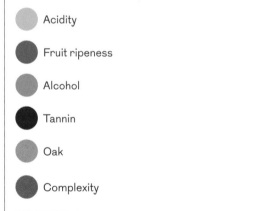

Acidity

Fruit ripeness

Alcohol

Tannin

Oak

Complexity

for example:

Sauvignon Blanc (Session 2) is grown in cooler climates, such as the Loire Valley, and warmer (or less-cool) ones, such as New Zealand. This, for example, is how the various factors balance in a good Sancerre from the Loire:

Contrast the Loire wine with a Sauvignon Blanc from the warmer climate of New Zealand. The Target shows that alcohol is much the same, but there is less acidity and more fruit.

COOLER CLIMATE
Loire Sancerre

Brisk and high acidity; moderate fruit ripeness; moderate alcohol

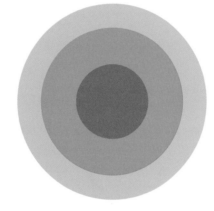

WARMER CLIMATE
New Zealand

More fruit ripeness; acidity less noticeable; high degree of aromatic intensity

The key difference in the balance between cool- and warm-climate Sauvignons is in fruit ripeness. Warmer versions stress this, and while there is always underlying acidity in these wines, it is not as noticeable with the warmer-climate ones as it is with those from cooler climates. Alcohol in both is moderate.

please note:

THE TARGETS ARE A PICTURE, NOT A GRAPH

It's important to note that our 'Targets' show **perceived** levels of the six factors – not measurable levels. If the Target for a wine shows a broader band for, say, acidity, or oak, it means that a taster will find the acidity or oak flavour more prominent. If a factor is missing entirely, it means that it is imperceptible in the taste of that wine – not necessarily that there is none present.

Remember, a good wine shows balance. It is not dominated by one factor; everything comes together to make a harmonious whole. For example, a wine made in a hot year from very ripe fruit will taste jammy and flabby without balancing acidity.

When you hear someone say 'ugh! I don't like dry wines/I don't like sweet wines', what they may well be finding are wines that are out of balance.

Looking at the components of balance one by one:

ACIDITY

Acidity is a positive in wine – it preserves the wine, gives it backbone, keeps it fresh.

Detect acidity through its mouthwatering effect, a tingling sharpness on the tongue.

Try tasting one glass of plain water, then a second with some lemon juice added: you'll notice the effect of the acidity in your mouth. Any fruit needs some acidity to be enjoyable, and wine – the juice of the grape, at heart – is no exception.

Too little acidity, and the wine will taste flabby and over-sweet. Too much, and it will be tart, astringent and sour (for more on this, see Climate and Wine Style on page 32.)

In general, the cooler the climate, the higher the acidity. For examples of high- and low-acidity wines, compare a Sauvignon Blanc wine with a Gewurztraminer.

FRUIT RIPENESS

Grapes in different climates, with more or less sunshine, ripen to different degrees – think of a green apple compared to a tropical fruit. Or compare a ripe, juicy peach with a hard, unripe one.

Fruit ripeness can be a good clue to whether the wine comes from a cool climate, or a warmer one: see the discussion on Old World and New World wines on page 46.

Ripe, fruity wines can be more immediately attractive than austere, mineral ones. But both sorts have their charms – and their uses.

You will find that acidity and fruit ripeness have an inverse relationship with each other.

ALCOHOL

The warming, weighty sensation in the back of the throat as you swallow is how you detect alcohol – apart, that is, from looking at the label.

That label will show that alcohol may be anything from 5 to 17 per cent of the wine, though most fall around 12-14 per cent. The amount of alcohol makes a big difference to the taste, the flavour, the entire sensation of a wine.

It can add weight and body to the wine. To comprehend weight, imagine drinking a glass of water, then imagine drinking olive oil (imagine it, don't try it...). The oil is weightier in the mouth.

The alcohol is natural. In essence, the sun on the vine creates sugar in the grapes. Yeasts (micro-organisms) found on the grape skins, or added to the vat by the winemaker, convert this sugar into alcohol. So the more sun, the more alcohol, and often the lower the acidity.

As with acidity, the place the wine is made has a big influence on alcohol level. Warmer climates lead to riper grapes with more sugar: thus higher alcohol.

Alcohol also tastes sweet: high-alcohol red wines show this.

SWEETNESS

Higher-alcohol wines can taste sweet. But some wines are sweet by nature. Apart from the sweetness from ripe fruit, the winemaker can decide to leave a little sugar in the wine by stopping the fermentation. Most reds are – or were – fully fermented out and therefore dry, though there's a trend to make everyday reds a touch sweet. Add to this the move to higher-alcohol wines, and we find more sweet-tasting wines than we used to.

TANNIN

Think of tea: drink a strong tea, and you feel a drying sensation, furring on gums and across the tongue.

This is tannin, a group of compounds found in tea – and in the skins of grapes. Lots of them are found in red grapes – and, as generally only red winemaking uses the skins, it's predominantly found in red wines.

Tannin adds body to wine and is an anti-oxidant preservative: thus it also aids its longevity. Red wines to be cellared benefit from tannin: it helps wine to age gracefully.

Wines made to be drunk young need lower tannins, and winemakers will steer the process to extract less tannin. Such wines may need, and get, more acidity to confer balance.

To see this, compare a Beaujolais (Gamay grape) and a Barbaresco (Nebbiolo grape).

How can you detect tannin? Swirl the wine around your mouth, and tannin will give a sensation of dryness to your gums and cheeks.

 ## OAK

Oak in winemaking is a choice: plenty of grapes get to be wine without it. Essentially, it is a choice of containers; the subtleties are set out in more detail on page 35.

The key is air, not just oak: an oak cask lets the young wine 'breathe', and this changes its development. Oak casks, especially new ones, also confer some flavours on the wine: when you smell or taste vanilla, or toast, that's oak.

You will find oak notes in many red and in some white wines.

Fresh, brisk wine, on the other hand, will generally indicate the absence of oak.

A useful comparison is between a Chablis (all are made from Chardonnay, and most are unoaked) and an oaked Australian Chardonnay.

 ## COMPLEXITY

Not all wines are intended to mature in bottle: most wine, in fact, is made to be drunk young and fresh. Those wines that are made to 'age' (as winespeak has it) gain complexity and interest in bottle.

This complexity is expressed via more interesting, persistent and nuanced scents and a broader and longer-lasting spectrum of flavours. Red wines will lose harshness and tannin, and develop softer, rounder, more savoury flavours. The acidity in whites will seem less apparent, and complex aromas and tastes will develop.

These factors stem from chemical reactions that go on beneath the cork. As these reactions proceed, the scents and flavours will subtly alter.

After a point, these reactions will slow and change, and the wine will fade, become less interesting, then go past its peak and will eventually turn to vinegar.

It is pointless to seek complexity in a simple wine: sadly, mere age will not make a very basic bottle into a classic.

WORDS AND MEMORIES...

The Flavour Spectrum

As we progress around the world of wine in the Course, you will meet the key grapes, each with their flavour spectrum. This is an aid to building memories.

Each grape's spectrum gives examples of commonly-found taste, flavour and scent notes in the wine, as prompts to help you describe, analyse, recognise and memorise. People vary: when you taste, expect to get somewhere on the spectrum, but not to duplicate our terms precisely.

Remembering sensations and using words to 'tag' them is how we build up a library of sensations, how we link other tastes and smells to help us to describe and remember wine.

As well as aroma/flavour 'tags' there are words to help describe the texture, or feel, of the wine. You might find it has grip, is soft, or plush, or crunchy or unctuous....

grass
peppermint
nettles
green apple
asparagus
kiwifruit
gooseberry
lime
pear
lemon verbena
lemon
orange
grapefruit
passionfruit
pineapple
banana
melon
coconut
white peach
peach
apricot
mango
tropical fruit
muscat grapes
lychees
roses
floral
hazelnut
almond
saffron
allspice
ginger
hay
'cats pee'
elderflower
acacia
honeysuckle
orange blossom
white flowers
wet wool
lanolin
candlewax
beeswax
marzipan
butter
honey
marmalade
caramel
butterscotch
syrup
toast
vanilla
smoky bacon
turkish delight
petrol
mineral
flint
stone
tea/earl grey

strawberry
raspberry
redcurrant
red fruit
summer fruit compote
cherry
black & red fruits
black cherry
fresh cherry compote
blackberry
blackcurrant
black fruit
ripe black fruit
plum
damson
fruit cake / plum pudding
baked dried fruit
dried fruit
bubblegum
chocolate
dark chocolate
bitter chocolate
grilled meat
meat
coffee
leather
smoked meat
autumnal
cedar
clove
cinnamon
spice
tobacco
cigar
toasted oak
truffle
mushroom
earthy
toast
oak
oak / vanilla
vanilla
pepper
liquorice
tea leaves
clay
graphite
smoke
floral
violets
eucalyptus
fennel, aniseed
thyme
wild herbs
dried herbs
forest floor
leafiness
green pepper
mint
grass

YOUR OWN REACTIONS

The language we use to describe our thinking and experience never fails to excite those who teach about wine, especially when the student feels it is all 'new'. While there is a scientific language for the chemical make-up of wine, it is not used for everyday parlance. As an example when we smell green pepper in a wine such as Sauvignon Blanc, we are actually smelling methoxypyrazines – but most of us would not use this in everyday language. The description of 'sweaty gym kit' is not uncommon in this session....

At the Wine School, we are huge believers that when we are getting to know wine and developing our interest and excitement we should use words that come to mind. If you are thinking 'Camden Town' when sniffing a Barolo, then we are keen that you say it – and we are equally keen that you listen to others' descriptions too. If someone says 'tar and roses' and someone else says 'paint remover' then we can see some kind of link – and it also usefully reminds that we all see, smell, hear, listen in different ways and have different interpretations.

WHAT WILL YOU FIND?

These commonly-found flavour and aroma notes will vary with culture and cuisine — and your own memories and associations.

AGE AND MATURITY

Age is how old the wine is. Maturity is whether or not it is ready to drink.

A wine can be mature while still young, as most wines (whites especially) are made to be drunk young and fresh. But some – and that includes whites as well as reds – are meant to progress to maturity in bottle.

Wines change as they age, even in a sealed bottle. The chemistry of this is challenging, and still being explored. Some of the aspects of wine that we get most pleasure from – complexity, subtle aromas – stem from this process.

Maturity reflects the effect of time on wine: is a wine at its best? Or over the hill? Maturity, like balance, is personal: some people like mature wines, others prefer the vigour of youth.

Colour is the first key to maturity: whites become yellower, darker, with age. Reds grow lighter, more tawny.

Use our blank square of paper opposite. Look at a red wine – glass held at waist level, tipped away from you at 45 degrees over the white square.

Is the wine light and translucent, or is deep and dark? Clear or opaque? Bright or dull?

Check out the colour of the rim – the edge of the wine – versus the core. The rim is where you will spot, in the colour and intensity of the wine, clear signs of youth or age.

As a very general rule, reds tend to get paler with age, whites get darker.

Red wines start off purple; as they get older, they lose pigmentation, and fade to brick-red, garnet, orange and finally tawny. Look for these clues at the rim.

Most whites start their lives clear and pale, and deepen to yellow and finally amber.

Look at a young white wine: the rim will be almost translucent and colourless

The heart of the glass has a pale lemon-yellow hue

The rim of a young red wine is intense, with purple hints

The bright, deep red colour reinforces the rim's message that this is a young wine, and a good one

TAKING A LOOK AT YOUR WINE

This is an important square:

- It has nothing in it, so you can hold your glass over it and look through the wine.
- Tilt the glass away from you over the blank square and look for three things:

COLOUR

For now, think in terms of a simple range, from light to dark, for both whites and reds. Whites range from pale lemon to deep gold; reds from deep purple to dark crimson or brick-toned.

Some wines have a signature colour, and experienced tasters can spot them across a crowded room.

With experience, you'll be able to spot faulty, out-of-condition wines by their colour alone: a lifeless, flat hue can be suspicious, and whites that are darker, or reds that are lighter, than their age would suggest should also raise concerns.

CLARITY

Can you see through it? There can be quite a range, from total clarity (some whites) to total opacity (some reds and fortified wines). Clarity can vary from wine to wine, and from young to old in the same wine. An older wine will be clearer, less dense. If it is hazy or cloudy, suspect a fault.

A wine in good condition will be brilliant, bright and clear.

SHADING

The edge of the wine, at the rim, will be a different colour to the heart of the glass: this is why we tilt the glass to look at the wine. Opacity matters here, but the shading also offers clues to a wine's age and character. A young red wine will be more purple than red. Older ones fade to brick-red, even orange, at the rim.

Young red wines will have a more intense colour at the rim; with time this becomes more muted.

White wines, when young, will be virtually colourless at the rim, shading to deeper hues at the heart. Whites vary in hue as much as reds: a sweet Sauternes or Muscat may be dark gold at the heart; a dry Sauvignon may be pale lemon.

THE PRACTICALITIES OF TASTING

Or, do try this at home

If you are to give yourself and your friends a fair chance when tasting, there are a few points to consider which will help the wines show to best advantage.

1. Choose a plain, clear glass so that you can see the colour and clarity/density of the wine. (Good light and a white background - a tablecloth? - is helpful too.)

2. The size is important: you need a glass big enough to swirl the wine, to get some air into it and release its aromas.

3. So, too, is the shape: a 'tulip', where the rim turns inwards, is better than a 'bell' shape: the tulip glass collects the aromas and funnels them to your nose.

4. It's best to rinse and dry the glasses before the tasting: this makes sure that there is no taste left from washing-up liquid - or from stale air if they've been stored upside-down in a cupboard. Cardboard boxes can also leave a discernible taint.

5. Have water, and perhaps some dry biscuits or bread, to hand to clear your palate before the next wine. A drop of water swilled round the glass helps, too.

6. A last tip: avoid wearing perfume or aftershave!

For more on this see Tasting at Home in the Appendix

TAKING NOTES

Is not vital. Wine professionals do it – as below – and when you remember that some taste a hundred wines in a day, you see why.

For most of us, the trick is to scribble down the very first impressions that cross your mind, without second-guessing yourself and noting what you think you **ought** to be tasting.

Writing really helps, but the mental note can be enough. The conscious effort to gather your thoughts, if only a couple of words, will help you to fix or tag the sensations in your memory.

Some tasters use technology as a shortcut to note-taking: a snapshot of the label on a device will save laborious scribbling in a notebook.

Beaune 1er Cru Perhuisots, Dom. Devevey
Lighter colour but bright + attractive. Oak a little prominent at the moment, but pretty, youthful fruit comes up behind, with some cherry notes.
Good finish. A lighter style of Beaune, but fine.

SUMMING UP

The balance factors come together to make a satisfying, interesting mouthful – or not

Flavour is not just in the mouth, it's in the nose as well. That's why a good sniff tells you lots, and adds to the pleasure. (To show how much, try tasting while holding your nose.)

How does your palate work? Hold the wine in your mouth: this heats the wine up and more character and flavours emerge. Don't be self-conscious: enjoying and tasting can be a symphony of slurping, sucking in air....

WHAT TO LOOK FOR

Think of the basics:

Swirl the glass to release the aromas

Sniff to experience the aromas

'Chew' the wine with a little air to bring out flavours and aromas

— First, what can you smell? Aromas of...?

— When you taste, can you detect:

- Dryness or sweetness?
- Acidity: high/medium/low?
- Tannin: none/a little/lots?
- Body: full/medium/light?
- Alcohol: high? low? Can you guess the percentage?

— What flavours do you find?

— What about the length: long/medium/short?

— Balance/satisfaction: would you recommend this wine to friends?

Remember, it always helps to **compare and contrast different wines** when tasting. Ask yourself questions like:

- Which wine has seen more sunshine?
- Which wine has more acidity?

Memory is your friend, because memory is strongly linked to your sense of smell.

As soon as you encounter the aromas, this sets off a series of thoughts about this wine:

- That was exciting
- That was dreary

HOW DO YOU CAPTURE THE THOUGHTS?

'That reminds me of.....' is a thought you will often return to: see Words and Memories on page 22.

What are you noticing that leads to this thought, or that thought? This is what this Course is all about.

Our flavour spectrums and balance targets give you an idea of the range of flavours and/or aromas that may spring to mind. What they don't tell you – and what you will note for yourself – are the subtleties of elegance, length, grip or smoothness... whether the wine's taste is, or is not, at variance with what you smelled before tasting; whether it explodes or sidles into your mouth....

As we move round the world of wine on the rest of the Course, you will find many reasons why wines taste as they do, from the character of the grape variety via the soil to the weather and the approach taken by the people who make the wine.

The summing up of all this comes in the glass in your hand –

'Is it good to drink?'

QUESTIONS

A quick quiz to help fix things in your memory

1. Name six factors that influence the balance of wine.

_____

2. How can you detect acidity when you are tasting wine?

_____

3. Is a wine high in acidity more likely to come from a cooler or a hotter climate?

_____

4. Is a wine high in alcohol more likely to come from a cooler or a hotter climate?

_____

5. How can you detect alcohol in wine?

_____

6. How can you detect that new oak was used in making wine?

_____

7. What is meant by the length of a wine?

_____

Answers on page 221

Right: How is the wine progressing? A winemaker takes a sample from the barrel.

GRAPE INTO GLASS: HOW TO MAKE WINE

This is the first of our Background pages: read these if you like, they are not essential to the basic plot. You can taste and enjoy wine without knowing any of it....

You have a vineyard. It's the one your grandfather, or his grandfather, planted. Or, if you have a blank canvas and can choose where to grow your grapes, then you first need to consider the site-selection factors that we discuss in Choices and Consequences.

For now, here are the vines. You are farming, there is a seasonal rhythm: prune in winter; tend, train, cosset and treat the vines; harvest in autumn. At every season, you'll face challenges: from spring (with its risk of frosts) through summer (hail... pests...) to autumn (rot...).

You have tools: chemical, physical, even biological, to fight back against the various creatures, diseases and blights that come between you and a healthy harvest.

In this introductory course, we'll grant you beginner's luck and a fine crop. You have chosen the right moment to pick; your grapes are plump and ripe, but still crisp and fresh with acidity.

What happens now?

continued...

SCIENCE SOUNDBITE: FERMENTATION
YEASTS + SUGARS → ALCOHOL, HEAT AND CO_2

Wine is made by adding yeasts to the juice of grapes. The yeasts — which need warmth to work — convert the sugars in the grape juice to alcohol, generating more heat and CO_2 (carbon dioxide) in the process. If all sugars are converted to alcohol the wine becomes 'dry'. Or the winemaker can stop the fermentation if he or she wants to leave some natural (residual) sugar in the wine. Methods used are lowering temperature, straining out yeasts, adding a controlled form of sulphur dioxide (SO_2) or a combination of the three.

The first choice is: white or red? Grape colour is a side-issue, for you can make white wine from red grapes (clue: the juice is colourless). Broadly, the basics are:

WHITE WINE

Grapes **come into the winery** in bunches. Check for and remove rotten grapes, leaves, 'MOG' (matter other than grapes). Crush the fruit to allow the juice to flow and (in the same process) strip the grapes from the stems. Throw away the stems.

Result: a pulp of crushed grapes and skins. Put this pulp into a **press** – a machine that applies enough force to release the juice without breaking the pips (they leave a bitter taste).

Leave the juice for a day, perhaps two, in a **tank to settle** so the solid matter (skins, mostly) falls to the bottom. Wineries use chilling, and/or sulphur dioxide, to protect the juice from oxidation and spoilage.

Now for the **fermentation**: pump the clear juice into a vat, add yeast, seal the lid, control the temperature with your cooling equipment. Fermentation converts the sugars in the juice into alcohol, carbon dioxide – and heat: thus the need for **cooling**.

There are waste-products from fermentation: the lees. These fall to the bottom, so the clear wine can be pumped off and then matured. Result: wine. It is filtered, then bottled.

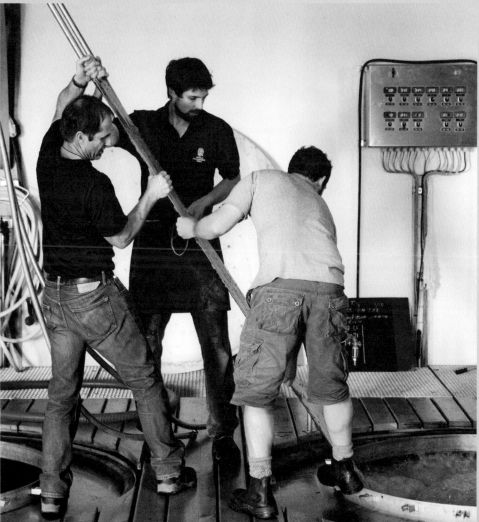

RED WINE

To make red, follow much the same process as for white, but keep the skins. You can choose to crush the grapes or leave the bunches whole, and to keep none, some or all of the stems.

Put the grapes, skins and all, into an open **vat**. (The press is a minor player in the process – see below.) Add yeast – or let the natural yeasts have free play.

Fermentation extracts **colour, tannins and flavour** from the skins. These skins tend to float up to the surface of the infant wine, pushed upwards by the carbon dioxide: they need to be pushed back down to keep the extraction going.

When the fermentation is over, pump the new wine into tanks, vats or barrels to **mature**.

The residue left in the vat can be pressed: this dark, tannic '**press wine**' can then be blended in to stiffen the main batch.

Your wine needs to mature for a time – how long depends on the sort of wine – before clarifying, filtering and bottling.

CHOICES, CHOICES...

So that's the recipe at its most basic. But long before a single grape hits the sorting-table, there are a myriad choices to consider....
See next page.

CHOICES AND CONSEQUENCES

Making wine means all sorts of decisions and actions, from the vineyard on to the cellar.

A broad-brush snapshot includes:

Site selection — Sloping or flat? High and windy or low and sheltered?

Soil — limestone or clay? Sand, schist, granite or gravel? Deep, or shallow? Well-drained or damp? Nutritious or poor?

Disease prevention and control — taking care the vines don't succumb to pests, or catch diseases that are incurable, and helping them to cope with ones that can be controlled (see biodynamics page 120)

Choice of grape variety — unless local laws make the choice for you

Choice of clone — within each variety are many choices: some clones of the grape are high-yielding, others ripen earlier or later, others offer more flavour....

Local laws enshrining traditions — see appellation law, page 78

Biodynamic? Organic? — see page 120

How many vines to plant per acre/hectare (density) — this will impact how much wine you can make, and its character

How severely to prune the vines, which will influence the yield

Harvesting: by machine, or by hand-picking?

Yield per hectare: decided by how many bunches you allow to develop

How much juice to extract from them

How gently to extract it

How long and at what temperature to ferment

What to ferment in: stainless steel? Concrete vat? Wooden barrel?

What vessel to mature the wine in — and for how long?

And that's before you consider all the advances in winery and cellar involving chemistry, biology and technology – changes beyond the dreams of a generation ago....
For reflections on this, see Making Wine Then and Now on page 34.

CLIMATE AND WINE STYLE

One thing the winemaker cannot change is the climate. Broadly, climate contributes to wine style like this:

- **Cooler climates** lead to higher acidity, more moderate alcohol; the wines tend to have less new oak contact
- **Warmer climates** lead to lower acidity, higher alcohol; wines frequently have more new oak contact

Grapes that grow in cooler climates keep their acidity until picking time. Their vines have produced a lower amount of sugar (through photosynthesis) at ripening, and acidity still dominates. The winemaker keeps the acidity in the wine and the sugar becomes the alcohol content. Acidity is dominant in the balance, producing crisp, dry wines, a style that many enjoy.

In warmer climates, grapes develop more sugar during ripening, which lessens the amount of acidity compared to the sugar level. When the juice becomes wine, the acidity has a different balance, with greater richness and alcohol.

You can work this out just by looking where the wine is made (such as when choosing from a restaurant wine list). Compare and contrast a wine from Northern France with a wine from California. The French wine will most likely have higher acidity and lower alcohol than the Californian.

TERROIR AND TECHNIQUE

Is wine made by Nature or by Man? Is terroir – the vineyard environment – the prime influence? Or is it technique, in vineyard and cellar? Rebecca Lamont explores.

Why are vineyards where they are? Are they the best spots – or just the most traditional? In lands like France or Italy, it's generally assumed that the best vineyards are those that already exist, and have done for hundreds of years. Indeed, laws dictate where grapes can, and can't, be grown.

But what of Chile, or New Zealand, or Canada? There are no traditions – or none with a lengthy track-record. There are no laws that say you can't devote a cow-pasture to grapes.

A French winemaker will, given this heritage, naturally assume that where the grape grows is the biggest factor in a wine's personality. His/her cousin in Canada or Chile may decide that good winemaking transcends place.

The first philosophy is summed up in one hard-to-translate French word: **terroir**. This brings together site, soil, slope, climate – everything that creates the vine's environment. A good wine, to a committed 'terroiriste' is one that shows you where it comes from. The second group asserts that as long as the grapes are healthy, it's what is done to them that matters. For them, it's about **technique**. At its extreme, this means a good wine is one that overcomes Nature's imperfections.

It is inevitable that wine producers in old and new countries have – generalising wildly – differing views on this terroir/technique debate. Luckily for wine-lovers, the debate is far more nuanced today than it was a generation ago, with New World winemakers exploring their lands for the most special sites, and French ones adopting novel approaches in the cellar.

How do we know how much nature is in the wine, and how much technique? The answer is rarely obvious, but there are producers working plots of land side by side in the same vineyard – Burgundy is a good example – who nevertheless produce entirely different wines thanks to their individual techniques and philosophies.

Winemakers often let us know about the philosophy and approach via back-labels, blogs and websites – or your wine-merchant may have the story.

It is so easy to take for granted all the effort that is put into making wine, but experience shows that there is usually a clear connection between passion for the subject, a love of, and respect for, the environment, and the quality of the end-product. The best wines tend to be made by those regarded as 'terroiristes' rather than technologists. Is it that easy to split the two?

QUANTITY AND QUALITY

For centuries, there has been an assumption that more means worse in wine: that the lower the yield, the better the quality.

Wine laws in, for example, France state the maximum amount of wine that can be made from a hectare of vines, the density at which vines can be planted, and in some cases the way vines must be pruned to limit the crop.

The shorthand way to measure yield is in hectolitres of wine per hectare: hl/ha. In France, around 50hl/ha is typical for quality wine.

Like most things in wine, this approach is being challenged: modern growers assert that by managing the vineyard, quality wines, whites in particular, can be made from yields up to 100hl/ha. They also point to the paradox that the best years for red Bordeaux are often the most abundant. The debate continues....

MAKING WINE THEN AND NOW
– AND THEN, AGAIN   *Demetri Walters MW reflects on what was, is – and will be.*

Wine, which is essentially fermented grape-juice, can make itself, entirely without the hand of Man, thanks to yeasts on the skins of grapes. Winemaking can be summed up as the intervention of humans in refining this process.

Historical mentions of winemaking go back a long way. Archaeological evidence is constantly winding back the birth of winemaking to before 3,500BC. In addition to its depiction in a number of ancient cultures, winemaking is frequently mentioned in the Old Testament of the Bible, where Noah is described as both the proto-winemaker and the first person to become intoxicated on the result.

Despite this long history, winemaking only became a scientific procedure in the late 19th century, with Louis Pasteur's discovery of the existence of yeasts and bacteria. Since that time winery hygiene has influenced quality and lent much greater control to winemakers. Today, a greater understanding of the chemistry of wine means that winery practices, as well as equipment, have become much more sophisticated.

This has substantially changed the complexion of winemaking at all levels. Scientific innovations (the use of cultured yeasts and enzymes, reverse osmosis, cryo-extraction and micro-oxygenation to name but a few) have enabled winemakers to manipulate their art, thereby delivering good-quality wines even in years affected by the vagaries of weather, or on sites formerly deemed unsuitable for high-quality wine.

But (as anyone reading the annual vintage reports from Burgundy, say, or Bordeaux will realise), such advances only go so far to even up the hand dealt by nature and, if technical advances can deliver more predictable results, one by-product has been the stylistic alteration in some wines once considered to be immutable in character.

Yet no top winemaker is aiming for a bland, industrial product. So now, seemingly in a bid to make more authentic wines, many producers are rediscovering old, even archaic, technologies, adding them to the modern winemaking mix in the crafting of their wines.

Some of these, still common in certain regions, are novel in others: the traditional basket press for example. Even far earlier equipment such as amphorae and stone fermentation basins have been resurrected from a rustic past and are once more employed, alongside modern techniques. Processes too from an earlier age, including the addition of pine resin to the fermenting grape juice and the non-disgorging of sparkling wines are becoming more fashionable.

Recent years have also seen the growth of the biodynamic movement (see page 120): this, though mainly in the vineyard, also seeks to employ traditional, super-organic methods in the winery in order to amplify a wine's sense of place.

The next stage of the story will be intriguing – with wines to match.

Left: An ancient style of vessel, the amphora, revived and in use at one South African estate
Right: Oak, however, has never gone away. The use of fire in barrel-making can add toast notes to wine.

THE INFLUENCE OF OAK

The kind of container you mature your wine in has a very important impact on its taste.

Choosing a stainless steel tank will prevent contact with the air: this has the effect of retaining the wine's vibrancy and fruit character.

If on the other hand you choose a wooden barrel (and oak has been the main wood of choice for centuries), then you will allow a small ingress of oxygen into the wine through the pores of the wood and the minuscule gaps between the barrel staves. This will 'soften' the wine, rounding it out and slightly diminishing the otherwise vibrant fruit character to give the wine a softer texture.

If the barrel that you use is a new one, it will also add some flavour to the wine. New oak contains vanillin and other sweet, spicy compounds, and these flavours will leach gradually into the wine.

Then, too, a barrel-maker (cooper) needs to bend the staves into the curved shape. They do this by toasting the inside of the stave with a flame; so as well as vanilla and spice, a new barrel will also add toasty flavours and sweetness to a wine. A winemaker can order the level of toasting they want in their barrels.

New oak barrels are extremely costly, so for lesser wines oak flavour can be gained by adding oak chips or staves to the vat.

Oak-ageing is usually associated with red wines; but some whites – primarily Chardonnay – gain from it too.

2

The first three grapes we shall compare are classic white varieties

SAUVIGNON BLANC
CHARDONNAY
SEMILLON

From their original homelands in France, these three have travelled across the world

---

SAUVIGNON BLANC
Zesty

The grape that makes Sancerre and Pouilly-Fumé in the Loire Valley, New Zealand whites and white Bordeaux

CHARDONNAY
Smooth

The grape of white Burgundy, for example Chablis or Meursault — and a key ingredient in Champagne

SEMILLON
Waxy

From Bordeaux, this makes the great sweet wine Sauternes and dry wines in Australia's Hunter Valley

Where the grapes grow

Wine grapes grow in the world's temperate zones, between 30 and 50 degrees north and south of the Equator. 'Cool' and 'warm' are relative: cool-climate grapes like Sauvignon Blanc will be planted in the cooler corners of a warm-climate country, where there is a moderating influence from, for example, ocean air. As the wine world expands, growers experiment with grapes in new places. These maps show the main zones where the classic grapes are grown.

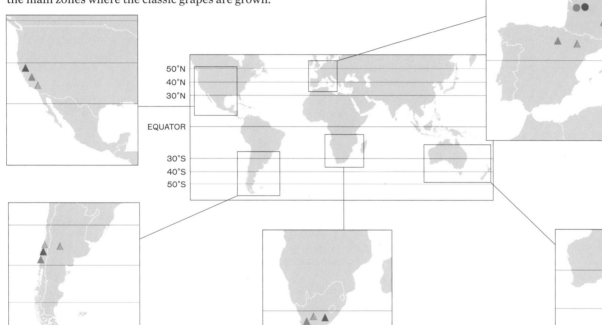

SAUVIGNON BLANC

● **Cooler climate**   ▲ **Warmer climate**

Upper Loire   Spain
Bordeaux   Chile
New Zealand   California
North-East Italy   South Africa
Slovenia
Austria

CHARDONNAY

● **Cooler climate**   ▲ **Warmer climate**

Burgundy   Southern France
Champagne   Northern Spain
England   California
Northern Italy   Chile
Austria   Argentina
New Zealand   Australia
                   South Africa

SEMILLON

● **Cooler climate**   ▲ **Warmer climate**

Bordeaux   California
                   Australia
                   South Africa
                   Chile

Sauvignon Blanc

KEY POINTS

- White grape
- Aromatic
- High acidity
- Likes a cool climate
- Rarely oaked
- Unblended in Loire and New Zealand
- Blended with Sémillon in Bordeaux

KEY REGIONS

Loire, Bordeaux, New Zealand, Chile

The distinctively aromatic scent of a Sauvignon Blanc wine – clean, bright, appetising – tells you that it should be drunk young and fresh. You will find aromas and flavours like gooseberries, asparagus, grass... even a hint of cat's pee.

This vine thrives in a cool climate: the wine it produces is brisk, and light- to medium-bodied. The Loire Valley in France is its homeland, and wines made here tend to have mineral – imagine the taste of flint – herby and floral notes.

This grape has transferred from its native France most successfully to New Zealand and California, but is widely grown around the world. In California it is sometimes known as Fumé Blanc. Warmer places, such as California, give riper grapes and fuller flavours – on the fruity rather than the herbal end of the range.

In Bordeaux, it is used alone, or blended with Sémillon, in dry whites; it can also be the minority partner to Sémillon in sweet wines such as Sauternes. Winemakers rarely use oak-ageing for Sauvignon: exceptions are some white Bordeaux and some Californians.

Wine suggestions for this session, page 216

AROMA & FLAVOUR

Depending on where they are made, Sauvignon Blanc wines have fruity and herbal notes. Cool-climate wines can show flinty notes.

When you try these wines, look out for:

- lots of aroma (aromatic grape)
- lots of acidity

Would you agree that these wines are:

- light-bodied wines, and mouthwatering? Do you see why we call them 'zesty'?

Which notes on the flavour spectrum do they evoke for you? Perhaps you have found some others of your own....

Maturity

Most Sauvignon Blancs are best when young, though top Loire whites can age for three-plus years. Other Sauvignons that gain from bottle-age are top New Zealand wines, and those where the grape is blended with Sémillon: white Bordeaux such as those from Pessac-Léognan are examples.

KEY AROMAS & FLAVOURS

- gooseberries
- 'cat's pee'
- asparagus

Cool climate
Warm climate

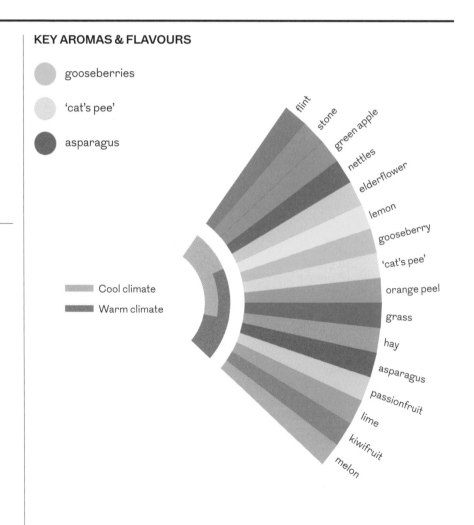

flint
stone
green apple
nettles
elderflower
lemon
gooseberry
'cat's pee'
orange peel
grass
hay
asparagus
passionfruit
lime
kiwifruit
melon

BALANCE

THE CHARACTER
OF THE WINE
IN YOUR GLASS

The key difference between cool- and warm-climate Sauvignons is in fruit ripeness. While there is always underlying acidity, you will notice more fruit ripeness and headier aromas in warm-climate wines. Here we compare a Sancerre from the Loire and a New Zealand Sauvignon.

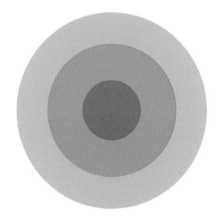

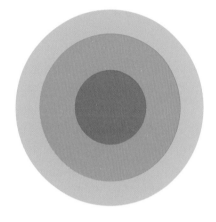

 Acidity

Alcohol

Fruit ripeness

COOLER CLIMATE

Loire Sancerre

Brisk and high acidity;
moderate fruit ripeness;
moderate alcohol

WARMER CLIMATE

New Zealand

More fruit ripeness;
acidity less noticeable; high degree
of aromatic intensity

Food matches

Cool-climate Sauvignons work well with fish and shellfish, piquant cheeses and Japanese food. More weighty wines match more complex fish and shellfish dishes, asparagus, substantial salads and pasta dishes; chicken works too. The acidity of these wines can either be used:

- to act as a foil to richness in a dish, or
- to match with more acidic dishes, e.g. those with a touch of lemon.

Some Sauvignon Blanc-friendly foods:

- Goats' cheese
- Fish and shellfish
- Thai green curry
- Pasta dishes
- Green salad
- Asparagus

FOOD & WINE

Some ideas for food matches
are given for each grape. For more
detailed advice see page 204.

KEY REGION:

The Upper Loire

The Loire, the longest river in France, flows right across the country all the way from the hills of the Massif Central to the Atlantic. This far north the climate is temperate, even cool: white wines predominate. The river links together a wide variety of vineyard areas in its thousand-kilometre journey: going downstream, from east to west, the first major vineyards are the homeland of Sauvignon Blanc.

SANCERRE & POUILLY

Sauvignon Blanc is the main grape around the famous wine villages of Sancerre and Pouilly-sur-Loire. Here in the Upper Loire, at 47 degreees north and far from the sea, it is cool in winter and warm in summer. The landscape is gentle, but dotted with modest hills: their steep slopes and rich Kimmeridgian clay soil (near-identical to that in Chablis, an hour's drive east) yield wines that – for Sauvignons – are fuller-bodied: the best, from ripe years, can develop in bottle.

Pouilly's Sauvignon wine is called Pouilly-Fumé, allegedly because of the smoky (fumé) note on the smell and taste. It is traditionally brisker, more austere, stonier than the more solid-bodied Sancerre wines from across the river.

In both Sancerre and Pouilly, growing popularity has led winemakers to offer selected bottlings from named vineyards – reflecting the individuality of their sites – and to age their wines in oak. These more complex (and costly) wines contrast with the straightforward, fruity styles that made the names of the twin villages.

The Loire Valley

Being just down the road from Paris did the Upper Loire wines no harm in the days when transport was a big slice of the cost of a barrel of wine. Burgundy is just off the right-hand edge of the map — so going east you cross a wine frontier where Sauvignon Blanc gets replaced by Chardonnay.

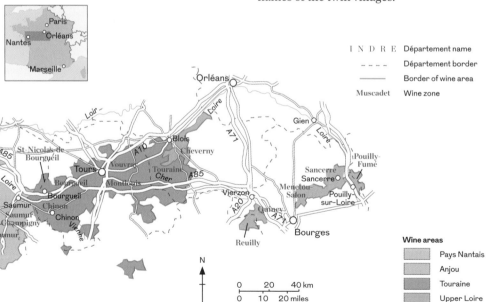

Above: The Sancerre vineyards are set amid rolling countryside; note how the slope is perfectly angled to catch the sun.

VINTAGES CAN VARY

This far north the climate can be marginal for ripening grapes, and wines vary markedly in character according to the vintage: in cool years they stress bright, floral acidity; in warmer years the wines gain body and fruit.

OTHER LOIRE SAUVIGNONS

While Pouilly-Fumé and Sancerre are the top names, Sauvignon is grown across the wider region:

- Simple, good-value wines can be found labelled **Sauvignon de Touraine** (around Tours, west of Sancerre and Pouilly).
- Close to Sancerre, but away from the river, a limestone outcrop lies behind the village of **Menetou-Salon**; the ten communes in this appellation benefit from the limestone and yield clean, crisp wines.
- Further west still, **Reuilly** has a range of soils and fleshier wines, while
- **Quincy**'s fresh, zippy style is attributed to soils with more sand and quartz.

SCIENCE SOUNDBITE: SAUVIGNON AROMAS

The characteristic aromas of Sauvignon Blanc come from identifiable chemical compounds known as methoxypyrazines (which contribute a grassy, green-pepper note) and thiols (flavours like passionfruit). The former develop only in the vineyard and decrease with more sun exposure, while the latter can also develop during winemaking and are affected by the type of yeast used.

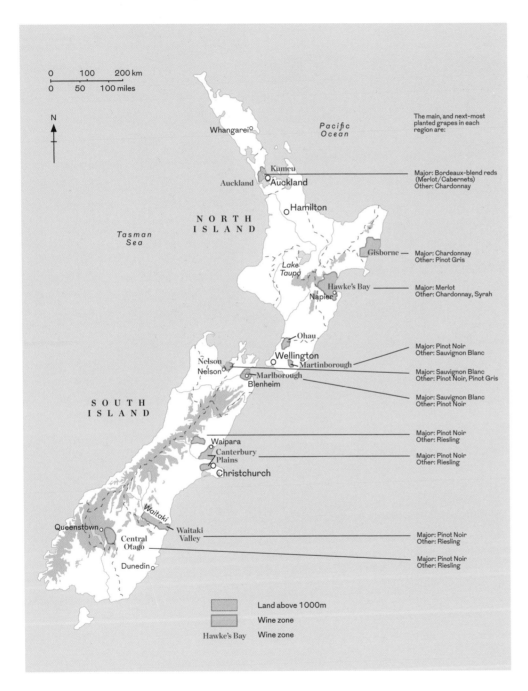

The main, and next-most planted grapes in each region are:

Major: Bordeaux-blend reds (Merlot/Cabernets)
Other: Chardonnay

Major: Chardonnay
Other: Pinot Gris

Major: Merlot
Other: Chardonnay, Syrah

Major: Pinot Noir
Other: Sauvignon Blanc

Major: Sauvignon Blanc
Other: Pinot Noir, Pinot Gris

Major: Sauvignon Blanc
Other: Pinot Noir

Major: Pinot Noir
Other: Riesling

Major: Pinot Noir
Other: Riesling

Major: Pinot Noir
Other: Riesling

Major: Pinot Noir
Other: Riesling

☐ Land above 1000m
☐ Wine zone
Hawke's Bay Wine zone

KEY REGION:

New Zealand

A generation ago, wine made from Sauvignon Blanc was known – if the grape-name was known at all – thanks to Sancerre and Pouilly-Fumé. Then New Zealand, in particular the South Island vineyards of Marlborough, burst on stage with wines that were sold primarily under the grape name. 'New Zealand Sauvignon' became a new heading on the world's wine-lists.

It brought a new flavour, too: vibrant, intensely fruity, upfront. From a standing start in the early 1970s, New Zealand has expanded its Sauvignon vineyards to the point where it has more than the Loire Valley – and seven New Zealand bottles in ten produced are Sauvignon.

Left: No-one — except the marketplace — tells New Zealanders which grapes to plant where. So a vine distribution map is beset by ifs and buts. Here we highlight the current state of play: it will change.

Sauvignon Blanc dominates where the climate is cooler. In the far north, where the climate is subtropical, red grapes are important — but even here, as we'll learn later, whites such as Chardonnay and Pinot Gris are grown in cooler corners. Hawke's Bay majors on reds such as Merlot, whereas Central Otago in the far South has a world-wide reputation for Pinot Noir — as does Martinborough in the North Island.

MARLBOROUGH

The **Wairau Valley**, in Marlborough county in the north-east corner of South Island, is the key zone. Here, around the little town of Blenheim, the climate is sunny and dry, the land flat and the soil well-drained. Irrigation can be needed in dry years. A key to this northern grape's success in these sunnier climes is the area's cool nights, caused by the cool Pacific Ocean air from the coast at Cloudy Bay. This keeps acidity in the ripening grapes.

In a wine district this new, growers are still seeking the best terroir, most recently exploring the side-valleys away from the river-bed. Another Marlborough zone that is showing much promise is the **Awatere Valley**, over the ridge to the south of Wairau. This valley, also opening onto the Pacific, at Clifford Bay, offers both stony river-bed soils on the valley floor and well-placed hillside sites. The Sauvignons from here are less assertive, more subtle, than the Marlborough norm.

New Zealand started to make Sauvignon Blanc just as the technology of winemaking underwent a revolution: in came stainless-steel vats, often with the means to keep the fermentation cool. Out went concrete or wooden vats where the temperature was set by nature, not man. The style for which Marlborough became known stems from technique as much as terroir – though the New Zealanders make much of their 'cool climate' credentials.

Elsewhere in New Zealand, Sauvignon Blanc plays second fiddle to Chardonnay, though some good bottles emerge from **Nelson** (also South Island) and **Hawke's Bay** in the North.

WHY THE WINES VARY: LOIRE AND NEW ZEALAND COMPARED

Get down among the small-print of the weather statistics, and Marlborough and Sancerre have very similar climates.

There are subtle differences that affect and mark the characters of the wines:

- It is **rainier** in the autumn in Marlborough, which can cause problems at grape harvest
- **Frost and hail** beset the Loire more than the South Island
- Marlborough is closer to the Equator (41°S compared to 47°N): that means **higher sun angles,** and thus more warmth, during the growing season

SAUVIGNON BLANC WORLDWIDE

California, **South Africa** and **Chile** are all significantly nearer to the Equator than either France or New Zealand: the warmer growing-season temperatures and much stronger sunlight lead to generally fuller, fatter wines with lower acidity.

That said, Chile, especially, finds cooler corners at higher altitudes and along the coast, giving conditions – and some wines – more akin to New Zealand's.

Chile's best Sauvignons come from the cool **Casablanca Valley**, with **Leyda Valley** up-and-coming among the even cooler coastal dictricts.

WHAT IS TERROIR?

Terroir is the sum of the natural, environmental factors — including soil, topography and climate — that influence how a wine tastes. For more, see page 33.

NEW WORLD VS. OLD WORLD

'New World' and 'Old World' are terms we often hear in the world of wine. What exactly do they mean? Anne McHale MW explains.

It's very straightforward. The term 'Old World' refers to the traditional wine-producing countries of Europe, while the 'New World' is everywhere else. So the best-known Old World countries include France, Spain, Italy, Germany and Portugal, to name but a few, while in the New World we might first think of Australia, New Zealand, Chile, Argentina, South Africa and the USA.

Traditionally there has always been a stylistic distinction between wines from the two camps. The typical New World wine will be forward, bright and all about fruit. It will leap from the glass, confident in its intensity; certainly no shrinking violet. Its grape variety or blend of varieties will be boldly stated on the label so that you know what you're getting when you buy it.

Contrast this with the archetypal Old World equivalent; the wine will usually be more muted – some say 'softer' – and exhibiting a certain restraint. Instead of being all about the fruit, there will be a savoury, even mineral aspect to this wine, which some would argue makes it a better match for food. In addition, on a traditional Old World wine label you will not find the name of the grape variety, but the name of the place where the grapes were grown (intrinsically linked to the important concept of terroir – see page 33). So in order to understand the style you might have to gain a little bit of background knowledge… which is why you're reading this Course.

These distinctions are, of course, generalisations; in the world of wine there are always –and increasingly – exceptions to the rule. There are New World wine producers who strive to sculpt a more restrained, savoury style of wine; there are Old World growers seeking a juicy, pungent, leap-out-of-the-glass mouthful of fruitiness.

The concept of terroir in the New World, perhaps overlooked in certain areas in the past, is very much in vogue these days – and, conversely, some Old World regions now look to blend from different vineyards,

A FEW WINE TERMS....

Keep one step ahead of your wine merchant by knowing a few key terms (more in the Glossary on page 222)

Appellation/AOC French official wine zone; see page 78 and Appendix.

Barrel, barrique oak cask for fermenting and/or maturing; affects taste and development of the wine

Biodynamic wine-growing and -making philosophy and techniques; page 120

Cépage grape variety

Claret red Bordeaux wine; page 75

Cru, Cru Classé: page 98; **Grand Cru, Premier Cru:** page 150

Fermentation conversion of grape sugars by yeast into alcohol; page 29

Lees the sediment left over after fermentation; page 57

Malolactic fermentation turns malic into lactic acid – softens a wine; page 57

Minerality appetising, stony, flinty character in some white wines; page 53

Noble rot (botrytis cinerea) a condition that creates great sweet wines page 62

New World/Old World page 46

Oak, use of page 35

Organic wine page 120

Terroir influence of site manifested in the taste of the wine; page 33

Varietal wine from a single grape variety

Vat large oak, stainless steel or cement vessel for fermenting and holding wine

Vieilles vignes old vines; generally speaking, these make finer wine

Yield amount of wine made per hectare or acre of vineyard; pages 32 & 33

rather than focusing on a single site.

Despite these exceptions, though, you will tend to find that when you focus on a single grape variety and taste two examples of it, one each from the Old and New Worlds, side by side (as you will be doing at various points throughout the Course), these stylistic divisions hold true.

Try giving each glass a quick sniff. Which leaps out of the glass? Which one

Above: The green of vines punctuates the tawny Australian landscape.

cries out 'drink me now' and seduces you with bagfuls of ripe juicy fruit? And which one is shy, more backward, with a subtle savoury twist? These will be your clues.

And remember – there is no wrong or right here. The most important thing of all is which one you prefer... and is it good to drink?

KEY REGION:

Bordeaux

France is reticent about grape varieties. Its tradition is that terroir, the hand of the maker and what goes on in the cellar play the key roles in wine, and that the names of the raw material should be – well, if not obscured, then relegated to the back label.

So it can come as a mild surprise to find that Bordeaux sells quite a lot of wine that is pure Sauvignon, and quite a bit more where the grape is blended with Sémillon. Increasingly, you will find wines with labels stressing 'Sauvignon Blanc' from Bordeaux rather than just 'Bordeaux Blanc': the Bordelais are perhaps responding to the high profile New Zealand has given the grape.

BORDEAUX: WHITE VS. RED

Bordeaux is best known for its red wines (to come, in Session 3) and it makes nine bottles of red to every one of white. But white wines, both dry and sweet, are among the most celebrated from this large region.

PESSAC-LÉOGNAN

The top dry white Bordeaux wines are Sauvignon-Sémillon blends. Their heartland is the Pessac-Léognan district of Graves. South of the city of Bordeaux, Graves – named for its gravel soils – was the site of the first, medieval, Bordeaux vineyards. (The châteaux here usually make reds, too: see Session 3.)

The best white wines are fermented and aged in oak casks, and for real concentration and long life yields must be kept low. Such wines are inevitably expensive – though they can seem good value compared to white Burgundies.

Like their Côte d'Or counterparts (see Chardonnay), these Pessac-Léognan whites can improve in bottle and last 10 to 20 years. Top-rank whites from Pessac-Léognan often do well in cool years when the reds disappoint: a climatic consolation prize.

A recent fashion has seen a few expensive, hand-crafted white wines emerge from the red-Bordeaux heartland of the Médoc. They carry the simple name 'Bordeaux', not the commune names (Pauillac, St-Julien etc) – but the name of a famous red-wine château will be prominent on the label.

At their best these, and the Pessac-Léognan white wines, offer a unique style: complex, full-bodied and yet with balancing acidity.

GRAVES & ENTRE-DEUX-MERS

Simpler Sauvignon Blancs and Sauvignon blends come from the basic Graves zone and from the large and varied Entre-Deux-Mers district. As with modest red Bordeaux, the sheer number of estates and producers offers both a delight and a challenge: there are lovely wines, but finding them....

Sauternes and Barsac (see pages 62-63) are renowned sweet wines made mostly from Sémillon; but there is usually a small amount of Sauvignon Blanc in the blends.

Chardonnay

KEY POINTS

- White grape
- Moderate or high acidity — depending on climate
- At home in cool and warm climates
- Takes on characteristics of winemaking
- Many are influenced by oak
- Grown world-wide

KEY REGIONS

Burgundy, Champagne, Australia, California

Chardonnay is a blank canvas: the smooth basic character of the grape mutates magically depending on where it travels to and how it is handled. The results are some of the world's greatest whites – this is the white grape of Burgundy, Chablis, Champagne –and equally many a cheerful everyday bottle.

It is easy to grow, easy to vinify. Consequently it has travelled around the world, and is made and sold at all price points. So popular it is almost a brand-name, it is to winemaking what good chicken is to cooking: endlessly versatile.... (But there are battery-farmed Chardonnays too!)

Chardonnay is successful on its own as a varietal wine, as in Burgundy, but is also blended (with Sémillon in the New World, with Pinot Noir and Pinot Meunier in Champagne). French wines that are all Chardonnay include white Burgundies such as Meursault, Mâcon, Montrachet, Pouilly-Fuissé.

Chardonnay wines can be everyday or premium; the former include simple wines from even the grandest places, the latter range right up to some of the costliest wines on the planet, such as treasured Burgundian Grands Crus and esoteric Champagnes. Rarity apart, fine Chardonnay wines offer complexity, ability to age and characters unique to their origins.

Chardonnays reflect winemaking techniques and decisions more than most wines: see notes on malolactic fermentation and lees on page 57. Many, especially the more serious ones, also show the influence of oak – from cask fermentation and/or ageing – in their personalities.

AROMA & FLAVOUR

Chardonnay can be the most difficult wine for the taster to describe, but always has a certain buttery smoothness of texture. If grown in a cool climate, for example in Chablis, the wine is steely, stony, appley, with good acidity. But a hot climate, such as Australia's Barossa Valley, will produce softer wines with notes of tropical fruit.

When you try these wines, look out for:

- smoothness and fullness
- clues to whether grown in a warm or cool climate: is it richer (warm) or leaner (cool)?
- any evidence of oak: i.e., the smell or taste of vanilla or toast.

Would you agree that these wines are:

- smoother and richer than the zesty Sauvignon Blancs, and that oak is noticeable on some?
- slightly deeper in colour than the Sauvignon Blancs? This is partly to do with the influence of air from oak ageing.

Maturity

Serious Chardonnays will age in bottle, especially those that have been matured in oak. At the pinnacle, a Grand Cru white Burgundy will improve for 12-20 years, but most white Burgundies, and New World equivalents, are at their best after five to eight years. Oak and age add more layers of complexity: age will add notes of mushrooms, nuts, honey, bruised apple. If it is also oaked: biscuit, toast, vanilla, smoke.

KEY AROMAS & FLAVOURS

- butter
- melon
- apple
- pineapple
- vanilla (if oaked)

Cool climate
Warm climate

lemon, green apple, pear, mineral, stony, grapefruit, white peach, apricot, butter, hazelnut, almond, honeysuckle, melon, pineapple, mango, banana, honey, coconut

THE POUILLY CONFUSION

Pouilly-Fuissé: white Burgundy, thus made from Chardonnay

Pouilly-Fumé: white Loire (see page 42), made from Sauvignon Blanc

BALANCE

THE CHARACTER
OF THE WINE
IN YOUR GLASS

Because of its neutral character, if Chardonnay is aged in oak – especially new oak – this will be obvious. Oak-ageing of any sort will soften the wine, restraining the fruit, as we learned in Session 1. The effect of new oak is to add another layer: vanilla, toast and spice.

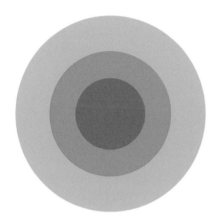

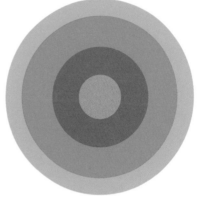

Acidity

Alcohol

Fruit ripeness

Oak

NO OAK
Chablis

Fruit and acidity in balance, with
moderately high alcohol

OAK
California

New oak adds its extra layer of
flavour and texture

Food matches

Chardonnay is a truly versatile food wine. It will match well with fish, poultry, cheeses and salads. Light, austere, cool-climate wines (like Chablis) go with unadorned shellfish, or simply-cooked white fish. Oaked ones work well with smoked fish and creamy sauces. Serious Chardonnays such as white Burgundies will match classic fish or shellfish dishes, chicken, mushroom-based sauces, or soft, washed-rind cheeses.

Some Chardonnay-friendly foods:

- Shellfish
- Fish dishes
- Cheeses
- Salads
- Chicken and other poultry

KEY REGION:

Burgundy

Like so many of the wine grapes in this Course, Chardonnay is of French descent. There is indeed a village called Chardonnay, buried in the countryside of southern Burgundy. Doubtless to the chagrin of the locals, its wine is only entitled to the lowly label Mâcon-Villages – but from starrier Burgundian vineyards come Chardonnays that are, at their finest, the greatest white wines in the world.

CÔTE DE BEAUNE

The heartland of Chardonnay wine is the world's most famous and expensive tract of vines, Burgundy's **Côte d'Or** or golden slope.

Here we encounter the Burgundy hierarchy or class-system, which we'll explore in Session 5. For now, bear in mind that 'Premier Cru' means seriously good, and 'Grand Cru' even better.

The Côte de Beaune sub-zone has the white Burgundy Grands Crus: **Corton-Charlemagne** and **Montrachet** – wines that are truly grand in quality, status and price.

Premier Cru comes next in the white-Burgundy ranks. These wines come from specific vineyards in villages such as **Meursault**, **Chassagne-Montrachet** and **Puligny-Montrachet**.

The point about Chardonnay in Burgundy is that it seems to match the terroir perfectly. Chardonnay thrives, does adequately to well, just about everywhere grapes will ripen; in Burgundy, and in Burgundian hands, it can and does transmit to our senses the subtle and exciting differences between vineyards, hillsides and villages – never mind vintages.

The Côte de Beaune is also the land of individuals: winegrowers whose quirks, skills and philosophies ring out from their wines. Here, the name of the maker is even more important than that of the vineyard.

The great white Burgundies – both Grands Crus and (increasingly) the Premiers Crus – are expensive: rarity, and the cost of small-scale, barrel-by-barrel, production and nurturing see to that. Luckily, there are plenty of Burgundian wines of lesser status at more accessible prices.

KIMMERIDGIAN

The name of the rock comes from a little village in, of all places, Dorset, England. Imagine the rocks at Chablis as the rim of a saucer: the opposite rim is 340 miles away at Kimmeridge. In between, below the Paris basin and the English Channel, many other strata of rock lie above this layer.

CHABLIS

For more affordability, look first to Chablis, an island of vines amid the rather northern-feeling forests and pastures of the Yonne. The rock beneath these modest hills is limestone and, in the heart of Chablis, clayey limestone (marl) of a special sort: Kimmeridgian.

The **Grands Crus** of Chablis rise above the town in an impressive sweep, sloping south into the sun. Their wines are stately and deep, and gain greatly from bottle-age.

Premier Cru Chablis is in far greater supply and is more variable, though the best are truly impressive and can be excellent value.

 Everyday Chablis is labelled, simply, 'Chablis' (see page 150 for how Burgundy labels its wines). It can be an excellent drink at one to three years old.

Chablis is a long way north (though not as far north as Champagne, another Chardonnay stronghold), and vintages can vary markedly in ripeness. Some Chablis-lovers say that their favourite wine loses some character in warm years. Others respond that the piercing acidity that marks poor-vintage Chablis is no loss.

OTHER WHITE BURGUNDIES

Chablis is clear-cut, in hierarchy and geography. The other, wider (i.e. non-Côte d'Or) Burgundies lack its brilliant precision, of both taste and nomenclature. Here are a few clues to the maze:

Pouilly-Fuissé The most famous 'other' white Burgundy has been a staple of restaurant wine-lists for a generation – perhaps because it is easy to remember and say. Once again limestone is the clue to this wine, which comes from the hilly vineyards around Pouilly and its neighbours: look too for **Pouilly-Loché** and **Pouilly-Vinzelles**. All three names spell wines that are softer and richer than Chablis, though the best of them have a nervous energy to balance the intense fruit.

Pouilly and its neighbours stand out from the wider **Mâconnais** crowd, though there are some enjoyable wines to be had from the **Viré-Clessé** district of the Mâconnais, where the limestone surfaces again.

Montagny and **Rully** are the main white-wine villages in the **Côte Chalonnaise**, a tract south of the Côte de Beaune. Search here for good-value wines that, at their best, are junior versions of their northern neighbours.

Chardonnay around France and Europe

Given that white Burgundy is expensive and prestigious and scarce, it would be a foolish vigneron who did not at least try to grow Chardonnay anywhere a vine will fit. French wine laws restrict its use in many appellation areas, but the more relaxed junior IGP wine-rules allow it in the **Languedoc**, where some interesting wines are made, and it thrives at Limoux beneath the Pyrenees. It is also grown in the **Jura**.

The other great French Chardonnay area, though many people do not realise it, is **Champagne**: the grape is a key component of the finest fizz, along with Pinot Noir.

It is hard to think of a European wine-growing country that has no Chardonnay. Even **England** has flourishing plantations, their fruit destined for the new wave of quality sparkling wines.

Much of this Euro-Chardonnay is uninspired, but look for interesting bottles from:

- **Northern Spain**, especially **Navarra**, and in a few top Cava sparklers
- **Austria**, especially **Styria** (Steirmark on the label)
- **Northern Italy**, especially **Lombardy** and **Piedmont**.

WINESPEAK: WHAT IS MINERALITY?

Minerality is a much-debated term: it refers to a kind of appetising, stony, flinty character which appears on certain wines. It's something one looks for in classic Burgundian Chardonnays. Some say that you can only notice it in whites; others find it in reds too. Wine experts continually debate this flavour and how it gets into wine. Does it come from the terroir, a lack of ripeness in the grapes, the winemaking methods or something else completely? There is no conclusive evidence.

KEY REGION:

The USA

Chardonnay the ubiquitous is as much at home in California as in Chablis. America does not make Chablis, of course – though the French had a long fight to stop California growers using the name. That said, emulation was a major force in the rise of Californian wine. Winemakers tasted the classics from Burgundy – and set out to make something as good, if not better. In 1976 the French wine world was rocked by the results of a blind tasting ('The Judgment of Paris') when several California Chardonnays outshone illustrious white Burgundies.

The period of emulation (and sometimes imitation) is past. California, and increasingly Oregon, yield Chardonnays that can be as subtle and challenging as anything from the Côte d'Or. But today, the wines are speaking their own language, not French.

CALIFORNIA'S TOP CHARDONNAYS

Soil is not what matters most in California: it is location, and the temperature of that location. See page 141 for how this works.

This means that many zones, most of them in the cooler Coastal belt, contribute fine Chardonnays:

- Mendocino's **Anderson Valley**
- **Russian River** and **Alexander River** in Sonoma County — a county where Chardonnay is the top grape
- **Carneros**, where cool air from San Francisco Bay moderates the climate
- **Napa Valley**, California's best-known wine area
- **Monterey** County's hillside vineyards
- Noted single-vineyard wines **Chalone** (near Monterey) and **Ridge Monte Bello** (Santa Cruz Mountains) are both on limestone
- Santa Barbara in the far south, within sight of Los Angeles — especially **Santa Maria Valley** and **Santa Rita**.

PACIFIC NORTHWEST

The quality and consistency of Oregon Pinot Noir and Chardonnay remind many of Burgundy. Look for wines from the various sub-zones of the **Willamette Valley**.

Washington State's **Columbia Gorge** is also promising Chardonnay country.

KEY REGION:

Australia

Australia followed a similar path, though its wines are much more in evidence on the world market (California, broadly, drinks what it grows, with a little help from the rest of the USA).

Australian Chardonnay has long ago buried the cliché of over-oaked fruit bombs: there are today wines in all styles, from a range of wine zones so broad that it's unwise to generalise about Australian wine at all.

The finest Australian wines are about special places and people, not brands and blends. Grape-growers and winemakers are searching out the best spots to plant fruit – for white-wine grapes, in a continent where 'it's too hot' is too often the complaint, the coolest spots. Match the right places and the most talented people, apply modern techniques, and some fascinating wines emerge. See the list, right, for some pointers.

AUSTRALIA'S WHITE-WINE REGIONS

Places that have made names for specific styles include:

Adelaide Hills (SA): Chardonnay
Barossa (SA): Chardonnay, Rhône varieties, Semillon
Clare Valley (SA): Riesling
Cowra (NSW): Sauvignon Blanc/Semillon
Eden Valley (SA): Riesling
Geelong (Vict): Chardonnay
Hunter (NSW): Semillon
Margaret River (WA): Sauvignon Blanc/Semillon, Chardonnay, Riesling, Sauvignon Blanc
Mornington Peninsula (Vict): Chardonnay
Mudgee (NSW): Chardonnay
Tasmania: sparkling wine from Chardonnay blended with Pinot Noir
Yarra Valley (Vict): Chardonnay

State names:
NSW – New South Wales
SA – South Australia
Vict – Victoria
WA – Western Australia

Left: The creation of fine New World Chardonnay depends upon cooling during fermentation. Stainless steel is the key material.

FASHIONS IN OAK

Oak casks and barrels are not just attractively folklorique containers. The wood contributes much more to a wine that is fermented, aged and stored in it. Today this short word carries a lot of meaning, as Simon Field MW explains.

After the amphorae and the animal skins and before the stainless steel, wood was ubiquitous in the making, maturation and transportation of wine.

Oak, supple yet water-tight, has remained the tree of choice for making vats and barrels – and its popularity at the fine-wine end of the spectrum has never been greater.

If imitation flatters, then the popularity of adding oak staves or oak chips to get the oak-barrel effect underlines the ubiquitous taste for wood-aged wine – and recognition of its relative expense. Nothing evokes the winemaker's art more than row upon row of expensive François Frères barriques, and nothing can scupper a vigneron's reputation (and bank balance) more than

---

Red wines are the ones that benefit from oak-ageing, maturing slowly in wood thanks to the tiny amounts of air the barrels let in: think the best Bordeauxs, Burgundies, Riojas, Barolos.... But there are also some top whites that are fermented and matured in oak: serious white Burgundies, a few traditional Champagnes — and their counterparts in the New World.

---

an unsuccessful adventure into the complex arena of wood treatment.

Why complex? There are a number of factors one has to consider if one wishes to age wines in wood, and a number of others if one also wishes to ferment the grape-juice in the same way. Oak, be it the American Quercus Alba or the European Quercus Robur, will enable the alchemistic and apparently contradictory chemical process known by the abbreviation of 'redox', whereby the liquid is both oxidised by the marginal intervention of air through the wood and protected ('reduced') by the interaction between yeasts and/or phenols in the finished wine.

Complexity is the aim – but it should be measured complexity, and not one which detracts from the inherent personality of a wine. Hence the huge importance that winemakers place on species of oak, and of how the oak is treated once the tree is felled. To summarise that American oak is loose-knit and lends rich creamy vanillin notes, as opposed to the tighter, spicier French-oaked wines, simplifies the discussion, but underlines the significance of the nature and extent of the intervention.

How the wood is sawn, dried and toasted are all variables which exercise the cooper and influence the wine; a wine's house-style is seldom more assured, indeed, than where there is an in-house cooperage. When I visit Vega Sicilia and López de Heredia in Spain this is a key part of the itinerary; it would, of course, be impossible to countenance the former's Unico made using American oak, or the latter's Tondonia with French.

This underlines the extent to which the medium really is the message, and explains the great ongoing fascination with the minutiae of the process. Tronçais or Allier oak, Hungarian or Russian, medium or low toast? There is plenty of choice.... Related to these questions are the murky scientific details of lactones, terpenes, aldehydes and many varied phenols inherent to the different oaks, all of which have a direct and significant influence on the style of the wine. And the selected oak framework of the wine must, most fundamentally, enhance the taste, and in no way undermine the sense of terroir to which all great wines aspire. Oak is of little use if it does not achieve both of these aims.

Right: Expensive new oak casks stand ready in an ancient Burgundian cellar.

MALOLACTIC FERMENTATION

After the yeasts convert the sugar in grape juice into alcohol (see fermentation note, page 29) there is the opportunity for another process — the malolactic fermentation. This time bacteria convert malic acid (the sharp-tasting acid of green apples, also present in grapes) into lactic acid (the acid of milk — smoother, softer). This takes place in all red wines, but in many whites it is suppressed in order to retain the wines' zingy freshness.

Chardonnay is one of the few exceptions where malolactic is frequently allowed to happen — this is partly what contributes to Chardonnay's smoothness. Also, some strains of bacteria produce a buttery-tasting substance, diacetyl, as a by-product, which is why we describe many Chardonnays as 'buttery'.

LEES

The 'lees' are the sediment left over after fermentation. This is made up of spent yeast cells and other matter, such as tiny bits of grape skins. Some winemakers choose to leave this sediment in contact with the wine as it ages in barrel or tank, as it helps protect against oxygen.

Another option is to stir the lees in the tank or barrel at various points during maturation; this will cause the spent yeast cells to release substances into the wine. Look out for subtle biscuity flavours and richness of texture. This technique is popular with Chardonnay.

CHARDONNAY, CHAMPAGNE & SPARKLING WINE

Chardonnay is one of the key grapes in Champagne, and the vine is grown around the world wherever winemakers aspire to make great sparkling wine. Simon Field MW explains.

Sparkling wine represents about ten per cent of all wine – and about one bottle of sparkling wine in ten is Champagne. The generic term 'sparkling' covers a gamut of techniques, from the somewhat perfunctory injection of carbon dioxide into wines made in a pressurised tank, all the way up to the appropriately grand-sounding Méthode Champenoise, which involves a second fermentation in bottle and the maturation of the resulting fizzy wine on its dying yeasts.

The decomposition of the yeast is called autolysis, and involves a poetic transmigration of flavour and a development of complexity which (or so the Champenois would have us believe) cannot be replicated elsewhere, such is the unique combination of its components, with soils, grape varieties and the marginal climate of this northerly French region all playing their part.

The key grape varieties of Champagne are Chardonnay and Pinot Noir – the

Burgundian stalwarts in other words; but here, a little further north, they are transformed by yeast-ageing into the greatest sparkling wines in the world.

Strictly defined Appellation laws – allied to unparalleled marketing nous – have allowed Champagne to command a premium over all pretenders, including Cava, Sekt and the currently fashionable Prosecco. But when one considers that it takes 1.5 kilos of grapes to make a bottle of Champagne and that the current price for a kilo of grapes is €6.50 and above, it becomes clear that the clever deal between those who grow the grapes (a.k.a. Récoltants Manipulants) and those who buy them and then sell and market them (Négociants Manipulants) has helped to uphold a mutually beneficial hegemony. Especially beneficial for those, such as the mighty LVMH, who have their feet in both camps.

The 'ancien régime' is being challenged around the world, however – as indeed should be the case – and this includes a more than promising threat from the vineyards of Southern England.

Left: Deep cellars cut out of the chalk bedrock provide perfect temperatures for the ageing of Champagne.

Sémillon

KEY POINTS

- White grape
- Not hugely aromatic
- Lower acidity than Sauvignon Blanc
- Thin skins
- Large berries
- Affected easily by noble rot
- Sweet and dry styles
- Can be influenced by oak

KEY REGIONS

Sauternes, Graves, Australia, South Africa

A big-berried grape with a thin skin, making wine moderate in acidity and deep in colour. It's a speciality of Bordeaux, where it is the core of sweet wines like Sauternes. It can also be made in a dry style – in France as well as the New World. Both variations age well in oak, and can age in bottle.

In Bordeaux's Graves district, especially in its Pessac-Léognan heartland, Sémillon is blended with Sauvignon Blanc to make characterful dry wines that are useful partners to classic cuisine.

Sémillon is affected easily by 'noble rot' (pourriture noble/botrytis cinerea: see page 62), which adds wonderful butterscotch, honey, marmalade and marzipan notes to its flavours. Noble rot-affected grapes are made into the great, naturally sweet, wines of Sauternes (the most famous, and expensive, is Château d'Yquem).

Australia specialises in making dry wine from Sémillon, either on its own or blended with Chardonnay. Look out for the very special Hunter Valley style which is picked early, is low in alcohol, high in acidity and not aged in oak – but which takes on some oak-like characteristics with bottle-age.

AROMA & FLAVOUR

Less pronounced in acidity, full and rich in flavour, both sweet and dry Sémillons need maturity to gain balance. Dry ones, especially when young, have citrus-fruit flavours. As they age, they gain a nutty richness. Sweet wines offer marzipan, apricot and – if noble rot is present – honey/raisin notes.

When you try these wines, look out for:

- richness, waxiness on the palate
- lime/lemon notes in young dry wines
- raisin/dried apricot/honey notes in top sweet wines

Would you agree that these wines:

- have a certain richness and citrus flavours?

Maturity

Sémillon, whether made to be dry or sweet, ages well in new oak, and both styles can gain considerably with bottle-age. Age brings balance. Quality dry wines from Bordeaux and Australia can improve for a decade and last for two; sweet Sauternes from fine vintages can age indefinitely.

KEY AROMAS & FLAVOURS

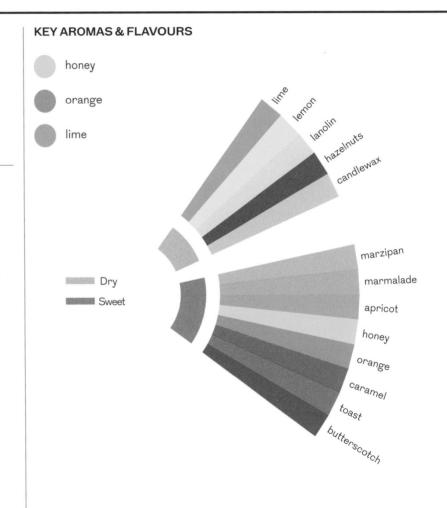

honey

orange

lime

Dry
Sweet

lime
lemon
lanolin
hazelnuts
candlewax

marzipan
marmalade
apricot
honey
orange
caramel
toast
butterscotch

BALANCE

THE CHARACTER
OF THE WINE
IN YOUR GLASS

Sémillon wines, dry or sweet, are comparatively low in acidity and alcohol. Fruit ripeness is there, but ripeness is perhaps the wrong term: it is richness, and a waxy, textured character even in dry wines, that tasters often comment on.

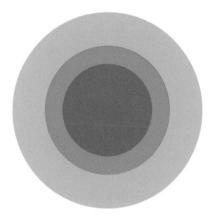

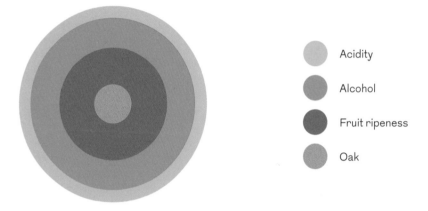

Acidity

Alcohol

Fruit ripeness

Oak

DRY

Hunter Valley, Australia

Balance and concentration,
with more acidity/lower alcohol than
most Sémillons, from early picking
and low yields

SWEET

Sauternes

The great sweet wine: more ripeness/
richness, including noble rot flavours
— but still with balancing acidity,
which prevents it from being cloying

Food matches

Dry styles work with many mildly-flavoured dishes; avoid strong flavours as the wine usually lacks acidity – though some Hunter Sémillons are exceptions. It is a fun lunch wine: dry Sémillon can go with aromatic salads. Sweet styles, too, are suprisingly versatile with food: as well as the obvious match with desserts, try them with rich pâté or powerful blue cheeses. Sauternes also works well with salty foods, and therefore can be good as an apéritif with, say, salted nuts.

Some Sémillon-friendly foods:

- Thai dishes
- Roast chicken
- Foie gras
- Roquefort and other blue cheeses
- Apricot tart

KEY REGION:

Sauternes, Bordeaux

One place – and the honeyed, subtle, long-lived sweet wine that comes from it – exemplifies Sémillon: Sauternes.

Sauternes the place lies at the southern edge of the great Bordeaux vineyards. Sauternes the wine is one of the world's greatest sweet wines – yet irresistibly appetising. Look out: those who find it tend to fall in love....

The way Sauternes is made is pretty odd, with the careful use of grapes that most winemakers would throw away. Sauternes is the world's best place for 'noble rot'.

NOBLE ROT

The French call it 'pourriture noble'. The grapes ripen and – in humid, warm, misty autumns – develop a form of fungus (botrytis cinerea) on their skins. As the Sémillon grape has a thin skin, the fungus punctures it. Result: the water in the grape evaporates, the flavour and sugars remain, and become highly concentrated. Pick and press these grapes – carefully – and the wine estate can make intensely sweet, honey-flavoured wine with balancing acidity and tremendous depth. Experienced tasters can spot the rot – extra subtlety of flavour, extra intensity. Needless to say, not all rot is noble: the grey, furry sort (which is much more common) just ruins grapes.

Noble rot happens in many places: it was first exploited in the Rhine vineyards. But Sauternes has probably the most perfect environment for its growth.

In some years, Sauternes sees no noble rot, and the châteaux make straightforward sweet wine. In noble-rot years, Sauternes deploys its second secret: selective picking. The most perfectionist estates – led by the famous Château d'Yquem – send their highly-skilled pickers through the vineyard time after time, plucking only the 'grains rôtis' – the individual shrivelled grapes, one by one. Some years, this involves five or six passes. One year, Yquem clocked up eleven – and despite this, the wine was not reckoned good enough for the château's label.

This of course costs a fortune. Add the cost of oak casks for fermentation, and the loss of revenue in years when the noble rot fails, and the burdens on the château bank-account can become crippling. So ask not why top Sauternes is expensive, but why it is so reasonable... it can in truth be cheaper than wines far less costly to make and far more predictable in their yield.

Luckily, modern Sauternes comes in more everyday guises as well as the top wines, and these can be splendid value for such unusual, adaptable bottles (or halves: enough for four).

Ch d'Yquem   First-growth château

————   Border of AOC Barsac

————   Border of AOC Sauternes

SAUTERNES

Why is Sauternes a place blessed by noble rot? The big river to the north of Sauternes, the Garonne, is tidal here and the water is relatively warm — see map above.

Into the Garonne flows the little River Ciron: this, arising from springs in the Landes forests, is cold. Cool water meets warm and mist forms, usually overnight and lasting into the day, until the sun burns through around noon. This alternation of morning mist and afternoon sun helps the botrytis to develop.

Above: Pickers in Sauternes need to be more than usually skilful: in noble-rot years, they have to select individual grapes.

BARSAC

Barsac, a sub-section of Sauternes, is the other name to look out for. The rules allow the wines of Barsac to use either Sauternes or Barsac on the label. Some find Barsac wines lighter in style, greener, with more acidity — but in truth styles vary far more between the individual châteaux and vintages.

OTHER SWEET WINES FROM SÉMILLON

- **Loupiac** and **St-Croix-du-Mont**, near Sauternes, offers lesser wines in the same style.
- **Monbazillac**, off to the east, is another enclave of noble-rot sweet wines from Sémillon (blended with Muscadelle).

Semillon worldwide*

Outside France, Semillon is known for dry wines rather than sweet. **South Africa** is making strides with Semillon, sometimes blended with Chardonnay or – more conventionally – Sauvignon Blanc to make wines with a Bordeaux-like density and structure.

Australia is the main outpost of the grape in the New World. The Hunter Valley (New South Wales) is a traditional source of complex, long-lived dry wines. The Barossa (South Australia) rivals the Hunter as a treasure-chest of old-vine Semillon: these wines can last 20 years.

Blends with Sauvignon offer a more modern, zingy style: look for these from Margaret River (Western Australia), from South Australia's Murray zone, and again from the Hunter Valley. In Australia generally, Semillon has lost ground to the ubiquitous Chardonnay and to more vogueish varieties such as the Rhône whites and Riesling – as well as Sauvignon Blanc.

The occasional bottle of fine Semillon also surfaces from **Chile**.

* The New World, by and large, does not use the accent on Semillon

WHAT IS 'SWEET?'

Don't let fashion deny you the pleasures of sweet wines, advises Barbara Drew.

A sweet wine is one which has some sugar in it. It can be a sweet component added after the fermentation is complete; but, more usually, it is natural grape sugars left in the wine by keeping in some unfermented juice.

But there are also wines often described as sweet which actually have no sugar in them: it has all been converted to alcohol by the fermentation.

Left: Grapes in Sauternes with the beginnings of noble rot.

The apparent sweetness of such wines is entirely due to the ripeness of the grapes. Think of a peach; a ripe peach is fruity, aromatic – and much sweeter than a green, unripe one. The link is so solid that our brains automatically associate ripe, fruity aromas and flavours with sweetness. In truth, we are not smelling sugar, we can only smell ripeness; but we automatically link the two, describing wines from warmer climates with soft, ripe-fruit flavours as 'sweeter' than their cool-climate counterparts.

The same fooling of our taste-buds works the other way about, too. There are many wines which are described as dry that may in fact have some sugar in them. Many Rieslings – a grape with very high acidity – have sugar left in them by the winemaker to balance that acidity and soften the wine. Often, everyday New World wines will have a little sweetness added to make the wine more appealing; as it is only a small amount, the overall effect is one of a 'dry' wine. (This difference between perception and reality is what our 'Balance' pages demonstrate.)

Truly sweet wines have been around for centuries; indeed sugar is a great preserver and some of the longest-lived wines in the world are sweet; think of the glorious Sauternes, Cotnari and Tokaji. However, more everyday sweet wines are not especially fashionable these days, often seen as 'low-brow', or associated with hybrid wine styles such as 'white' Zinfandel. And German mass-produced wines of the previous generation, like Liebfraumilch, gained sweet wines a reputation for poor quality that is being slow to dissipate.

Don't deny yourself these pleasures, though. Sweet wines are very versatile; they are excellent with desserts, but also contrast beautifully with a whole range of savoury foods – try them with terrines, cold meats, strong cheeses…. Medium-sweet wines, meanwhile, are classic matches for spicier dishes, such as those of Asian or Persian cuisines.

SWEET WINES TO TRY

It is not always easy to tell whether a wine will be sweet or not, though some bottles have scales on the label to indicate the level of sweetness. For guidance on German wines, see pages 110-11. Other good sources of sweet wines discussed in this Course are the Loire (Chenin Blanc, pages 123-127), Alsace (Riesling and Gewürztraminer, pages 118-9) and Austria.

TASTING NOTES
Record your own impressions

Prompts: you are looking out for

Sauvignon Blanc: Aromatic, zesty, mouth-watering

Chardonnay: Smooth, range of aromas/flavours (green fruit or tropical fruit, maybe vanilla/toast)

Sémillon: A waxy richness, lime in young dry wines, raisin/dried apricot/honey in sweet wines

SAUVIGNON BLANC

1 _____

_____

2 _____

_____

CHARDONNAY

3 _____

_____

4 _____

_____

SEMILLON

5 _____

_____

6 _____

_____

BLIND TASTING

7 _____

_____

8 _____

_____

9 _____

_____

10 _____

_____

TIP

Your first thoughts are the best —
your second thoughts are
usually what you think you **ought**
to be tasting!

QUESTIONS

In Session 2 we have looked at three grape varieties: Sauvignon Blanc, Chardonnay and Sémillon:

1. Which variety makes Pouilly-Fuissé and where does this wine come from?

2. Which variety makes Pouilly-Fumé and where does this wine come from?

3. What is the name of the 'good' rot on grapes which is useful in making sweet wine?

4. Which of the three grape varieties is the most aromatic?

Which variety might have aromas often described as:

5. – butter, cream, vanilla?

6. – marmalade, honey, apricot and marzipan?

7. – cat's pee on a gooseberry bush?

8. – asparagus, grass, hay and flint?

9. Which one is often made into sweet wine?

10. Which two out of the three varieties are often blended together?

Name the grape variety beside each description, and if possible the area it might be from:

11. – high acidity, moderate fruit ripeness with aromas of green apple, grass, flint/minerals and moderate alcohol

12. – high acidity, intense fruit ripeness and very intense aromas of cat's pee, gooseberry and passion fruit

13. – moderate acidity, high alcohol, intense fruit ripeness with aromas of tropical fruit, toast and vanilla, full-bodied and smooth

14. – high acidity, moderate fruit ripeness and moderate alcohol, smooth texture with no toast or vanilla and aromas of lemon, green apple and minerals

15. – high acidity, quite low alcohol, dry with notes of lime and candlewax

16. – sweet with rich texture and notes of honey, apricot and marzipan as well as balancing acidity

Answers on page 221

Right: Harvesting in the Loire Valley.

Overleaf: Vineyards shrouded against birds add surprising textures to a New World landscape.

3

Three red grapes that make red Bordeaux and have spread around the world

CABERNET FRANC
MERLOT
CABERNET SAUVIGNON

*These three grapes live together as well as apart: a successful ménage à trois.
Combined in various proportions, they form the 'Bordeaux blend' that is the recipe
not just for red Bordeaux itself – Claret – but for wines from as far apart
as Chile and Western Australia.*

CABERNET FRANC
perfumed

On its own in the Loire, and blended in Bordeaux, it has perfume and finesse

MERLOT
hedonistic

Ripe, rich and full on its own, it brings the fruit to complement Cabernet Sauvignon's structure in blends

CABERNET SAUVIGNON
structured

Tannic and dark, with fruit flavours in youth and complexity with age

Where the grapes grow

These red grapes thrive in a narrower range of temperatures, and thus latitudes, than the whites in Session 2. Cabernet Sauvignon ripens later than the whites, and thus has a longer growing season. Cabernet Franc ripens earlier than its Cabernet cousin, and Merlot earlier still.

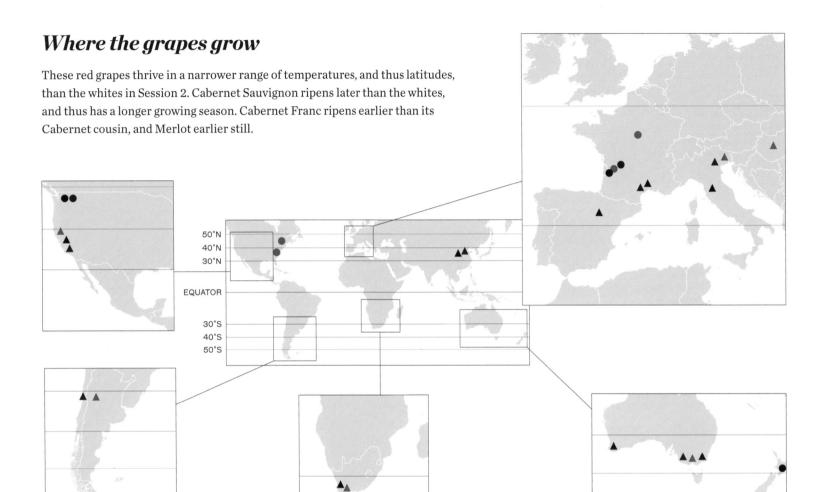

CABERNET FRANC

● **Cooler climate**
  Central Loire
  Bordeaux
  Virginia
  Canada

▲ **Warmer climate**
  Southern France
  Italy
  Hungary
  California
  Argentina
  Australia
  South Africa

MERLOT

● **Cooler climate**
  Bordeaux
  Washington

▲ **Warmer climate**
  Southern France
  Italy
  California
  Chile
  Australia
  China

CABERNET SAUVIGNON

● **Cooler climate**
  Bordeaux
  New Zealand
  Washington

▲ **Warmer climate**
  Southern France
  Italy
  Spain
  Bulgaria
  California
  South Africa
  Australia
  China

Cabernet Franc

KEY POINTS

- Red grape
- Aromatic
- High acidity
- Likes a cool climate
- Thickish skins
- Medium tannins
- Blended in Bordeaux
- Unblended in the Loire: light, crisp, early-drinking

KEY REGIONS

Bordeaux, Loire, Australia, Chile, California

Cabernet Franc makes wine that is fragrant, refreshing and appetising. A cool-climate grape, it is at home in the Loire and Bordeaux.

Alone, Cabernet Franc makes Loire wines such as Bourgueil, Saumur-Champigny and Chinon. These Loire vineyards lie at 47 degrees north, so it takes a warm year to make long-lived, structured wines: most vintages are at their best drunk young – and cool. These are the customary wines of the Paris bistros. Still in France, look out for riper, softer Cabernet Franc wines from the Languedoc, in the warmer south.

It is a key, if minor, player in the 'Bordeaux blend', added to the dominant Cabernet Sauvignon and Merlot. As such it has been planted around the world wherever winemakers hope to emulate and surpass the Bordeaux prototype.

Cabernet Franc has higher acidity than its Cabernet Sauvignon cousin, though it is less tannic. It ripens earlier, and in Bordeaux is usually used as a counterpoint to Left Bank (Médoc and Graves) Cabernet Sauvignon, adding perfume and delicacy, but rarely rising above 15 per cent in a blend.

It plays an increasingly important role on Bordeaux's Right Bank, performing the same role with Merlot but as an equal partner at some of the very top châteaux, most famously at Cheval Blanc and Ausone in St-Emilion.

In fact Cabernet Franc was St-Emilion's most important quality grape variety before the devastating frosts of 1956. Replanting with Merlot became an economic necessity, providing generous and more reliable quantities for the then-impoverished vignerons.

Wine suggestions for this session, page 216

AROMA & FLAVOUR

When tasted unblended, Cabernet Franc's perfumed, crunchy fruit, brisk acidity and tannin come to the fore. It contributes the same attributes to Bordeaux blends.

When you try these wines, look out for:

- high acidity
- medium but grippy tannins
- medium body
- crunchy red fruit aromas and flavours

Would you agree that these wines are:

- the antithesis of typical, everyday, soft red wines — higher in acidity and tannins?

Maturity

Traditionally, Loire Cabernet Franc wines only age well in warm years. This is less the rule today, as new techniques in the vineyard help to improve ripeness, and winemaking techniques extract more tannin.

A good Chinon or Bourgueil can age 5-7 years, when it will have plum and herbal notes and show a touch of savoury complexity. Top wines – top producers, best vintages – can age 20 years.

KEY AROMAS & FLAVOURS

- raspberry
- tobacco
- grass

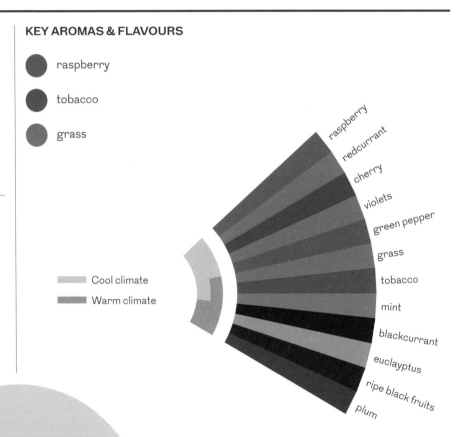

Cool climate
Warm climate

raspberry
redcurrant
cherry
violets
green pepper
grass
tobacco
mint
blackcurrant
euclayptus
ripe black fruits
plum

TOP TIP

Keep your Loire Cabernet Franc wines from good, ripe vintages: in a few years, you'd have something special for a modest outlay.

BALANCE

THE CHARACTER
OF THE WINE
IN YOUR GLASS

When grown in a cool-climate zone such as the Loire Valley, Cabernet Franc has high acidity and noticeable tannins, balanced by fruit. Warmer zones mean higher alcohol, riper fruit, moderate acidity and smoother tannins.

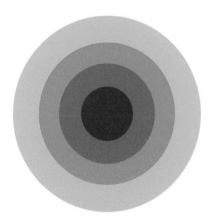

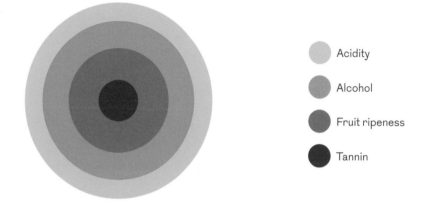

Acidity

Alcohol

Fruit ripeness

Tannin

COOL CLIMATE

Chinon, Loire

Brisk, refreshing acidity is the most prominent factor

WARM CLIMATE

Argentina

Riper fruit and alcohol spell a softer wine

Food matches

Young wines show fruit and moderate alcohol: they make refreshing apéritifs or partners to simple, lighter, not heavily sauced, foods. More serious, mature wines will match classic French country dishes: because of their tannins and fruit balance, these are good food wines.

Some Cabernet Franc-friendly foods:

- River fish
- Pork dishes
- Rabbit
- Cold meats
- Salads

KEY REGION:

The Central Loire

KEY REGION:

Bordeaux

Follow the river west from the Sauvignon Blanc vineyards around Sancerre and Pouilly, and you come to Tours, an ancient city and capital of the main red-wine zone of the Loire (see map page 42). Cabernet Franc is the most important grape here, and around Saumur in the neighbouring Anjou region.

In Touraine and Anjou, the wines are named after districts rather than villages. **Bourgueil** is generally thought the best, with **St-Nicholas-de-Bourgueil** and **Chinon** in the next rank, followed by the wide zone of **Saumur** and (slightly superior) **Saumur-Champigny**.

Once again, limestone subsoil is important: much of Bourgueil is on tuffeaux, the local name for the deep beds of limestone, though good wine is also made on the river-bed gravels. Cabernet Franc thrives here, because it ripens early and the Touraine vineyards are well to the north – even by autoroute, it is a three-hours-plus drive (335km) south across virtually vine-free country until you reach the Bordeaux winelands, where Cabernet Franc plays a minor but useful part.

Cabernet Franc may ripen early, but in many of the vintages from the 1960s to the 1980s it failed to ripen properly or at all, and the red wines of the Loire faced decline. There has been a turnaround in weather patterns, allied to greater sophistication in winemaking, and the last three decades have seen a far greater proportion of successful years. Indeed, 1990 was a standout vintage that set the tone for the next 25 years.

There are few grand wine estates in the Touraine country: the best wines come from small-scale family concerns – and not all the best are in the most prestigious appellations. Those who come to love this unusual but delicious style of red wine learn to follow the fortunes of vintages (still variable) and growers (some rise, some fall). You will have competition: much wine is sold direct to Parisians.

Of the three grapes that make red Bordeaux, Cabernet Franc has the lowest profile. It is rare for a Bordeaux estate to be driven by Cabernet Franc, but one star château, Cheval Blanc in **St-Emilion**, gives it the prime role in the blend in certain years. Vieux Château Certan in Pomerol has 30 per cent of this variety in its vineyard. Yet without Cabernet Franc, many a Claret would be leaner, less interesting – and in some vintages, in rather shorter supply.

We talk about the way Bordeaux blends its palette of three red grapes overleaf. In most Right Bank districts, Cabernet Franc is blended with the predominant Merlot. Over the river in the **Médoc** and **Graves**, the grape does double-duty: as an insurance against possible poor ripening of Merlot and Cabernet Sauvignon, and as a bringer of bouquet and delicacy. These Left Bank vineyards may have up to 15 per cent Cabernet Franc, though some estates have none at all.

SCIENCE SOUNDBITE: pH AND PURPLE PIGMENTS

Cabernet Franc makes wines which generally have a low pH (i.e. high acidity) — especially so in the Loire Valley. At lower pHs, the blue-purple hues of a wine's colour pigments are preserved, accounting for the vibrant youthful-looking colour of many Loire reds.

Cabernet Franc worldwide

Above: Cabernet Franc flourishes high in a valley near Stellenbosch, South Africa.

Ambitious winemakers who want to market a 'Bordeaux blend' have planted Cabernet Franc, alongside Cabernet Sauvignon and Merlot, in places from **Tuscany** to **Chile** via **California** and **Argentina**. Its presence in blends will only be apparent through a careful look at the back-label, if at all.

As a majority or sole partner, it is grown in northern and central **Italy** (Friuli is one place to look for it), in **Hungary** and in **South Africa**.

Back in France, Cabernet Franc wines can be found from St-Chinian (limestone again...) in **Languedoc-Roussillon**.

Just as in its Loire heartland, Cabernet Franc does well in cool places where most red-wine grapes struggle to ripen. Thus it crops up on wine lists in the **USA**'s East Coast, in **Canada** and in **China**.

It shows promise in **New Zealand**, is making rapid strides in **Argentina**, and is quite widespread in **Australia**.

CLARET
The term came originally from the French 'Clairet' — a dark rosé wine still produced today. The English borrowed the word and changed it to Claret, which refers not to rosé but to any red wine made in Bordeaux.

BLENDING GRAPE VARIETIES

In recent decades the wine world went mad for 'varietals': wines made from a single grape variety. But many of the classic wines marry varieties to produce wines far greater than the sum of their parts, as Martin Hudson MW explains.

The Bordeaux wine region, stretching inland from France's western, Atlantic, coast, is famous for red wines made from a blend of grape varieties – unlike, for example, Burgundy and the Northern Rhône. Arguably the Bordelais have made a virtue of a necessity thrust upon them by the variable maritime climate and soils of their region.

The grape varieties that constitute Claret – Merlot, Cabernet Franc and Cabernet Sauvignon – become ripe in that order, so each can potentially see different weather at harvest time. The difference in ripening time can mean that Merlot is harvested in ideal sunny conditions while Cabernet Sauvignon is picked in the rain – or vice versa; so having a blend of grapes can act as an insurance against the downpours which frequently bedevil the region in September and October.

Then, too, the grapes will thrive in different soils, Merlot tolerating cooler, wetter clay ground than the Cabernets, which need free-draining gravel or sandy soils – hence the dominance of Merlot on the Right Bank and Cabernet Sauvignon on the Left.

Are there other advantages to making a blended wine? The difference in ripening times of the grapes certainly makes life easier for picking teams; also for staggering the use of grape reception equipment, including sorting tables and crusher/destemmers, at the winery.

This timing difference means that the grape varieties have to be vinified separately, so that the final blend can be created after the wines have completed both fermentation and their maturation. This allows a much greater control over the quality of the final blend, as any parcels that do not seem up to the required quality for the 'grand vin' after maturation can be used in the second wine or sold off in bulk.

The other great advantage of blends is that inevitably they have additional layers of flavour and texture when compared with a single-variety wine. In Bordeaux this manifests itself in the range of aromas and flavours found in the wine, the balance that can be achieved between the acidity and tannin from the Cabernets and the generosity of the Merlot, and the generally restrained level of alcohol.

Blends can be much greater than the sum of their parts – but the grape varieties need to be carefully selected to complement, rather than clash, with each other.

BORDEAUX WHITES

In this cool-climate, Atlantic-influenced region, white wines, too, are often blended. Even for dry white wines, it is by no means the rule that Sauvignon Blanc dominates: indeed, some of the most illustrious dry-white-wine châteaux habitually use more Sémillon than Sauvignon.

Both Sauvignon and Sémillon are vigorous vines, and can over-crop – yield a lot of grapes with little flavour – unless carefully managed. Sometimes, this management is forced on the vigneron by the weather, which is one reason why poor, cool vintages in Bordeaux that make unmemorable reds can produce good dry whites.

In the sweet-wine districts, Sémillon is the senior partner – though once again vintages can, and do, vary the recipe. At some Sauternes châteaux, Sémillon makes up 90 per cent or more of the blend. A third grape, Muscadelle, is a frequent minority contributor.

Right: Merlot grapes ripening in St-Emilion.

BLENDED WINES AROUND THE WORLD

Some of the most notable include:

Bordeaux blends Inspired by Bordeaux, many wine producers in California, Australia, New Zealand, South Africa, Argentina and Chile offer Cabernet Sauvignon/Cabernet Franc/Merlot blends.

GSM Southern Rhône-style reds made from Grenache, Syrah and Mourvèdre are dubbed 'GSM' in Australia, California and South Africa.

Superior fizz Champagne is usually a blend of Chardonnay, Pinot Noir and Pinot Meunier, and when ambitious winemakers around the world want to make a high-quality sparkler, they tend to plant at least the first two of the three.

Semillon/Sauvignon Blanc As in Bordeaux, these two white grapes are blended in places such as Australia and South Africa.

Marsanne/Rousanne These Southern Rhône white grapes are blended in their homeland, in the Languedoc and in Australia.

GRAPE OR PLACE ON THE LABEL?

Why does a typical French wine label not name the grape variety, like wines from Australia, the USA or Chile? Here we explain a little about the French wine laws.

The red wines from Chinon and Bourgueil are made from Cabernet Franc (see page 74) but they don't often say so: the names of the area and the grower are prominent. Today, the wine laws allow the label to name the grape as well. Until recently, it was actually forbidden for most Appellation d'Origine Contrôlée (AOC) wines, but it is still not common.

The reason for this is buried deep in the French wine laws. The whole point of the laws is to defend authenticity. The wine producer needs protection against fraudulent use of his or her identity. As everywhere, the law comes down hard on those who pretend their wine is someone else's – stealing the ID of, say, Château X.

In France (and nearly all wine countries have followed France down this road) the law goes further. It recognises that Bourgueil, for example, is a valuable name: wine from there is highly thought of, and the name on the label commands a higher price than wine from lesser villages. A wine from Bourgueil must, if it is to carry the coveted name, stick to the rules as laid down in the AOC regulations. This of course protects the consumer as well as the producer.

The main points the French rules cover are:

- **ORIGIN:** the grapes must be from a specific area
- **GRAPES:** each AOC sets out which varieties can be grown, and all others are forbidden
- **YIELD:** only so much wine can be made from each hectare of vines
- **VINTAGE:** 85 per cent of the wine must come from the year stated

Many AOC rules go further into details like pruning, picking dates and bottling. Some wine zones also taste and appraise wines. But the big four are those noted above.

AOC/AOP

These acronyms can get confusing...

AOP – Appellation d'Origine Protégée – is the updated term for AOC in the 2009 European Union wine law reforms. You'll see either AOP or AOC on the label.

IGP – Indication Géographique Protégée – replaces Vin de Pays.

See **Appendix II** for more on the wine rules in France and elsewhere in the EU.

So you can be pretty certain that a French wine with AOC/Appellation Contrôlée on the label is what it says it is. And that the grapes are grown, and the wine made, to an approved 'recipe'.

Broadly put, an AOC guarantees origin, not quality. The reputation of the producer is all-important: within the rules, there's wide scope for some winemakers to make splendid wine and others to turn out boring, indifferent bottles. Both will have the appellation on the label, but within every appellation some vineyards are better than others – and the bigger the wine zone the wider the variation.

The law sets the minimum standards: it does not – cannot – guarantee excellence. Finding that is down to you the consumer and your wine merchant.

Right: Here in Burgundy, the 33 Grands Crus are separate appellations, and dispense with the village name. The 635 Premiers Crus are defined within villages, and so both village and cru name goes on the label.

REMIERS & GRANDS CRUS

WHO MADE THE RULES?

The Italians, more particularly the Tuscans, say they thought of it first....
In 1716 the Duke of Tuscany made a law stating which villages Chianti could come from. The list of top vineyards in Tokaji, Hungary, dates from a royal decree of 1737. In Portugal, lawmakers set out the borders of the Port country in 1756. French wine districts began to define their zones at the end of the 19th century, and the French national AOC system dates from 1935.

...AND HOW TO GET ROUND THEM

Does authentic mean old-fashioned? Critics of the French (and other nations') quality-wine systems complain that the rules set wines in stone: you have to make your wine the way your grandfather did, and experiments with new grapes or techniques are forbidden.

In truth, there are ways for a free-thinking winemaker to sidestep the rules – for instance by 'demoting' their wines to the lesser, but freer, quality-level formerly known as Vins de Pays (in modern Euro-speak, Indication Géographique Protégée or IGP) and building a reputation unfettered by the terms of the local AOC.

ALSO TRY...

Malbec and Carmenère

Carmenère and Malbec are two grapes that have found more favour in their adopted South American homes than they currently enjoy in Bordeaux, whence they were exported. They were both useful, if secondary, grapes before the ravages of the phylloxera pest devastated the vineyards in the 19th century.

In Chile, Carmenère was at first mistaken for Merlot but now, correctly identified, its wines with their crunchy red and black fruit and spicy top-notes have become Chile's signature style, particularly from Maipo and Colchagua. It also masquerades as Cabernet Gernischt in China.

In Argentina, Malbec has found a home that enables it to mature fully without the risks of the astringent tannins often associated with its original home in Cahors. The limpid skies in Mendoza allow the wines to bring out the full damson-and-sloe fruit characteristic of this grape, and ripen the tannins that enable it to age gracefully. Its success there has caused a shift in attitude in its native France – the wines of Cahors are far more likely to say Malbec on the back label than the traditional name, Côt, although Côt is still used in that unlikely outpost for this grape, the Loire. Consumers' love affair with the grape has also caused a resurgence of planting in Bordeaux.

Left: Harvesting Malbec in Argentina.

Merlot

KEY POINTS

- Red grape
- Thin skins
- Soft, supple tannins
- Moderate to high alcohol
- Influenced by oak
- Blended in Bordeaux: softens wines

KEY REGIONS

Bordeaux, Languedoc, Italy, Chile, California, Washington

Merlot has become a byword for velvety texture, mouthfilling fruit and soft tannins. This reputation downplays its importance, both as a key part of the 'Bordeaux blend' and as a single-variety wine.

The variety is a mirror-image of its partner Cabernet Sauvignon. Merlot ripens early and yields large, thin-skinned grapes, whereas its partner does the opposite.

Merlot wine is typically low in tannin, and higher in alcohol than Cabernet Franc. High-quality Merlot can be aged in oak, though much simple wine is made to drink young.

In Bordeaux, Merlot dominates on the Right Bank, the country of Pomerol and St-Emilion. Pomerol is nearly all Merlot; at some estates it is 95 per cent.

Across the Gironde in the Médoc, top winemakers view Merlot as a minor player, though it is rare to find a serious château where there is none. Indeed, at the smaller, less prestigious estates it may predominate. Much of the everyday wine sold as Bordeaux and Bordeaux Supérieur is Merlot.

Elsewhere, Merlot on its own makes large amounts of soft, approachable wine around the world. In warm-climate zones, it has a tendency to become 'hot' and jammy.

Like Cabernet Franc, it is often grown to be blended with Cabernet Sauvignon in winelands from South Africa via Tuscany to California. Some of the most interesting 'straight' Merlots come from Chile and Washington State, and it is widespread in Spain, south-eastern Europe and in southern France.

AROMA & FLAVOUR

Soft, sweet, fruity flavours – damsons and chocolate – low tannins and moderate acidity make appealing wine at the simple level. Top Merlots, aged in oak, display a widening range of flavours, moving towards mushrooms and truffles. Merlot softens and fattens Bordeaux blends, balancing Cabernet Sauvignon's austerity.

When you try these wines, look out for:

- richness and smoothness
- warm alcohol
- mouthfilling plum fruit

Would you agree that these wines are:

- smoother, softer and richer than the Cabernet Franc wines?

Maturity

Most Merlots are designed to be drunk young; or, in the case of Right Bank Bordeaux, at 5-10 years depending upon the vintage and producer. A few classic Pomerols and St-Emilions can age for decades, and can gain unrivalled complexity and depth. Ageing capacity of New World Merlots depends upon the maker and the style they aim at: oak, once again, can make the difference (see Cabernet Sauvignon).

KEY AROMAS & FLAVOURS

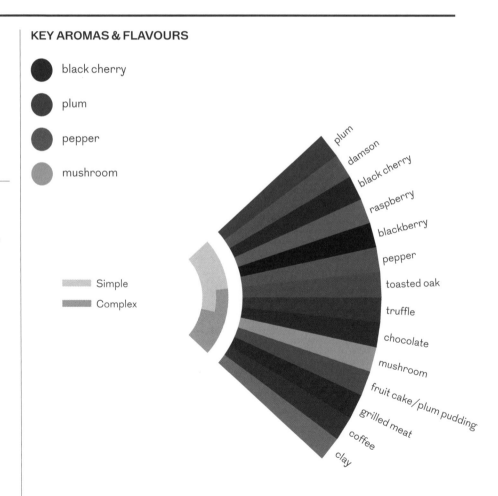

- black cherry
- plum
- pepper
- mushroom

Simple
Complex

plum
damson
black cherry
raspberry
blackberry
pepper
toasted oak
truffle
chocolate
mushroom
fruit cake/plum pudding
grilled meat
coffee
clay

BALANCE

THE CHARACTER
OF THE WINE
IN YOUR GLASS

Most Merlot made around the world is simple, and designed to be drunk young. Its key attributes are velvety texture and soft tannins. Acidity is low, fruit and alcohol are dominant. But it also makes serious, structured wines, such as those top Bordeaux Pomerols aged in new oak. These have more moderate levels of fruit, gain tannins from the oak and develop complex flavours from the mushroom end of the spectrum.

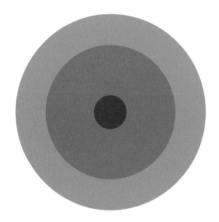

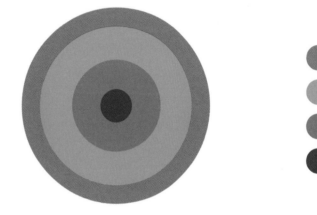

- Complexity
- Alcohol
- Fruit ripeness
- Tannins

SIMPLE
Chilean

Merlot wines are usually high in alcohol, which — with the fruit — conveys sweetness

SERIOUS
Pomerol

Typical Merlot fruit, tannins and alcohol are balanced by extra complexity

Food matches

Versatile, smooth and rich, Merlots are lower in acidity than Cabernet Sauvignon-based wines. These are soft, grapey, fruitier reds that partner grilled red meats rather than roasts, and cuisine that moves more towards the hearty and away from the elegant: think rich casseroles, sauces, meaty pasta dishes, dishes with a touch of sweetness about them. More mature, serious Merlots are good with with well-hung meats.

Some Merlot-friendly foods:

- Red meats
- Pork, duck, turkey
- Sauced dishes
- Mediterranean dishes
- Italian cuisine
- Gently-spiced food
- Chocolate

KEY REGION:

Right Bank Bordeaux

The wine-lands on the Right Bank of the broad Gironde estuary look to Libourne rather than Bordeaux as their capital, and have Merlot rather than Cabernet Sauvignon as their chief grape. Behind these simple facts is some venerable and tangled history, whose effects are still apparent today.

The Right Bank's big names are St-Emilion – by far the most productive district – and Pomerol. The prices and status of their top wines rival and sometimes exceed those of the Médoc, across the Gironde. One difference is in the size of the properties: St-Emilion is a country of modest farms, not expansive estates as in the Médoc. Compare the two top St-Emilion châteaux, Ch Ausone at just seven hectares and Ch Cheval-Blanc at 36, with their Pauillac (Left Bank) counterparts: Ch Latour has 65 hectares, Lafite 94ha, Mouton 79ha.

Pomerol's top properties are even smaller: Pétrus is a seventh the size of Lafite; Ch Le Pin is a mere two hectares, with a typical production of 600 12-bottle cases. Pomerol itself is a small place, its total area a sixth that of St-Emilion, and less than the smallest of the Médoc star communes, St-Julien.

These differences stem from history but have real results today: Right Bank wines are more diverse; the noted ones are harder to find because in shorter supply; there is a more rapid rise (and fall) in status as small wine estates emerge into fashion or, sometimes, fall from favour.

The Merlot basis of the Right Bank wines makes them richer, deeper, fleshier and sometimes easier to like than the Cabernet Sauvignon-dominated Médocs. In general, they mature more quickly – but there are important exceptions. The aim of the winemaker can matter here as much as the grape varieties grown, and in Pomerol and St-Emilion some châteaux aim for structure and tannin, and thus a long life. The Merlot

NOTE: ST-EMILION GRAND CRU

It is often thought that the term 'Grand Cru' is part of the St-Emilion classification; not so. Nor is it equal in status to the Grands Crus of Burgundy or Alsace. 'AOC St-Emilion Grand Cru' is simply another St-Emilion appellation, albeit one that covers the same area. The 600 or so châteaux that use the term on their labels just have to produce wines with 0.5 per cent more potential alcohol and a slightly lower yield than basic St-Emilion. It would be more helpful if the wines were referred to as 'St-Emilion Supérieur' rather than 'St-Emilion Grand Cru' (see facing page).

Left: The town of St-Emilion stands on a crest overlooking the wide vineyards of the Right Bank: the countryside here is considerably hillier than the Médoc and Graves districts of the Left Bank.

can mask these attributes in youth, but time will show that they are there.

Most Right Bank wines – from St-Emilion and its satellites (places that add St-Emilion to their names), from Fronsac and Canon-Fronsac, from the Côtes of Castillon and Francs – are designed to mature in three to five years. These are not 'investment' wines, but the enjoyable staples, stocking cellars across France and the wider world. However, the handful of top châteaux – a list recently augmented by fashionable 'garagiste' wines made in minuscule amounts by star winemakers and consultants – sell for prices as high as any in Bordeaux.

CLASSIFICATION

In the upper range, St-Emilion's wines are classified according to quality and (unlike in the Médoc, where the list is frozen at what was decided in 1855) the classification is regularly reappraised, wines are tasted, and châteaux are promoted and demoted. The top rank is **Premier Grand Cru Classé A**, with four estates; then 14 ditto '**B**'; then 64 **Grands Crus Classés**. For more on classifications see pages 98-9.

Then there is 'Grand Cru' used on its own: see note on facing page.

Merlot worldwide

Merlot's international fame was firmly cemented even before its moment of stardom in California. It is widely grown across the southern half of **France**, both up-river from Bordeaux – Bergerac in particular – and in the Languedoc. Its name on a label is a reliable signal here of a soft, fruity red, though some producers with higher ambitions offer wines with more grip and interest. It is found, too, in northern and central **Italy**: inexpensive wines in the north-east, and more serious ones in Tuscany.

In the **USA**, California grows Merlot in quantity. A proportion goes into 'Bordeaux blends' (with the Cabernets), but most is bottled as a 'varietal' (wine from a single grape variety). Styles range from the bland to the fascinating: the latter sort, signalled by price as much as anything, balance the dark, opulent and rich aspects of ripe Merlot with fine tannins and spice. These wines tend to come from the cooler parts of the state: Sonoma for example. Washington State is another source of good US Merlot.

As with Cabernet Sauvignon, **Chile** has had success with Merlot. The wines are typically soft and approachable.

THE WORKINGS OF THE WINE TRADE

How does the wine get from the grower to your glass? Mark Pardoe MW gives us an insider's account of sourcing wines from Bordeaux and Burgundy.

It's April. There isn't a hotel room free in Bordeaux. The world's wine trade has descended on the city, and the region, for a week of 'en primeur' tastings of the new vintage. Tasters arrive at the châteaux all day, every day, often as little as 15 minutes apart and with little time to engage, other than to taste inky, un-knit cask samples of two or three wines and make their rapid assessments of how the wines will develop. They'll be constantly aware that their judgment will only be proved right – or wrong – in a decade's time.

But these buyers cannot buy what they have tasted from the châteaux themselves, for the Bordeaux market, known locally as 'La Place', works like no other.

At the top of the tree are the châteaux. Often substantial in size and producing many thousands of bottles each year, these were mainly established during the growth of the city's merchant classes during the 17th and 18th centuries. They take their names from past or current owners and the best, or most famous, can be considered as brands – a rare concept in the fragmented wine market. Although taking as their heart the vineyards surrounding each château, there is no barrier to the addition of further land to the estate – as long as the appellation of the new vineyard matches that of its new owner.

Once the château has its wine ready for sale, the courtier (broker) and négociant (merchant) come into play. There are about one hundred courtier companies in Bordeaux: their role is one of liaison, both between the châteaux and the 400 or so négociants, and between the négociants themselves. They have privileged access to who has what stock and what the market is

Left: It's not just a case of picking up the phone and ordering. Bordeaux buyer Max Lalondrelle gets down and dirty in the vineyards.

looking for. With the new vintage release, allocations of wine are requested (by the négociants) and made (by the châteaux), and the courtiers smooth the process for their two per cent commission.

Once the négociants have the wine, they offer it to the global market. Loyal customers are rewarded with the most desirable names, and the wines are traded rapidly or slowly, depending on the demand for the vintage. The stock-holders are the châteaux, who may choose not to release all their wine at once; the négociants, who will keep whatever they cannot sell; and their eventual customers.

To the outsider the system seems unnecessarily involved, but the advantages of linkage provided by the courtiers, and the négociants' instant access to a global market once the wine is released, benefits everyone in some way. Without this system, each château would need to employ its own sales team to cover every market, although the facility to control distribution more closely by leaving La Place does hold an allure for some of the biggest names....

But Bordeaux is not just about the big names. The produce of the great Crus Classés accounts for only about five per cent of the area's wine; there are another 5,000 châteaux spread throughout this enormous region, which makes about the same amount of red wine each year as the whole of Australia. These producers fight it out on the open market, but their bounty in no way matches that of the great names.

Left: Jasper Morris MW, Burgundy director, gets hands-on with the selection of grapes for the new vintage.

Now it's November, and the scene changes. A wine-buyer is in a cellar with one of his Burgundian producers. It's cold and misty outside, but the cellar is colder. The buyer has his heavy boots on; he doesn't need them when he's in Bordeaux.

The vigneron dips his pipette into a barrel of new wine. He doesn't say what it is. He lets pour a few dessert-spoonfuls of a translucent, shimmering red liquid into the grubby glass provided. They exchange glances; the producer says nothing. It's a test; the buyer tastes, then spits the wine

out onto the gravel between the barrels (something he would never do in manicured Bordeaux).

The wine is good, very good, but doesn't resonate with the usual range from this cellar. The buyer is being tested – on his understanding of the wine, the cellar and the producer, because away from the commercial gloss of brands and Bordeaux, the art and skill of the buyer is to forge a connection and empathy with each of his suppliers, adjusting his approach to each circumstance and personality.

Passing the test will enhance the buyer's standing in the eyes of the grower, and strengthen the bond. The answer given to the test doesn't have to be correct, but must demonstrate a fundamental understanding of place, person and wine.

Burgundy's Côte d'Or is the apogee of complexity and, while the buying process in all regions other than Bordeaux follow the same principles, none are as challenging. A mesmerizing network of intermarried families, patchworks of vineyards under multiple ownerships, all squeezed into a region about the size of 5,000 football pitches, it remains a mystery to many, lacking the touchstones of familiarity provided by the Bordeaux châteaux.

In Burgundy, and often elsewhere, the key words are not only the name of the wine, but also the name of the person who made it.

6 x 0,375L
BORDEAUX
BORDEAUX
6 x 0,375L
BORDEAUX
BORDEAUX
6 x 0,375L
BORDEAUX
6 x 0,375L

Cabernet Sauvignon

KEY POINTS

- Red grape
- High acidity
- Thick skins
- Small berries
- Firm tannins
- Lean where Merlot is plump
- Influenced by new oak
- Blended, in Bordeaux, with Merlot and Cabernet Franc
- Quality wines age well
- Most widely-grown grape in the world

KEY REGIONS

Bordeaux, Italy, Australia, Chile, California, South Africa

Prestige attaches to Cabernet Sauvignon from its dominant role in the great red wines of Bordeaux's Médoc. With Châteaux Lafite and Latour among its roll-call, its reputation for excellence is hard to match.

This status, and the grape's inherent character and ability to mature for decades, have propelled Cabernet Sauvignon around the world. Everywhere from Chile to Bulgaria, it is a variety that producers of red wine aspire to master.

They face a challenge, for the vine's virtues are matched by its drawbacks: it is late to ripen, and in cool years can struggle to do so at all; it is thick-skinned and yields initially austere, tannic wine.

Bordeaux is its homeland, and there it is the senior partner (to Merlot and Cabernet Franc) in the Left Bank vineyards of the Graves and the Médoc – notably the latter. The great châteaux of the Pauillac and St-Julien districts are typically 75 per cent Cabernet Sauvignon, though it is not so dominant in less august vineyards.

The variety's high level of tannins and concentrated flavour allows ageing in oak casks for the finer wines – and the combination of grape and oak makes wines that can go on maturing, and gaining complexity and interest, in bottle.

Great Cabernet Sauvignon-dominant Clarets – as Bordeaux's red wines are traditionally known – can be enjoyed at half a century old.

'New World' equivalents can show equally compelling patterns of evolution: California and Australia have now established track-records for great Cabernets.

Around the world, in cool climates and warm, Cabernet Sauvignon makes distinctive wines. Warmer places encourage fruit ripeness; cooler ones tend towards acidity, even austerity – but its character always shines through. Winemakers in warmer climates increasingly blend this variety with its Bordeaux partners in a quest for balance.

AROMA & FLAVOUR

Fruit in balance with acidity and tannin: in its original French homeland, Cabernet Sauvignon – and blends dominated by it – is made to go with food. As it moves round the world, warmer climates give it more soft-fruit ripeness but, if made with a view to balance, it remains subtle and appetising. In cool vintages it can be austere, explaining the Bordeaux habit of blending it with Merlot and Cabernet Franc.

When you try these wines, look out for:

- blackcurrant flavours in young wines; cedar, leather and dried fruits in older ones
- lots of tannin
- noticeable acidity

Would you agree that these wines are:

- less plump and rich than the Merlot wines, and slightly leaner and more austere, with higher tannins?

Maturity

Cabernet Sauvignon wines can last for decades, as Bordeaux's Médoc First Growths show. New World Cabernets have also shown the ability to age.

Not all Cabernet is designed to be cellared, but the best – those with structure and concentration and aged in oak – can develop marvellous complexity with age. In young wines you can taste the oak: this can make them positively unpalatable. But as the wines undergo bottle-ageing the effect of oak falls away.

KEY AROMAS & FLAVOURS

- blackcurrant
- chocolate
- mint
- tobacco

Cool climate
Warm climate

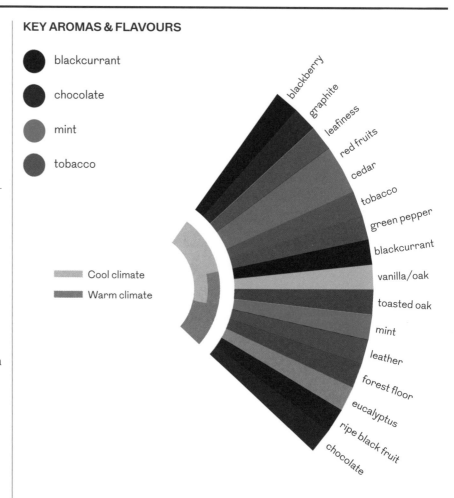

blackberry
graphite
leafiness
red fruits
cedar
tobacco
green pepper
blackcurrant
vanilla/oak
toasted oak
mint
leather
forest floor
eucalyptus
ripe black fruit
chocolate

BALANCE

THE CHARACTER
OF THE WINE
IN YOUR GLASS

Wines from cool and warm climates differ in their youth, and in the ways they mature: see how they develop a sense of balance as they age.

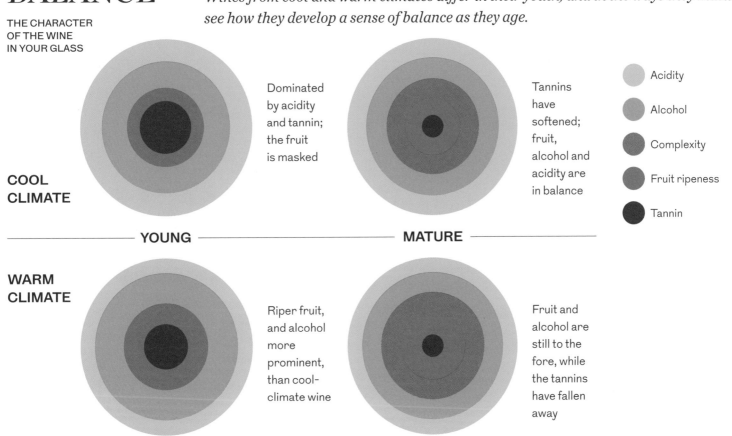

COOL CLIMATE

Dominated by acidity and tannin; the fruit is masked

Tannins have softened; fruit, alcohol and acidity are in balance

YOUNG ———————— MATURE

WARM CLIMATE

Riper fruit, and alcohol more prominent, than cool-climate wine

Fruit and alcohol are still to the fore, while the tannins have fallen away

- ● Acidity
- ● Alcohol
- ● Complexity
- ● Fruit ripeness
- ● Tannin

Food matches

Choose Cabernet Sauvignon wines for the meat course, though they will go on to partner cheeses. In its homeland of the Médoc, lamb is the classic match: the appetising acidity and tannin will cut through the richness. The more mature wines partner beef or venison superbly. Top wines, when at their peak, deserve to take the limelight with simpler, subtler fare.

Some Cabernet Sauvignon-friendly foods:

- Roast meats, especially lamb
- Beef
- Game, such as venison
- Grilled meats
- Hard cheeses such as aged gouda

KEY REGION:

Left Bank Bordeaux

Cabernet Sauvignon rose to international wine stardom thanks to an almost perfect CV. Its referees include the Bordeaux châteaux everyone on the planet with a corkscrew has heard of: Château Lafite, Château Latour, Château Margaux. As the wine world became global in the late 20th century, any winemaker with ambition wanted to match these French greats, to conjure up the Napa Valley's, or wherever's, riposte to the great Clarets of the Left Bank's Médoc and Graves districts.

Those eager New World pioneers were, and are, in luck: the Cabernet Sauvignon grape is adaptable. Given a reasonably warm climate, it can and does flourish from Bulgaria to Chile. Compare and contrast the frustrating time Burgundy-lovers have in coaxing Pinot Noir to grow outside its native heath (see Session 5).

Despite its worldwide spread, no-one and nowhere has really matched the Bordeaux prototypes. Excellent and enticing bottles of Cabernet Sauvignon flow from California, Australia, Chile and a dozen other places (see following pages); but most wine-lovers agree that they never quite topple the stars of the Médoc and Graves.

Cabernet Sauvignon came quite late to the Médoc. It emerged by accident (see Science Soundbite page 97), but once they'd discovered it, the Bordeaux châteaux realised that it suited their terroir – and, more important, their pattern of business. For the Médoc invented the idea of long-lived wine (OK, the Romans had a stab at it, too...); wine that spends its infancy in oak casks and grows to maturity in bottle.

Left: The map shows how the large region of Bordeaux splits into Right and Left Bank zones (with Entre-deux-Mers in the middle).

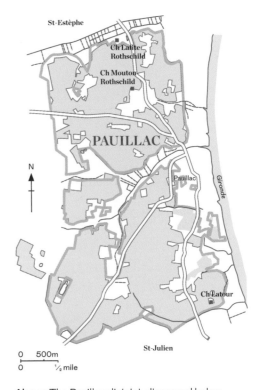

Above: The Pauillac district, discussed below, has three of the top wine estates of the Médoc within its bounds. Vineyards are shown in green.

Cabernet has the tannins, the structure, the interesting flavours to suit this process. Result: wine that needs time, that does not have to be sold as soon as it is made.

Today's Clarets from the Médoc and Graves are dominated by Cabernet Sauvignon. The more illustrious, the bigger the proportion: it rises to 75 per cent at Latour. As discussed on page 98, there are many ranks of Bordeaux wine estates: down at the base of the pyramid among the 'petits châteaux', even in the Médoc, Merlot takes first place.

Above: Gravel soil in the vineyards of the Médoc.

The terroir at the top Médoc estates has been studied intensely, down to and including the drains. Gravel is the key to success here. It forms the gentle – sometimes almost imperceptible – slopes and dunes, pictured above, that stud the otherwise flat landscape. Glance at any map of the Médoc (see for instance Pauillac, left) and you'll note that where the blue lines of the streams are, the vines are not. The streams are really drainage channels, for the landscape between the gravel hillocks would be tidal marshland were it not for the engineers of three centuries. The best gravel banks are those highest and nearest to the

Gironde estuary. Here, the drainage is best: Cabernet Sauvignon needs a well-drained site and gravel provides it. (Merlot will cope with damper feet.)

Of the five top châteaux – the First Growths – three 'look at the river' from Pauillac's gravel (see map); Ch Haut-Brion occupies a superb bank of gravel in the Graves district (the clue is in the name), and Ch Margaux too sits atop a low but definite gravel rise. At all five the gravel is remarkably similar, with large stones on the surface that reflect the sun upwards onto the ripening grapes.

GRAVEL VERSUS CLAY

Bordeaux is of course more than the Left Bank Médoc: the Right Bank vineyards, already discussed in the Merlot pages, make a different style of Claret. Here, the recipe is more Merlot and clay than Cabernet Sauvignon and gravel. Clay is not the only sub-soil found on the Right Bank: some of the best St-Emilion châteaux sit on a limestone ridge, and there is gravel here too. Geographers, and wine students, have endless fun matching the character of the wines to the various soils – only to find that a new winemaker at a château turns out something quite different from an unchanging terroir.

HEIGHT IS RELATIVE

Visitors to the Médoc often look bemused when locals talk about gravel slopes and banks: to the outsider, the whole place looks flat. The vertical difference between a sodden marsh and well-drained gravel can be as little as five metres (16 ft). The best gravel banks rise to a dizzying 25m. Wine anoraks treasure the detailed French survey maps that show the five-metre contour, for this line divides the vines from the pasture, and the border of the official appellation follows it with uncanny precision. Such a detailed map can be a real aid in spotting potential among the myriad 'petits châteaux' of the northern Médoc and the Graves.

Cabernet Sauvignon worldwide

The original motive for the worldwide planting of 'Cab Sauv' (as the New World generally abbreviates it) may have been imitation, but that phase is well past. The grape's adaptability means that it makes wines of many styles according to local conditions and decisions. There's a common character, as discussed on the Flavour and Balance pages: its wine has plenty of structure; with enough sun it has good fruit; it can age in an interesting way.

Where does Cab Sauv do best? Australia and California dispute the prize. **Australia**'s winemakers blend it with Shiraz (a pastime generally frowned upon in France), use it in 'Bordeaux blends', and make 100 per cent Cabernets in areas such as Coonawarra (S Australia), perhaps the best Cab Sauv location in the country. Other favoured districts are Margaret River (W Australia) and Clare Valley (S Australia).

In the **USA**, California's Napa Valley and its various sub-zones, including most famously Stag's Leap and the 'Rutherford Bench', leads the pack. Indeed, Napa has been growing Cabernet Sauvignon for 140 years and has a track-record to challenge the Médoc.

Both Australia and California offer Cabernets in styles and at price-points from the simple and everyday to the sophisticated and (very) expensive: you can pay Bordeaux classed-growth prices for a top Coonawarra or Napa wine.

Chile and **South Africa** rival the top two. Chilean Cabernet is typically bold with fruit, higher in alcohol than a Claret. The Cape offers an increasingly interesting list of Bordeaux blends built around Cabernet Sauvignon. **New Zealand**, too, is making increasingly good Cabernet blends.

Back in Europe, **Spain**, **Italy** and southern **France** offer Cabernets that tend to graft local flavours and approaches onto the grape's fundamental character.

The latest frontier? **China**. Bordeaux has made a great success of exporting to China the notion that Bordeaux red wines are a benchmark for excellence. The results include several new châteaux in China, complete with turrets both on the label and in the vineyard, and wide new plantings of Cabernet Sauvignon. China is working hard to establish, amid its many climates and soils, the best terroirs for Cabernet. Watch this space....

Right: Vines in the Napa Valley, California.

VINTAGE VARIATIONS

What makes a great vintage? Mark Pardoe MW discusses how – and why – wines vary from year to year.

Sometimes Bordeaux is even busier than usual for the 'en primeur' tastings, because the word is out that it's a great vintage. For the Anglophone, 'vintage' is a problematic word, with its connotations of age and venerability; but in its original French, and in use throughout the wine trade, it just means the production of a single, identified year.

The creation of any wine is the culmination of an agricultural process. Each autumn, grapes ripen on vines, are harvested and then turned into wine. The quality of that wine depends on where those vineyards are situated, and on what the weather did that year.

The success of any given vintage will depend on the ripeness of the grapes – not just in terms of sugar levels, but how the tannins and acidities have 'ripened' as well. Unripe tannins make red wines too bitter; unripe (high) acidity shows as sharpness.

The ideal time to harvest is when all these elements are in prime condition – but a cool spring or a wet August may mitigate success, and so the skill of the vigneron is to judge the moment to pick, to maximize success.

In regions with reliable and predictable weather patterns, the variations can be less marked; but more marginal regions, where the grapes creep more slowly towards full maturity, demonstrate greater variations. This gentle, final fulfillment of maturity is also vital for the accumulation of complexity in the final product.

On a broader scale, the vintage is the measure of a wine's age. Some wines require maturation to show all that they are capable of, and the length of maturation will depend on the quality and style of the vintage. Others wines demand enjoyment earlier in their life-cycle. The knowledge of the vintage is the key to this fulfillment.

Technical understanding of both grape-growing and winemaking is now at such a level that the concept of a poor year is becoming almost (but not quite) inconceivable. Certainly the big names of the wine world are in a position of such security that the sacrifices necessary to discard any fruit deemed unsuitable are well within their compass, so that whatever is produced will be worthy of the name.

So, what is a 'great' vintage? It is one where all these elements have come together under near-ideal conditions. But great vintages are not normal vintages; it would be more accurate to label them as 'exceptional', as they only tend to occur two or three times per decade.

For the rest of the time, any wine's true personality is better expressed by the more frequent 'lesser' vintages. These may be marked by a greater or lesser perception of some of the wine's typical characteristics, but all should be treated as representative of each wine's heritage.

Fundamentally, every wine that is produced, great or small, is an expression of one year in time – a snapshot of history and a reflection of life and its vicissitudes.

Opposite: Winemakers everywhere have one eye permanently on the weather: storms at the wrong time can destroy an entire vintage. In spring, as here, frost can kill the emerging buds, or a hailstorm can strip them right off.

THICK SKIN? SMALL GRAPE? WHY DOES SIZE MATTER?

The thickness of a grape's skin has an important impact on the finished wine. The Cabernet Sauvignon vine, for instance, produces small grapes with thick skins; when the grapes are crushed, the skin:juice ratio is high, meaning that the resultant wines are usually deep in colour and high in tannin.

Merlot, on the other hand, produces bigger grapes with thinner skins. This results in wines that are not quite as intense in colour and have less tannin. The two therefore complement each other well in a blend.

SCIENCE SOUNDBITE: DNA PROFILING

Great strides in the DNA profiling of grape varieties have been made in recent decades. One of the most interesting discoveries has been that Cabernet Sauvignon is indeed, as its name hints, the offspring of two famous parents: Cabernet Franc and Sauvignon Blanc. One could surmise that it exhibits characteristics of both: when grown in a cool climate it has some of the green-pepper notes of Sauvignon Blanc, and also the high acidity of Cabernet Franc, although it has developed much firmer tannins than the latter.

CLASSIFICATIONS AND RANKINGS

What is a Cru Classé – a Classed Growth? Why do parts of Bordeaux have a rigid pecking-order, and others not? Martin Hudson MW explains.

In 1855 the Bordeaux Chamber of Commerce drew up a new classification of the red wines of the Médoc and the sweet wines of Sauternes and Barsac, which they presented at the Universal Exhibition in Paris. The red wines were ranked by the price they commanded into five levels, or 'crus', with Châteaux Haut-Brion (the only wine included from outside the Médoc peninsula), Lafite, Latour and Margaux occupying the top tier.

The sweet whites were split into two levels, first and second – but with Yquem above the list as the sole Premier Grand Cru.

The only significant change to the 1855 list was in 1973, when Ch Mouton-Rothschild was promoted from Second- to First-Growth status: that took a Presidential decree.

The classification is now over 150 years old, so has some anomalies, with châteaux like Palmer (Third Growth), Lynch-Bages (Fifth) and Pontet-Canet (Fifth) among others, performing above their supposed status; however, few people would argue with the status of the top tier.

If the exercise were to be repeated – based again on market price – there would, though, be surprisingly few changes. That said, the market recognises a clutch of 'Super-Seconds' that can challenge the Firsts in price. These include Léoville-Las-Cases, Léoville-Barton, Montrose, Palmer, Cos d'Estournel....

(If anyone offers to sell you a case of Third-Growth Ch Dubignon, refuse: the wine is indeed on the 1855 list, but its land was sold off decades ago to other châteaux.)

Exactly a century after the Médoc list, in 1955, St-Emilion introduced a classification based on the results of a tasting panel. Any property producing wine of St-Emilion Grand Cru status (a status attained simply by a slightly higher alcohol level and lower yield than straightforward AOC St-Emilion) could apply, and potentially be classified – in ascending order of merit – Grand Cru Classé,

Premier Grand Cru Classé B or Premier Grand Cru Classé A. This classification is reviewed (notionally) every decade, with the possibility of promotion and demotion, the most recent update being in 2012.

Graves decided to follow suit in 1959, with both red and dry white wines having the chance to become Cru Classé. Thus far, there has been no review of this classification other than the addition of Haut-Brion white in 1961.

A point to note is that all these Bordeaux classifications, with the exception of the relatively lowly St-Emilion Grand Cru, are not enshrined in the AOC rules, unlike Premier Cru and Grand Cru vineyards in Burgundy and Chablis.

Note, too, that in Bordeaux it is the châteaux that are ranked, but in Burgundy it is the land. A Bordeaux château can expand its vineyard (as long as it buys land of the same AOC) without changing its classification – and some have done just that. In Burgundy, by contrast, it is forbidden to expand a Grand Cru by even a row of vines.

CRU

'Cru' is a difficult word to translate into English: 'growth' seems somewhat unsatisfactory, but the inference is wine grown on a particular, ranked, patch of land — though in some areas it can mean an entire village.

TASTING NOTES
Record your own impressions

Prompts: you are looking out for

Cabernet Franc: Crunchy red fruits, high acidity

Merlot: Rich, plummy smoothness

Cabernet Sauvignon: Blackcurrant and lots of tannin

CABERNET FRANC

1 _____

_____

2 _____

_____

MERLOT

3 _____

_____

4 _____

_____

CABERNET SAUVIGNON

5 _____

_____

6 _____

_____

BLIND TASTING

7 _____

_____

8 _____

_____

9 _____

_____

10 _____

_____

QUESTIONS

In Session 3 we have looked at three red varieties – Cabernet Franc, Merlot and Cabernet Sauvignon:

1. Which variety makes Chinon and from what region does this wine come?

   _____

2. Which is the main variety in St-Emilion and from what region does this wine come?

   _____

3. Which variety gives grapes which are small and thick-skinned?

   _____

4. Which variety gives grapes which are large and thin-skinned?

   _____

Which might have aromas often described as:

5. – blackcurrants?

   _____

6. – plums?

   _____

7. – fresh raspberries?

   _____

8. In which Old World region are these three grape varieties blended together?

   _____

Name the grape variety beside each description:

9. – plummy with good acidity, soft tannin; full-bodied with richness and warm alcohol

   _____

10. – medium-bodied with high acidity and crunchy red-fruit flavours

    _____

11. – cedar, leather and dried-fruits aromas with a lean mouthfeel and high tannins

    _____

Bordeaux

12. – name two wine communes on the Left Bank.

    _____

13. – name two wine communes on the Right Bank.

    _____

Answers on page 221

Opposite: Cold work in the winter vineyards: pruning the vines.

Overleaf: High-trained vines in Argentina, overlooked by the snow-covered Andes.

4

These three aromatic white grapes offer contrasting styles and personalities

RIESLING
GEWURZTRAMINER
CHENIN BLANC

RIESLING
aristocratic

The source of great German wines, it also makes fine dry and sweet wines in Alsace, Austria and Australia

GEWURZTRAMINER
exotic

Highly aromatic, conjuring lychees and rose-petals from the glass, with a unique spicy flavour: its homeland is Alsace

CHENIN BLANC
energetic

High acidity and honeyed fruit combine to make wines that can be drunk young and fresh or — from its Loire homeland — aged for decades. It can be all styles: dry or sweet, still or sparkling

Where the grapes grow

Riesling is the quintessential cool-climate grape, having its heartland in the German vineyards at almost 50 degrees north. While it does well in warmer places (Australia's Eden and Clare Valleys) it does not thrive in truly warm zones. Gewurztraminer follows its example, though its main home is Alsace. Chenin Blanc's origins lie in the Central Loire, and it does well in South Africa.

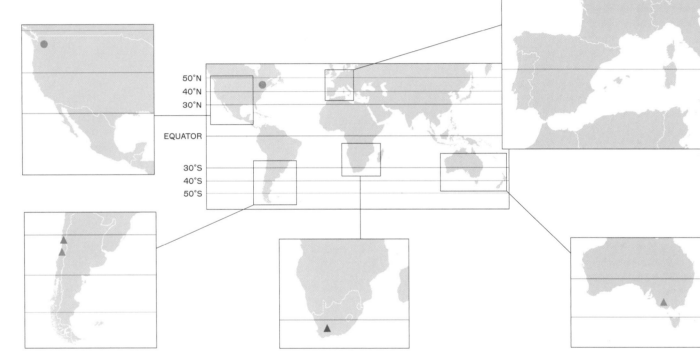

RIESLING

● **Cooler climate**   ▲ **Warmer climate**

  Germany   Australia
  Alsace   Chile
  Austria
  New Zealand
  Washington
  Canada

GEWURZTRAMINER

● **Cooler climate**   ▲ **Warmer climate**

  Alsace   Chile
  Germany
  New Zealand

CHENIN BLANC

● **Cooler climate**   ▲ **Warmer climate**

  Central Loire   South Africa

Riesling

KEY POINTS

- White grape
- Aromatic
- High acidity
- Likes a cool climate
- Rarely (if ever) aged in new oak
- Wines range from dry to very sweet
- Can age very well

KEY REGIONS

Germany, Alsace, Austria, New Zealand, Australia

Is this the best white-wine grape of them all? It's a bit of an insiders' secret, but judged by Riesling's excellence in places as far apart as Germany and Australia, and by its versatility in making wines from bone-dry to sweet, the answer is yes. Its true trump cards are its unmistakeable aromatic character, high acidity and ability to gain haunting complexity with age.

Riesling (say 'Reesling') originated in Germany, where the Mosel and Rhein valleys go on yielding world-class examples. It is found in Alsace, where the French made a deliberately different, food-friendly style; in Austria, South-East Europe, Australia, New Zealand, Chile.

How it is made can radically alter the character of a Riesling wine; but whatever technique is used, winemakers find that the variety yields a wider range of unique flavour compounds than any other. A cool-climate wine will be floral; a warm-climate one suggests lime.

German Rieslings are typically made with low alcohol and at least some sweetness: in quality wines, this sweetness comes from the grapes, as fermentation is halted before all the natural sugar is consumed. So a Mosel Riesling can be just eight per cent alcohol. In their home valleys, the tall, slim bottles – green on the Mosel, brown on the Rhein – are opened as apéritifs, or just to enjoy on a sunny afternoon....

Wines made in warmer places, from Alsace southwards, are typically lower in sweetness and higher in alcohol. In some warm-climate wines, Riesling's aromatic signature is masked by ripeness.

Riesling grapes ripen late, and growers in Germany, Alsace and Austria let them go on ripening in fine autumns to reach very high levels of natural sugar. The results – see page 111 for names and sweetness levels – are among the world's best sweet wines, yet always with the grape's underlying acidity to prevent them from being cloying.

Wine suggestions for this session, page 216

AROMA & FLAVOUR

Germany's aromatic key grape runs the gamut from green apple to honey and flowers, and can be beautifully sweet – or bone-dry. Even when sweet, it is balanced by appetising acidity. One of the best grapes at reflecting terroir, it conjures complexity and finesse from austere slate hillsides in Germany, and depth and flavour from sunny slopes in Alsace. New Zealand makes an off-dry, higher-alcohol style.

When you try these wines, look out for:

- lots of balancing acidity
- when young: fresh, floral fruit — peach and elderflower in cool climates, lime and toast in warm
- with age: aromatic, complex, petrolly notes

Would you agree that these wines are:

- mouthwatering and aromatic? If sweet, do you notice that the sweetness is balanced by high acidity?

Maturity

Quality wines are enjoyable young, yet can age superbly for decades – equally true of dry wines and sweet. The underlying acidity keeps fine Rieslings beautifully in balance while they age. Look out for older Rieslings: since most other whites don't gain from ageing, you may find bargains.

SCIENCE SOUNDBITE: THAT PETROL AROMA

Distinct petrolly aromas in Riesling are caused by a compound called TDN. In German Rieslings this compound develops during bottle-age, but in some Rieslings from warmer climates (such as the Clare Valley in South Australia) it appears in youth. Its early presence is thought to be influenced by riper grapes and more sun.

KEY AROMAS & FLAVOURS

- citrus fruits
- green apple
- petrol
- honey

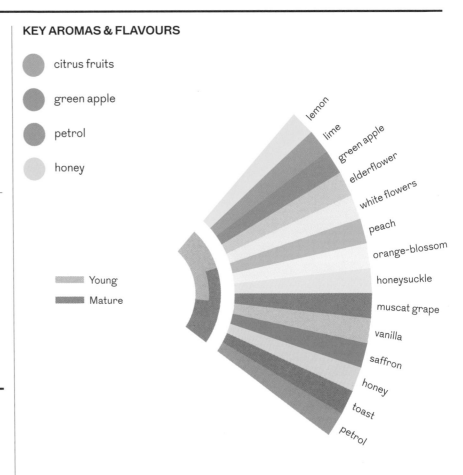

Young
Mature

lemon
lime
green apple
elderflower
white flowers
peach
orange-blossom
honeysuckle
muscat grape
vanilla
saffron
honey
toast
petrol

BALANCE

THE CHARACTER
OF THE WINE
IN YOUR GLASS

Riesling grows in warm climates – Australia, California – as well as in Germany's chilly northern valleys. Warm-climate wines are typically aromatic, fruity yet dry. Alsace – warmer than the Mosel – aims for drier wines with higher alcohol.
Here we show how a Mosel wine ages, gaining complexity while acidity and fruit stay in equilibrium.

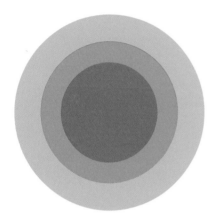

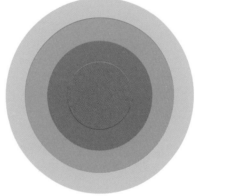

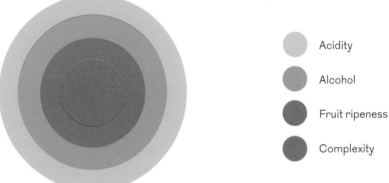

Acidity

Alcohol

Fruit ripeness

Complexity

YOUNG

Fruit and acidity to the fore, fresh
rather than complex

MATURE

Complex honey-and-petrol aromas
overlay balancing acidity

Food matches

Riesling's versatility can make it a puzzle to match with food. Go by origin: Mosel and Rhein Kabinetts and Spätleses are good alone, as apéritifs; low in alcohol, these are also fine wines to enjoy on their own on a summer afternoon. Auslese and sweeter wines pair well with ripe fruit or desserts. Drier German styles (see pages 110-11) match many dishes. Alsace, Austrian and Australian Rieslings will generally be meal-time wines: drier yet fruity, and with enough body to partner food.

Some Riesling-friendly foods:

- Crab, lobster
- Goose
- Duck, and pork, with fruit-based stuffings or sauces
- Spicy foods
- Desserts

KEY REGION:

Germany

Riesling's identity was forged in the steep valleys of western Germany. On the terraces above the rivers Rhein and Mosel ('Rhine' and 'Moselle', as they were anglicised) the grape variety was prized as early as the Middle Ages. It was – and is – given the top sites: the sunniest slopes. Here, it makes the best wines Germany can offer: some of the finest white wines in the world.

These valleys are a long way north – Koblenz, where the two rivers meet, is at 50.30°N, a hundred miles (160km) further north than chilly Champagne, and about the same latitude as the Isle of Wight on the south coast of England. In Germany, this means cool summers and harsh winters: sunlight to ripen the grapes is at a premium.

Successful German vintages – those where the Riesling ripens properly – used to happen once or twice a decade. Recently, the success-rate has shot up to perhaps seven years out of ten. Is this climate change? Or better viticulture and choice of vine clones (see page 32)? Only time will tell, but meanwhile there are many more fine Riesling bottles to enjoy.

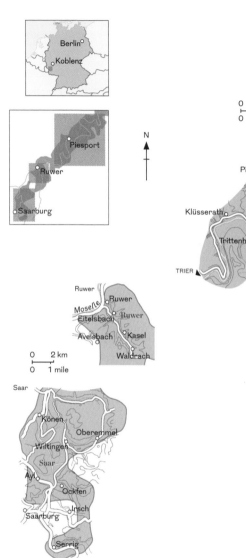

The maps **above** pinpont the best stretches of the Mosel Valley. The top vineyards are in the villages marked: you'll often find villages named on the label, with '-er' added: this means 'from'. The second word in a name is that of the vineyard ('Wehlener Sonnenuhr' for example).

THE MOSEL

The best spots for vines in these northern valleys are the south-facing slopes, tilted into the sun (much as a solar panel is aligned on a roof-top). As the Mosel meanders through the wooded hills of the Eifel, it has cut a deep valley. The curves shown on the map mean that sometimes the left bank, sometimes the right is best exposed to the south – so there is nothing as simple as a 'right bank/left bank' contrast in the wines.

There is more to the Mosel than slope and aspect, crucial as they are. The soil (see picture) makes a major contribution: slate is the best, and some of the top vineyards resemble nothing so much as a slate quarry: the vines poke out of a steep scree-slope of blue-grey fragments. This slate provides excellent drainage, plenty of reflected heat and (maybe it is just association of ideas?) a stony, steely, slaty note in the wine.

As well as Mosel, you will also see the names Saar and Ruwer – these are tributaries of the main river. The top wines come from the valleys of the Saar and the Mittel (middle) Mosel. The source of the grapes, the vineyard, will be on the label, along with (in bigger type, usually) the name of the estate or grower. The village (the best are on the map) is sometimes missing, as the vineyard is supposed to speak for itself.

The word 'Riesling' will be relegated to the back-label, if it is there at all. The assumption is that this is the grape that is grown. As in many fine-wine districts, getting to know the names of the best growers is the route to the finest bottles: some estates have track-records dating back eight centuries.

THE RHEINGAU

The Rheingau was, historically, the region's top wine district. Here, the great river makes a helpful jink in its mostly south-to-north flow, and runs east-west. The Taunus hills rise up on the north bank, providing a splendid sweep of gently-tilting vineyard sites, with Riesling predominant.

Look out here for names of the great, venerable estates: Schloss Johannisberg, Schloss Vollrads. The villages with the best reputations are **Rüdesheim**, **Oestrich**,

Left: The slate soil helps the grapes to ripen by reflecting sun and heat onto them.

Hallgarten, **Erbach** and, off to the east, **Hochheim** – which claims to be the source of the word 'hock': Victorian English for Rhine-wine (Queen Victoria was a fan).

REST OF GERMANY

Every German wine region grows Riesling: the **Pfalz** specialises in drier wines, rich and balanced. **Rheinhessen**, like the Pfalz seeing a revival in estate wines, has a growing name for long-lived, intense Rieslings; the **Nahe** is known for delicate wines from Mosel-like steep slopes.

Other German white grapes include Silvaner, the signature grape in Franken. The Pinots Gris and Blanc – Grauburgunder and Weissburgunder on the labels – do well in the Rheinhessen and in Baden in southern Germany, where the climate is akin to that of Alsace. And – as noted below – German red wines are increasingly common, and good.

Alsace: see page 119 for Alsace Rieslings

RHEIN CAN BE RED...

Riesling rules the Rhein – but not totally: the red wines from Rheingau village Assmannshausen, made from Spätburgunder (Pinot Noir), are famously good, if scarce. Good reds also come from Pfalz, Ahr and Baden.

'GERMAN? IT MUST BE SWEET – I WON'T LIKE IT....'

Many wine-drinkers make this leap –and miss some stunning wines. Modern German wines range from dry and appetising to gloriously sweet... but which is which? Catriona Felstead MW has the key.

Knowing what's in a tall, elegant Alsace or German bottle used to be easy: Alsace wines were nearly always dry, Germany's predictably sweet. However, this simple rule no longer applies; dry German wines are increasingly common, while some Alsace wines (see page 118) now have high levels of residual sugar. Result: a puzzle when trying to match wines with food. Both have tried to clarify sweetness on the label; whether their efforts have reduced or increased the confusion is somewhat debatable....

The German Wine Law of 1971 categorised (controversially) the quality of a wine by the sugar-ripeness level ('**must weight**') of the grapes at harvest. So, in theory, the levels go:

Deutscher Wein and **Deutscher Landwein** are the lowest (driest) categories, followed by **Qualitätswein bestimmter Anbaugebiete** (QbA), the first 'quality wine' level, which often comprises simple, fruity, slightly off-dry wines.

Prädikatswein If you see any of the terms defined on the facing page on the label, then you are looking at the higher quality level, Prädikatswein. There are six levels, in increasing order of ripeness.

This all sounds like good German logic – however, grape ripeness and wine sweetness do not necessarily correlate. It would be reasonable to expect a Kabinett to be fruity and off-dry, a Spätlese to be a touch riper with greater intensity, and an Auslese (my personal favourite) to have noticeable sweetness and concentration.

However, any wine from Deutscher Wein to Auslese can actually be made in a dry, medium-dry or sweet style, according to the winemaker's preference in that vintage. Beerenauslese (BA), Eiswein and Trockenbeerenauslese (TBA) are always reassuringly sweet.

If you are wanting a dry wine, all is not lost. Look for **trocken** (dry), **halbtrocken** (medium-dry), **Classic** or **Selection** on the label: the wine should taste dry (Classic being of QbA level, and Selection essentially a dry Spätlese).

Feinherb generally means a slightly sweeter style than halbtrocken – but be aware, this is an unofficial term.

Secondly, look for an eagle logo on the bottle's capsule. This winemaker belongs to the **VDP (**Verband Deutscher Prädikatsweingüter**)**, an association of specialist producers who have broken away from the German wine law and categorize quality by terroir, as in Burgundy, not by grape ripeness. They have a much clearer distinction between sweet and dry wines.

VDP **Grosse Lage** is their equivalent of Grand Cru; VDP **Erste Lage** of Premier Cru and VDP **Ortswein** of a Village wine. If any of these are sweet, they will have one of the Prädikatswein terms (see right) on the label. If they are dry they will have 'Qualitätswein Trocken' on the label.

A dry VDP Grosse Lage wine also has its own special designation: VDP **Grosses Gewächs** ('great growth' is a rough translation).

My advice? If you are looking for a specific style, then always ask your wine merchant for an opinion – and then, if you pour a glass which is not to your taste and has no sweetness indication on the label (or on the merchant's website), do not be afraid to take the bottle back and ask for a different style. But please, do not be deterred from trying a bottle; these can be amongst the finest and most rewarding wines in the world.

Opposite: In the Mosel, steep means steep....

GERMAN PRÄDIKATSWEIN TERMS

Kabinett Fresh and fruity in style; often off-dry but can be dry, medium-dry or sweet.

Spätlese From grapes that are picked later, after the rest of the harvest. Can have more richness than QbA or Kabinett wines; often medium-dry but can also be dry, medium-sweet or sweet.

Auslese From selected bunches, these wines can be concentrated and intense. Often medium-sweet but can also be dry, medium-dry or sweet.

Beerenauslese (BA) Meaning 'selected berries', these are produced from overripe grapes, often affected by noble rot, and can produce rich, sweet dessert wines.

Eiswein 'Ice wines' are rare. They are made from grapes of the same minimum sweetness as BA wines — but this sweetness is due to their being picked so late that they have frozen on the vine. They tend not to be affected by noble rot, so the result is a very pure, sweet style that can have delicious freshness.

Trockenbeerenauslese (TBA) 'Selected dry berries' produce the highest sweetness level of Prädikatswein. Grapes affected by noble rot are individually picked so late in the autumn that they have dried and shrivelled on the vine and are almost like raisins; lusciously sweet wines.

See page **118** for **Alsace** terms

KEY REGION:

Austria

Austria makes a lot of wine, red as well as the white wines for which it is chiefly known. Riesling is grown in just four per cent of its vineyard, but its wine can be so long-lived and delicious that – in export markets especially – it gets much of the attention.

WACHAU

Lift a visitor blindfolded into the Wachau, Austria's prime valley for Riesling, and they'd think themselves beside the Rhein or Mosel. Here, too, steep hills rise from the river (the Donau, or Danube), vineyards cling to the slopes, romantically-ruined castles crown the crags. The wine-cellars and taverns are perhaps even more hospitable.

But to the wine-lover accustomed to the Mosel, Austrian Riesling offers a different slant on the grape. We are in a subtly different climate here: a long way inland, with hot, dry summers. The hills are higher: many vineyards are at 400m above sea level, whereas the Mosel's rarely attain half that. The high slopes are cool at night, balancing the warmth of the days. Autumns are long.

The resulting Wachau Rieslings are typically higher in alcohol than the Mosel's, but balance the extra weight with a dry finish. As in Germany, fine autumns can yield great sweet wines: terms such as Auslese are in use in Austria, too, but the natural sugar levels are higher. Wachau wines tend to be lower in acidity than German Rieslings, which may curb their ageing potential – but only relatively. It is well worth keeping the best wines for six years or more.

KREMSTAL AND KAMPTAL

'Tal' means valley, and these two districts, east of the Wachau, have gentler landscapes with wide, productive vineyards. Riesling is important here too, though Grüner Veltliner (see right) makes the most wine. Labels on Kamptal wines (and others from Austria) sometimes mention 'loess' – a type of deep, loose sandy-limestone soil, not a place. It's reckoned locally that Riesling does best on the rocky hills, Grüner Veltliner on the loess.

Rieslings from these two valleys may not be able to compete at the very top level – the Wachau wines usually excel – but they are reliable and share the Wachau wines' broad character. Drink them younger.

ALSO TRY:

Grüner Veltliner

Not a name that trips off the non-German-speaking tongue, but one worth remembering. This is Austria's most-planted white grape, and its most individual wine.

Grüner Veltliner is grown virtually nowhere else but Austria and places (Slovenia, parts of Hungary) that border it – which surprises anyone who tries its wine. It is always lively, always appetising, but ranges in style from brisk and tart to generous and round.

Some tasters find a white-pepper note in 'Grüner', others talk of spice. It needs care in grape-growing and winemaking, for it can over-crop, leading to insipid wine, or can be blowsy and over-perfumed. Most modern wines avoid these extremes.

Grüner Veltliner is a fine all-rounder, interesting without food and sympathetic with it. Drink it when it's young and fresh – though top wines from ambitious estates can age.

KEY REGION:

Australia

EDEN VALLEY

The name 'Eden' is a good start: wine pioneers discovered this high, comparatively cool corner of South Australia in the 1850s. But it was only in the late 20th century that Riesling vines were found to excel in this favoured spot.

Today, Eden vies with Clare (see below) as the southern hemisphere's Riesling heartland. Eden lies east of the bigger, lower-lying Barossa Valley region; confusingly, the two together make up the zone named 'Barossa' (without the 'Valley'). Riesling is important in the Eden Valley, but Shiraz (see Session 5) is more widely grown.

Eden Valley Rieslings are typically elegant and floral, showing a stony purity. Most wines are made dry, but some growers pick late into the autumn to gain richness and complexity.

Above: The well-named Eden Valley in South Australia produces a range of grapes, but is best-known for Riesling and Shiraz.

CLARE VALLEY

Clare Valley is some 100km further north, thus warmer; but it is also high up, and in parts feels the cooling influence of the ocean. There is a range of landscapes, including stony hills of limestone and shale that suit Riesling well; Cabernet Sauvignon and Shiraz thrive, too, in other corners.

Rieslings from Clare can vie with the best in the world. They can have a long life, but with their high acidity are often closed and dumb in youth. Wine-lovers with patience are rewarded after five or ten years by bottles that balance taut mineral notes with rich lime flavours. These wines are usually dry, but balance any austerity with delicious mid-palate richness.

WESTERN AUSTRALIA

Cold ocean currents temper the heat in Australia's south-west corner, and cool-climate grapes do well. Riesling is a minority grape here – much of the enthusiasm has been for Chardonnay and Sauvignon Blanc – but convincing bottles emerge from wineries in the Great Southern and Margaret River districts.

Riesling worldwide

New Zealand, despite its cool-climate credentials, has shown less interest in Riesling than in Chardonnay (and of course Sauvignon Blanc). Riesling accounts for only one per cent of New Zealand's wine production. However, Central Otago, tucked away in the middle of the South Island, shows promise for the grape, as do Waitaki Valley, Waipara, Canterbury Plains and Nelson, where the free-draining stony soils suit it well.

Chile has made a name for Rieslings, especially from its southernmost (coolest) vineyards. The characteristic style is fresh and aromatic.

In the **USA**, look to Washington State for a range of interesting Rieslings, some grown on a very large scale; also to California's select group of growers who persevere with sweet (sometimes botrytis) styles. Over the border, **Canada** too has success with late-harvest sweet Rieslings, up to and including Ice Wine (see 'Eiswein', page 111).

Right: A belt of strategically-planted trees can give wind protection to the vines.

Gewurztraminer

KEY POINTS

- White grape
- Aromatic: distinctive perfume
- Low acidity
- High alcohol
- Full-bodied
- Quality wines can age well

KEY REGIONS

Alsace, New Zealand, Australia, Pacific North-West, Chile

An oddball of a vine, Gewurztraminer makes white wines that are perhaps the easiest of all to identify with one sniff. Indeed, its rich, unctuous, oily texture in the glass, with 'legs' of glycerol showing on the sides as you swirl it, can suggest the grape even before the nose has a chance to register its heady, hot-house perfume.

Another visual clue is its colour: deep rose-gold, not the watery brilliance of Sauvignon Blanc.

Gewurztraminer (say Gevurztraminer) makes low-acidity wines of rich, aromatic character. They are high in alcohol for a white wine – 13-14 per cent is typical – and good ones can age well. The low acidity increases our perception of sweetness in the wines.

Its heartland is Alsace, in the belt of vineyards sheltering in the lee of the Vosges mountains. Here, in one of the driest corners of France, vines ripen in long, sunny autumns to yield sweet fruit that can, in good years, make rich 'Vendange Tardive' (late-harvest) wines.

Most Gewurztraminer is however off-dry – though it can be hard to tell from the label: vintages vary widely in ripeness, and producers differ both in their interpretations and in the way they label sweetness (see page 118).

Gewurztraminer thrives in New Zealand, Chile and West Coast USA, but demands a relatively cool site if it is to reproduce the benchmark Alsace character. Closer to home, it grows in Germany and Austria (spelt 'Gewürztraminer' with the accent: Alsace and New World countries tend to omit it).

As a food wine, Gewurztraminer partners the cuisine of its native Alsace, and has gained a world role as a match to spicy foods from China to Thailand.

AROMA & FLAVOUR

Powerful, individual, unmistakeable: this perfumed grape is hard to miss, with its aromas and flavours of roses and lychees. Some find it difficult to like this wine that is more about fragrance than fruit; to others it's quite irresistible. Generally low in acidity and full-bodied, a fine one will be beautifully aromatic, with a clean, refreshing finish. A lesser wine can be positively overpowering on the nose.

WHEN YOU TRY THESE WINES, LOOK OUT FOR:

- rich texture on the palate
- low acidity
- very distinctive aromas and flavours of lychees and rose petals
- nearly always some sweetness

Would you agree that these wines are:

- very perfumed and floral, and that they have noticeably lower acidity than the Rieslings?

Maturity

Though nearly always drunk at one to four years old, quality Gewurztraminer can age – especially the sweeter ones, and those with noble rot. In Alsace, Vendange Tardive – late-picked – will indicate a sweeter wine; Sélection de Grains Nobles the sweetest (and potentially longest-lived).

TOP TIP

As well as 'Gewurz', look out for Alsace's Pinot Noir red wines: they are starting to gain respect — and exports — as warmer summers and new techniques yield wines that are delicate, yet full of cherry/raspberry fruit.

KEY AROMAS & FLAVOURS

- rose petals
- lychee
- spice
- turkish delight

Dry
Sweet

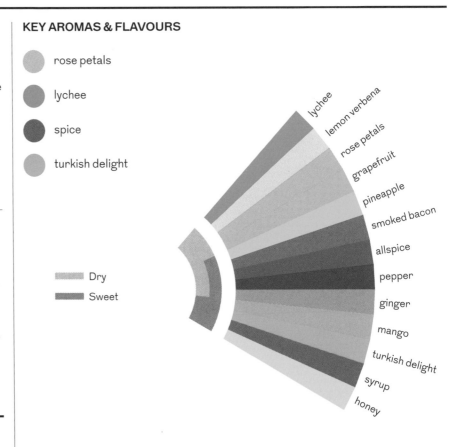

lychee
lemon verbena
rose petals
grapefruit
pineapple
smoked bacon
allspice
pepper
ginger
mango
turkish delight
syrup
honey

BALANCE

THE CHARACTER
OF THE WINE
IN YOUR GLASS

Ripeness and alcohol, plus low acidity, combine to give an impression of sweetness to most Gewurztraminers.

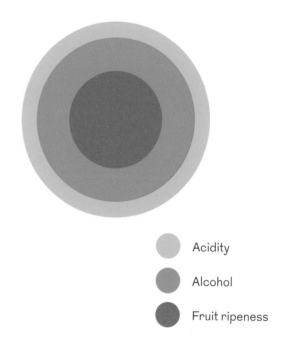

Acidity

Alcohol

Fruit ripeness

ALSO TRY: OTHER ALSACE GRAPES

Here – unusually for France – wines are labelled by grape variety. Apart from Gewurztraminer and Riesling (see page 119), you will see:

MUSCAT Even more floral and fruity than Gewurztraminer, the wine is akin to fresh muscat grapes. It can be made very sweet, though most in Alsace are light and dry.

PINOT GRIS Alsace wines from this grape are a far cry from cheap, dilute Pinot Grigios (the same grape in Italy): here, Pinot Gris spells richly honeyed, dry whites as well as superb sweet late-harvest wines. More acidity than Gewurztraminer.

PINOT BLANC Used in Alsace for everyday white wines: light- to medium-bodied, crisp and dry, with hints of apples, honey and yeast and a refreshingly pure and clean finish.

PINOT NOIR The red Burgundy grape: see Top Tip.

SYLVANER Neutral whites, tending to crisp acidity; rarely seen alone these days.

Food matches

Savoury, salty foods temper the fullness and/or sweetness of Gewurztraminer wines: try them with the Munster cheese traditional in Alsace. Or match them with oriental cuisine.

Some Gewurztraminer-friendly foods:

- Creamy-sauced pork dishes
- Pâté
- Mould-ripened soft cheeses
- Gently-spiced dishes

KEY REGION:

Alsace

The vineyards here look east to the Rhine; pine-forested hills shelter them, the grapes go by names like Riesling, Gewurztraminer, Sylvaner.... Yet we are in France, not Germany.

Tangled history and shifting frontiers made Alsace a unique blend of both countries. Firmly French in its love of gastronomy (it shelters a remarkable concentration of fine restaurants), it is also French in its wine laws and approach to winemaking. The bottles may be tall, the wines white (though reds are made), but the accent is on depth and body, with dry wines at around 12-13 degrees rather than the more ethereal Rieslings of the Mosel.

Gewurztraminer is a key grape of Alsace. It comes second to Riesling in rankings by area planted, but nowhere else in the wine world succeeds so well with this quirky, fascinating variety. Alsace enjoys a dry, sunny climate (see below) and 'gewurz' ripens in the long autumns to naturally high sugar levels far in excess of Riesling.

SWEET OR DRY?

It can be a puzzle sometimes to tell if a Gewurztraminer – or indeed any Alsace wine – is dry or sweet. Alsace labels may appear simple by comparison with German ones. However, they are potentially even more confusing due to the complete lack (with a few notable exceptions) of any official sweetness category on the label at all. The problem with Alsace wines is that their high levels of minerality (see page 53) can offset our perception of sweetness, so some very mineral wines with residual sugar can taste dry while drier, less mineral wines can taste sweet. It is an incredibly complex issue that has resulted in most producers (unhelpfully) not giving an indication of sweetness on the label at all.

There are some pointers, though. If you see the term **Sélection des Grains Nobles (SGN)** on the label, then you are looking at the rarest, sweetest, most concentrated level of Alsace wines, sometimes with grapes affected by noble rot. Note, though, that some SGN wines can be a lot sweeter than others....

Vendange Tardive (late harvest) is the level below SGN and would suggest a dessert wine – however, as with German Auslese Rieslings, some Vendange Tardive wines can be almost dry. The best have great potential for ageing.

If you are really looking for a dry Alsace wine, you are in trouble – unless you know the producer's house style. The following (EU-approved) terms may guide you, but are not widely used and are by no means definitive: **Sec** (dry), **Demi-Sec** (medium-dry), **Moelleux** (sweet) or **Doux** (sweeter).

However, now some producers are using a sweetness scale on the label, which attempts to convey the taste of sweetness in the wine, rather than the actual residual sugar level. This is by far the best method of assessing the taste of the wine without opening the bottle. That said, there are a few different types of scale in use, none of which correlates with each other, and none of these is obligatory – hence, for now at least, the confusion continues....

GRAND CRU

The 51 top vineyards in Alsace are ranked as **Grand Cru**. On a label, this signals a wine from a single vineyard, from a single vintage, and from one of the four permitted varieties; Riesling, Muscat, Gewurztraminer, or Pinot Gris. Yield must be lower than usual.

ALSO TRY:

Riesling in Alsace

Compare, if you get the chance, a Riesling from Alsace with one from the Mosel and a third from South Australia. Three very different wines, but all sharing the character of the grape. Alsace believes in powerful, dry wines; earthier, weightier and fuller than in Germany. Dry Alsace Rieslings can be austere and steely, yet with balancing hints of honey. The Australian will typically be drier, with more acidity and more intense lime character.

Riesling's character in Alsace stems in large part from climate and terroir (see caption); but tradition, in the shape of gastronomy, plays a part, too. Alsace wines seem designed for the table, and to partner the powerful flavours the region traditionally enjoys.

Today, there is a widening range of styles, with some producers pushing the steely subtlety of the grape, others aiming for a more voluptuous character. This is a region where – above the everyday level – it pays to know the producer's approach to their wine.

See page 117 for other Alsace grapes

Left: Vineyards clothe the foothill slopes of the Vosges mountains. They face east, south-east or south, enjoying the long sunny days of this northern (47.5°N) latitude and continental climate. The Vosges confer shelter from the rain-bearing west winds, making Alsace one of the driest as well as sunniest corners of France. The slopes provide good drainage and tilt the vines towards the sun.

Gewurztraminer worldwide

Germany also grows this grape, usually under the name Traminer: look for it in the more southern wine regions such as Baden and the Pfalz. You can follow the grape across south Germany and into **Austria**, where it is a speciality of Styria (Steiermark) and on into **Hungary** and other South-East Europe winelands.

The best-known Gewurztraminers outside Europe come from **New Zealand**. It has been tried just about everywhere that is cool enough – **Chile** is gaining a name for it. Good examples have emerged from **Australia**, the Pacific North-West and elsewhere in the **USA** – but it is a minority taste.

TRAMINER/SAVAGNIN

Gewurztraminer, the spicy Traminer, is in fact an example of the ancient Savagnin grape, which is now less well known under its original name — except in the Jura mountains of Eastern France. There it makes an extraordinarily tangy wine, often produced in a sherrified form after ageing in casks without topping up. The prime example is the unique appellation of Château-Chalon, 100 per cent Savagnin, which may not be released until its seventh year.

BIODYNAMIC AND ORGANIC: CAN YOU TASTE THE DIFFERENCE?

Some embrace these techniques, some think they're pure moonshine; but noticeably fine wines are resulting, finds Jasper Morris MW.

Organics and biodynamics are labels which incite fascination or cynicism in equal measures. Those in favour feel that these methods improve the quality of the wine as well as being ecologically and environmentally sound. The nay-sayers deplore what they see as a lack of scientific rigour, and suspect that the labels are sometimes being used purely for marketing purposes.

Organic vineyards are farmed without the use of chemical intervention, though such naturally-occurring elements as copper and sulphur may be used in compound form (copper sulphate) as a fungicide. There are, though, worries about the possible build-up of copper deposits in the soil, as it does not biodegrade easily. Since 2012 the EU has introduced the concept of Organic Wine, though the regulations in the winery (as opposed to vineyard) are not stringent.

Many producers talk blithely about being organic, but do not seek certification from such organisations as ECOCERT. Others do, but prefer not to say so on the bottle, as they think that the prime message should be the producer, appellation/variety and vintage. Some do also make their certification clear on the label: helpful to restaurateurs and retailers who wish to promote this category, or to consumers who wish to support it.

Biodynamics takes organic farming to a more spiritual level. The father of the movement is widely regarded as being Rudolf Steiner, who gave a series of agricultural lectures in 1924 setting out the broad principles. His best-known follower since then has been Maria Thun (1922-2012), who published an annual biodynamic gardening calendar. Nicolas Joly of Savennières in the Loire Valley was one of the earliest French vigneron proponents of the biodynamic movement, since when the idea has spread widely in Alsace, Burgundy and many other parts of the world. Biodynamic accreditation is through DEMETER (whose French base is in Colmar, Alsace) or BIODYVIN.

continued...

Opposite: Vines at Chile's Alcohuaz estate, high in the Andes, grow in virtual desert. The wines here are made using biodynamic techniques.

Biodynamic ideas combine Man, the Earth and the Cosmos. Some of the ideas are quite straightforward and link easily enough to other belief systems; others seem absolutely out where the buses don't run. The former include aligning wine-growing and -making to the moon's progress through the constellations, and essentially homeopathic treatments; the latter planting cow's horns in the ground (though there is evidence of this in viticulture as far back as the 17th century).

Biodynamicists, like organic winemakers, are accused of using the label as a marketing tool – and doubtless there are exponents who prefer the public relations benefits of biodynamics to the detailed practice. But it is worth pointing out that many of the producers who were quick to espouse this new idea (Zind Humbrecht in Alsace, Leroy, Leflaive, Lafon and many more in Burgundy) were already at the top of the quality tree and had much more to lose than to gain in terms of reputation.

It would be a bold move to ascribe specific qualitative aspects to the wines made by organic or biodynamic methods compared to their conventional counterparts. But watching a number of already high-quality producers across the years as they switch to biodynamic farming, I have observed an enhanced crystalline purity in their wines and a more precise definition of vineyard characteristics.

Below: This Argentine estate leaves you in no doubt.

Chenin Blanc

KEY POINTS

- White grape
- Aromatic
- Very high acidity
- Thin skins — susceptible to noble rot
- All styles from dry to sweet, also sparkling
- Can age for decades

KEY REGIONS

Loire Valley, South Africa

Here is a grape with a split personality. Much (very) ordinary and unmemorable white wine is made from it around the globe; yet, in its heartland along the gentle slopes of France's Loire Valley, it makes some of the world's longest-lived and finest white wines.

Not just split, but varied: from the same area – Vouvray, in the Loire – Chenin Blanc becomes still or sparkling; can be bone-dry or 'moelleux' (sweet), semi-sweet or botrytis-sweet.

For all variations of Loire Chenin, the very high initial acidity is the key to character and development.

Most Chenin Blanc, though, aspires to nothing like this sophistication. From places as varied as South Africa, Argentina and California, it makes straightforward dry white wine, often with a floral note. Growers applauded its high yields and its high acidity – even in warmer climates than its northern homeland of the Loire; but world-beating quality has not been their aim.

Now, however, interesting Chenin Blancs are emerging from South Africa and other New World winelands. As in the Loire, there's a range of styles from dry to sweet.

The pinnacle of Chenin Blanc is still the Vouvray district of the middle Loire, where wines are made that can last a century.

Vouvray can be pétillant – gently, subtly fizzy. In contrast, a whole industry of Loire sparkling-wine producers relies on Chenin Blanc for sparkling Saumur: clean, correct and rarely more than bland unless Chardonnay is added to the mix, when it becomes Crémant de Loire.

AROMA & FLAVOUR

Perhaps the hardest white grape to generalise about: its personality is in the hands of the winemaker. Far less aromatic than Gewurztraminer or Riesling, the evanescent scent of a fine cool-climate Loire example may remind you of an orchard, or honey, beeswax and flowers. In some cases, wet wool or lanolin may come to mind....

When you try these wines, look out for:

- green apple aromas and flavours
- very high acidity
- sometimes a distinctive whiff of wet wool/lanolin
- occasionally hints of toast/vanilla from oak on South African examples

Would you agree that these wines are:

- very high in acidity (often balanced out by some sweetness in the sweeter styles), and that they have noticeable green apple flavours?

Maturity

Most Chenin Blanc is made to drink young, but the grape makes some of the world's longest-lived white wines in the right place. The sweetness in the wine is masked by very high acidity in youth – but the acidity confers longevity. Serious Vouvrays, both dry and sweet, can not only last but can evolve for decades: wines from the 1920s are still glorious. As with Sauternes, top sweet wines are from vintages where noble rot develops.

KEY AROMAS & FLAVOURS

- green apple
- wet wool/lanolin
- honey
- quince

Cool climate
Warm climate

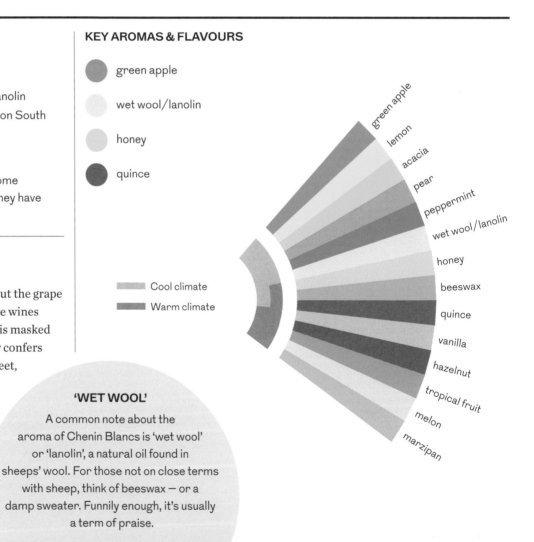

green apple
lemon
acacia
pear
peppermint
wet wool/lanolin
honey
beeswax
quince
vanilla
hazelnut
tropical fruit
melon
marzipan

'WET WOOL'

A common note about the aroma of Chenin Blancs is 'wet wool' or 'lanolin', a natural oil found in sheeps' wool. For those not on close terms with sheep, think of beeswax — or a damp sweater. Funnily enough, it's usually a term of praise.

BALANCE

THE CHARACTER
OF THE WINE
IN YOUR GLASS

Young cool-climate Chenin Blanc is acidic, dry, even austere: the acidity masks the inherent fruitiness. As the wine ages, it can – alone among wines – taste sweeter as the acidity softens out. Here we show the contrast between top examples of cool- and warm-climate styles.

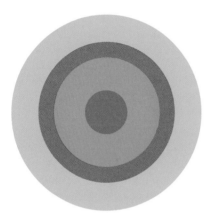

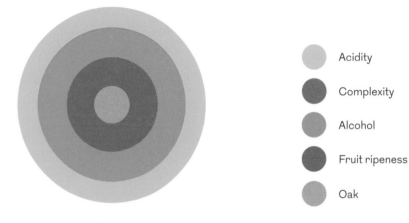

Acidity

Complexity

Alcohol

Fruit ripeness

Oak

COOL

Dry Vouvray from the Loire

Acidity masks the fruitiness

WARM

Oaked, South Africa

More upfront tropical-fruit flavours
balance oak and higher alcohol

Food matches

It is hard to generalise because of the wide sweep of styles, but as well as the ideas to the right try Chenin Blancs as an apéritif, and with strong cheeses or rich terrines. Medium-sweet styles are good on their own.

Some Chenin Blanc-friendly foods:

- Dry-style wines: fish, salads
- Medium styles: seafood, fish in rich sauces
- Sweeter versions: desserts - fruit tarts and pastries, particularly almond- or apple-based ones
- Cheeses

KEY REGION:

Loire: Anjou and Vouvray

The valley of the River Loire – see map on page 42 – links a wide range of wine styles. Among the most unusual, and fascinating, are the Chenin Blanc wines made in the central tract: Anjou and the Vouvray district of Touraine.

Whereas a white Sancerre is a predictable matter – dry, and clearly Sauvignon Blanc – an Anjou Chenin wine can be anything. Depending upon the vintage conditions and the maker's desires, it can be bone-dry, intensely sweet, or anywhere in between. The age of the wine is yet another variable: among whites, only Rieslings last as long and change so much in bottle.

Vintages vary because the Loire is well north, and because the Atlantic winds bring mild, rainy air up the valley, to meet the colder, drier weather of central France. One year is rarely like another.... To make sweet wines, especially those from noble rot-affected grapes (see page 62) growers hope for a long, warm, misty autumn.

The geography and organisation of these vineyards is as quirky as the wines. **Anjou**, the winelands south of the city of Angers, makes mostly Chenin Blanc whites. Enclaves such as Coteaux du Layon – and even more special districts such as Bonnezeaux and Quarts de Chaume – benefit from special terroirs. The sweet wines used to be the only bottles worthy of note, but modern dry Anjou is a reliable standby. Savennières is a favoured riverside zone for long-lived dry whites.

Upriver to the east, **Vouvray** is the heart of another Chenin Blanc district: here are made perhaps the finest sweet whites the Loire offers. Once again, the best of these demand and benefit from years (decades, even) in bottle. **Montlouis** offers a similar style, perhaps less intense.

In between Anjou and Vouvray the **Saumur** country, scattered around the castle and town, is known not only for its red wines (which we met in the Cabernet Franc chapter), but is also the heartland for Chenin Blanc sparkling wines, the best of which are labelled Crémant de Loire.

DRY AND SWEET ON THE LABEL

Clues to the style of Anjou and Vouvray whites will be found on labels, but note that the level of acidity – which varies from vintage to vintage, and between producers – can make the wines taste far drier than their sugar levels would imply:

- **Sec** Dry
- **Sec-Tendre** Off-dry
- **Demi-Sec** Medium dry – but moderately sweet to most tastes
- **Moelleux** Sweet
- **Doux** Sweetest of all
- **Liquoreux** As Doux

You will also see the term **pétillant**, meaning gently sparkling.

Opposite: Vineyards above the Loire at Savennières.

KEY REGION:

South Africa

Chenin Blanc used to be the workhorse grape of the Cape vineyards, prized as much for its neutral character and reliability as for any specific virtue. The fashion for reds, and for more recognisable 'international' whites, put Chenin in the shade. But its virtues – acidity, concentration – are being rediscovered.

Chenin vines that survived the rush to plant Sauvignon are now fêted as 'old bush vines', and their wine appears under some fashionable labels from Stellenbosch and Swartland. Producers are blending Chenin Blanc with minority proportions of Clairette (for an aromatic lift), Viognier and other Southern Rhône varieties, and some are ageing the result in old oak.

Some producers are also trying new oak for fermentation, adding spice and vanilla notes that enhance the essentially neutral character of the Chenin.

TASTING NOTES
Record your own impressions

Prompts: you are looking out for

Riesling: Fresh fruit and floral aromas, lime, toast and possibly petrol
Gewurztraminer: Lychee and rose petals, full body
Chenin Blanc: Green apples and very high acidity

RIESLING

1 _____

_____

2 _____

_____

GEWURZTRAMINER

3 _____

_____

4 _____

_____

CHENIN BLANC

5 _____

_____

6 _____

_____

BLIND TASTING

7 _____

_____

8 _____

_____

9 _____

_____

10 _____

_____

Opposite: Old vintages in the cellars at an estate in Germany (the fungus enjoys the fumes, but is entirely harmless...).

QUESTIONS

In session 4 we have looked at three grape varieties: Riesling, Gewurztraminer and Chenin Blanc.

1. Which variety makes Vouvray and from which region does this wine come?

2. Which of these varieties are found in Alsace?

3. Where in the New World might you find Riesling growing?

4. Where in the New World might you find Gewurztraminer growing?

5. Where in the New World might you find Chenin Blanc growing?

6. Which of these varieties is most often made into a range of styles including sparkling?

7. Which of these varieties has the lowest acidity?

Which might have aromas often described as:

8. — green apples and wet wool?

9. — citrus fruits and even a hint of petrol?

10. — rose petals and lychees?

Name the grape variety beside each description:

11. — full-bodied with rich, unctuous texture, off-dry with low acidity and intense floral aromas?

12. — very high acidity, sweet or dry, with green apple flavours and a touch of honey and quince?

13. — aromatic, high acidity, intense citrus and white flower flavours with a touch of petrol?

Answers on page 221

Opposite: Large old barrel in the traditional oval shape in use for fermentation in the Mosel.

5

Three classic red grapes of France whose highly individual characters, allied to their particular environments, make for three very distinct styles.

GAMAY
PINOT NOIR
SYRAH/SHIRAZ

GAMAY
fun & fruity

The grape of Beaujolais: crisp, fruit-laden, juicy wines that bring immediate pleasure, though the best can age gracefully.

PINOT NOIR
prima donna

The source of red Burgundy: capricious, exacting, delicious — at its greatest, sublime. Winemakers worldwide battle to master its subtle character.

SYRAH/SHIRAZ
peppery

Syrah produces long-lived Rhône reds such as Hermitage and Côte-Rôtie; it has travelled well and makes warm, generous wines around the world.

Where the grapes grow

Pinot Noir is fussy about its growing conditions, insisting on a cool climate, while Syrah is the opposite, demanding warmth. Both are found around the globe where conditions permit. Gamay is one of the few grapes we discuss that has a dominant homeland: Beaujolais in central France.

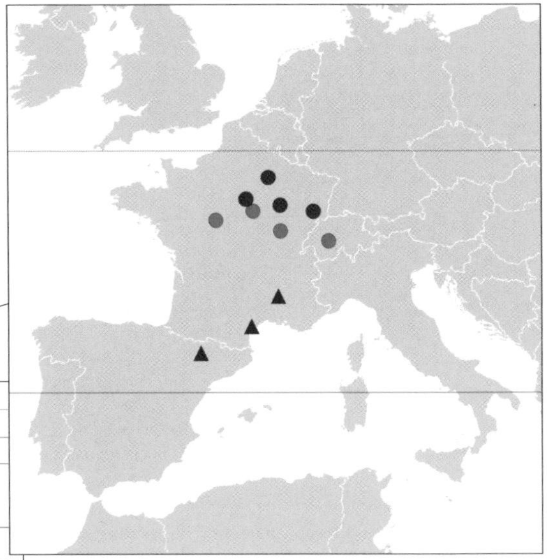

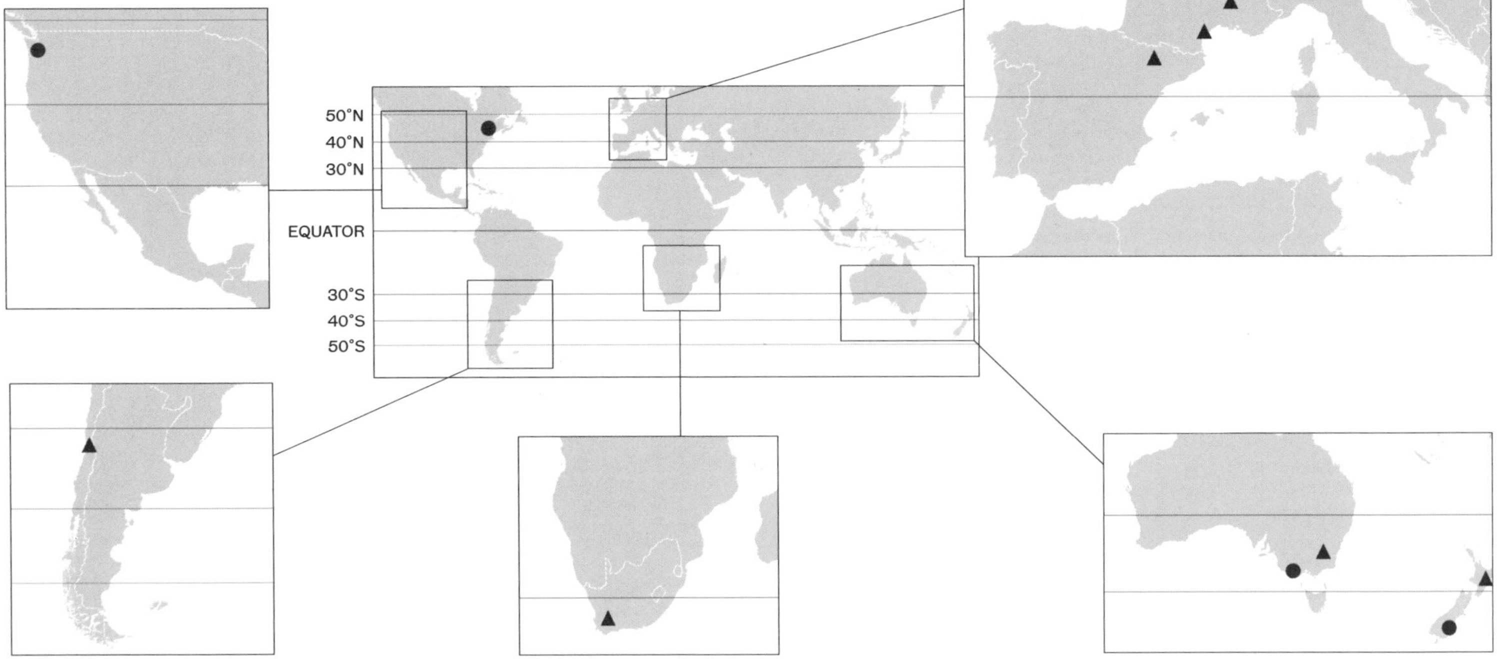

50°N
40°N
30°N

EQUATOR

30°S
40°S
50°S

GAMAY

● **Cooler climate**

Beaujolais
Upper & Central Loire
Switzerland

PINOT NOIR

● **Cooler climate**

Burgundy
Champagne
Upper Loire
Jura
Oregon
Canada
New Zealand
Australia

SYRAH/SHIRAZ

▲ **Warmer climate**

Rhône Valley
Southern France
Spain
Australia
California
South Africa
New Zealand
Chile

Gamay

KEY POINTS

- Red
- Fruity
- High acidity
- Moderate alcohol
- Low tannins in most wines
- Moderate tannins in Cru wines
- Rarely blended
- Most are to drink young

KEY REGIONS

Beaujolais, Loire, Switzerland

Gamay shows its personality as the sole grape of Beaujolais, a charming, hilly district of central France. The wine named after the district has one of the clearest-cut characters on the list of French reds. Drink it young – only the best will age; drink it with food – its appetising acidity is balanced by ample fresh, fruity flavours; drink it chilled on a summer's day.

Because Beaujolais is so much the benchmark for Gamay, most notes about that wine refer equally to the grape. It is grown elsewhere, in the Loire, in corners of rural France and in Switzerland, and it has been tested around the world; but in terms of sheer quantity Gamay equals Beaujolais.

In the glass, the wines are typically clear and light to look at: none of the opacity and density of, say, a Syrah or a Cabernet. The colour ranges from the startling lipstick-pink of new Beaujolais, through purple, to the brick-red of a mature Morgon.

Beaujolais demonstrates the hierarchy of French wine – and how this marries with terroir, the special character of the place the wine comes from.

At the base of the pyramid is straight Beaujolais: simple wine from anywhere in a wide area.

Beaujolais-Villages comes from a clutch of communes – villages – in the north of the zone. Here the soil is reckoned better, and the wine has more structure and staying-power. It drinks well at one to two years old.

The top rank, Beaujolais's first division, is made up of ten defined areas or 'Crus' – Morgon, Fleurie and the like – that are appraised as having the best terroirs, and characters of their own.

So much, so logical. And here the logic slides in typically French fashion: it is not mandatory to print the word 'Beaujolais' on a Cru label – and frequently it is not.

Wine suggestions for this session, page 216

AROMA & FLAVOUR

Gamay equals Beaujolais, and at their simplest these are wines to drink young and cool, brimming with summer fruit and refreshing acidity, and low in tannin. Further up the quality scale, Beaujolais from one of the Crus gains more complexity with a little bottle-age. All Gamays are at their best with food.

When you try these wines, look out for:

- bright, lipstick-pink to purple colour
- fresh summer-fruit aromas and flavours
- occasionally, aromas of bubblegum and banana: these show it's made using carbonic maceration (page 148)
- earthy notes on some

Would you agree that these wines have:

- high acidity and juicy summer-fruit aromas, with spicy, earthy notes on certain examples?

Maturity

In general, don't mature! Young and cool is the rule. Simple Beaujolais: drink the most recent vintage. Beaujolais-Villages: drink the most recent or the vintage before last. The only Gamays that age well are the Beaujolais Crus, which can be good at 3-5 years; up to 10 in the best vintages and vineyards.

TOP TIP: BEAUJOLAIS AND VALUE

Beaujolais Nouveau is new wine, bottled and sold just weeks after the harvest. It can be fun, but is certainly not great, and it colours perceptions of Beaujolais as a whole. The nouveau fashion has waned in some markets, but one side-effect lingers: quality Beaujolais is good value.

KEY AROMAS & FLAVOURS

- bubblegum
- strawberry
- earthy

Basic
Cru

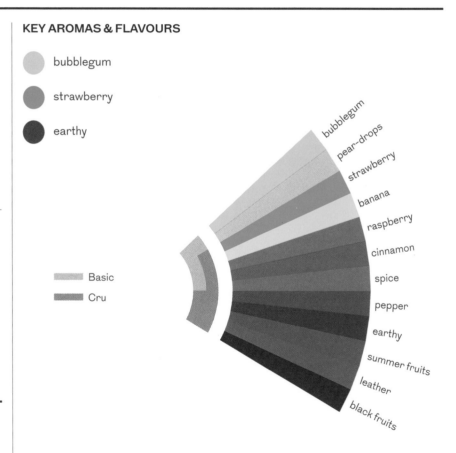

BALANCE

THE CHARACTER
OF THE WINE
IN YOUR GLASS

The contrast between a simple Beaujolais – labelled just 'Beaujolais' – and wine from one of the ten special, named, zones is apparent from the start: the Cru wine will have far more tannin and structure. By five years old, it can develop complex, mature notes.

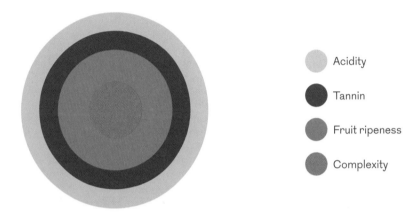

BASIC BEAUJOLAIS

Simple Beaujolais, around a year old

CRU BEAUJOLAIS

More concentrated from the start,
5 years' maturity adds savoury depth

○ Acidity

● Tannin

● Fruit ripeness

● Complexity

Food matches

These are great food wines: 'Some can strike you as half of nothing on their own, but put them with food and the lights go on...'

In France, Beaujolais is a staple of restaurant wine lists at the simple level – for good reason, as its vibrant fruit and acidity partners assertive, hearty dishes. The more serious, Cru, wines work with classic Burgundian cuisine.

Some Gamay-friendly foods:

- Charcuterie: salami, ham, terrines
- Roast poultry
- Salmon
- Soft cheese
- Cherries
- Rustic dishes: casseroles, sausages

KEY REGION:

Beaujolais

SOILS AND STYLES

Beaujolais, as we learned on page 135, comes in three levels – defined by one expert as 'weekday, Friday and weekend' wines:

- Ordinary **Beaujolais** is labelled as just that, and comes from the biggest zone (see map opposite), so there is more of it.
- **Beaujolais-Villages** again carries that name on the labels, and is made in 38 communes in a selected tract of land.
- The **Crus** are the wines from the top ten zones: look for these names, not 'Beaujolais', in large type on the labels.

Beaujolais is a textbook example of the influence of terroir. Here, the everyday wine is grown on sandy soil, with some clay, whereas the '-Villages' communes are on sand and schist. The 'top ten' Cru vineyards enjoy well-placed, sunny sites on granite, so they get extra bonus points in the terroir stakes.

What's special about granite? The soil here is not granite rock, but a mix of decomposed granite and red-sandstone topsoil and other, mostly organic, matter. Granite soil is poor in nutrients and drains well: two factors that vines love. Granite soil is also disliked by Pinot Noir, which prefers limestone – but Gamay is well content.

THE CRUS

The Beaujolais Crus, mapped lower right, are best enjoyed at two to three years old; exceptions are noted below.

From north to south:

St-Amour Light, charming, with soft juicy fruit. The best wines benefit from some ageing.

Juliénas High overall standards, perhaps under-rated. Reminiscent of Fleurie (with added spice and flesh) when young, it shows a velvety class and depth as it ages. Its structure allows ageing up to and beyond its fifth birthday.

Chénas Limited production of weighty wines that can be full, generous and rich. Some producers oak-age their wines, others don't; both styles can be equally successful. Most is at its best in its first five years, but the finer 'vins de garde' easily age over a decade.

Moulin-à-Vent (pictured left) Worlds away from light, fluffy Beaujolais, when fully mature (often at 10 years or more) it can resembles more a Burgundy, or even a Rhône, than Beaujolais.

Fleurie Perfumed, silky, fresh, floral. Approachable almost immediately but, despite initial impressions, a wine with a depth and concentration that allows it to age as well as any in the region.

Chiroubles The lightest of the Crus and most refreshing too, with silky fruit and great charm. Best drunk young – although the very finest can age well.

Morgon Morgon needs more time than other Crus – wait two to three years for the most serious to develop their rich, savoury flavours.

Regnié Sandy soils here yield wines with an attractive, supple character and lots of aromatics. Most are best drunk young.

Côte de Brouilly Fruity, round, textured wines that can be reasonably tannic and often show earthy notes. Most should be drunk in three to four years, but the most age-worthy styles from top producers in top vintages can last up to a decade.

Brouilly As Côte de Brouilly

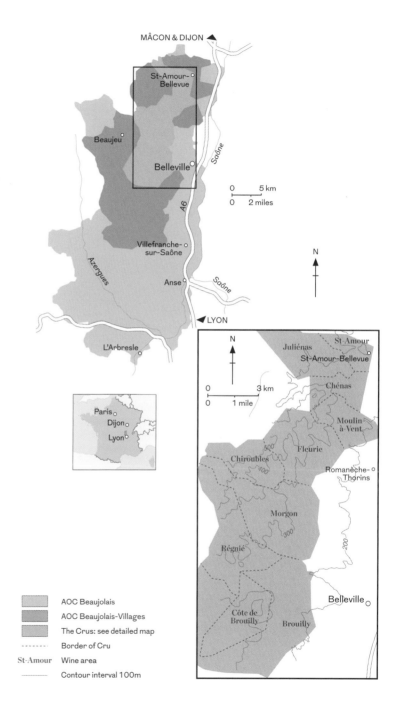

- AOC Beaujolais
- AOC Beaujolais-Villages
- The Crus: see detailed map
- - - - - - - Border of Cru
- St-Amour Wine area
- ——————— Contour interval 100m

HOW WARMTH AFFECTS GRAPES

Four key red-wine grapes – Pinot Noir, Gamay, Syrah and Grenache – are grown in this swathe of Eastern France. To thrive, each requires a subtly different range of temperatures.

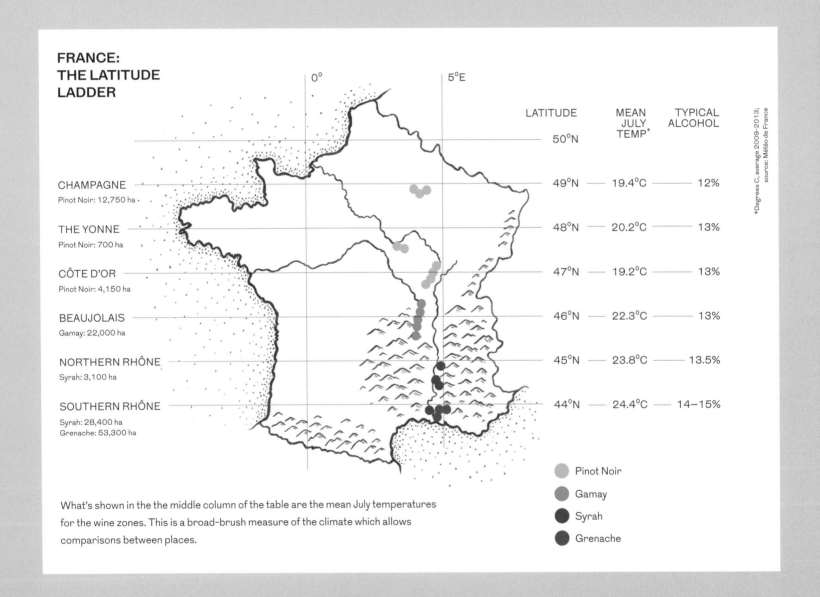

FRANCE: THE LATITUDE LADDER

	LATITUDE	MEAN JULY TEMP*	TYPICAL ALCOHOL
	50°N		
CHAMPAGNE Pinot Noir: 12,750 ha	49°N	19.4°C	12%
THE YONNE Pinot Noir: 700 ha	48°N	20.2°C	13%
CÔTE D'OR Pinot Noir: 4,150 ha	47°N	19.2°C	13%
BEAUJOLAIS Gamay: 22,000 ha	46°N	22.3°C	13%
NORTHERN RHÔNE Syrah: 3,100 ha	45°N	23.8°C	13.5%
SOUTHERN RHÔNE Syrah: 28,400 ha Grenache: 53,300 ha	44°N	24.4°C	14–15%

*Degrees C, average 2009-2013; source: Météo de France

● Pinot Noir
● Gamay
● Syrah
● Grenache

What's shown in the the middle column of the table are the mean July temperatures for the wine zones. This is a broad-brush measure of the climate which allows comparisons between places.

Follow the Latitude Ladder southwards: at the top, in the chilly **Champagne** region just a couple of hours from the English Channel, Pinot Noir is grown at latitude 49 degrees north. It continues to dominate in the **Côte d'Or** near Dijon, and in the **Yonne** – the countryside around Chablis, where they make reds as well as its more famous whites. Pinot needs cool conditions: too warm, and the wine is blowsy and uninteresting.

Moving on south, Gamay takes over. Villefranche, at 46 degrees north, is in the **Beaujolais** zone. The mean July temperature here is a crucial three degrees higher.

In the **Northern Rhône**, temperatures rise further: Valence, close to the great vineyards of Hermitage, is at 45 degrees north, and 1.5°C warmer. The key red grape here is Syrah. Near the Mediterranean in the **Southern Rhône**, Avignon is too warm for Syrah except in cooler, high-placed vineyards. Here Grenache takes over: a vine that thrives in hot conditions and is found on into Spain.

There is more to the picture than average temperature, of course. Longer summer days in the north mean more sunshine hours. And further north, site selection is crucial. In Champagne and Burgundy, the vineyards are on slopes which confer shelter and helpful exposure to sunlight. The best Syrah vineyards are on south-facing hillsides: Syrah loves to soak up the sun. In the Southern Rhône, flat land is not considered a drawback as there's enough sun for even the heat-loving Grenache.

CALIFORNIA: EFFECTS OF THE OCEAN

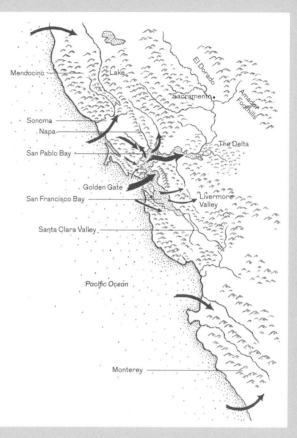

This map shows the topography of coastal California. Ranges of hills run broadly parallel to the Pacific, with gaps formed by rivers — most notably, San Francisco Bay.

The arrows show how cool air from the ocean flows inland through the gaps. As the land is warmed by the sun, so the air above it rises and cool air flows in from the Pacific to take its place. In some spots, fog forms; if so, summer daytime temperatures are chilly.

The 'fog gaps' lead to the paradox that northern Napa and Sonoma Counties are quite a lot warmer than their southern parts, which are cooled by San Pablo Bay, one arm of the great San Francisco inlet. Thus Carneros, on the Bay shores, is a better spot for cool-climate grapes than the main Napa Valley to the north.

FINE WINE FROM HOT LATITUDES

As the map above demonstrates, in coastal California the temperature contrast comes not from latitude (as in France) but from distance from the ocean. At around 38 degrees north – the latitude of North Africa – the area is naturally hot: go inland, around Sacramento in the Central Valley, and hot it indeed is, with over 100 days a year rising above 32°C. By contrast, the ocean shore, cooled by the Pacific Ocean currents, sees fewer than 20 days at this level.

The coastal zone, and the areas where ocean air reaches through the gaps in the Coastal Range – most notably the Bay itself – are by far the coolest. And that's where the best wines are grown. **Napa**, **Sonoma** and – recently – the Sierra foothills of **El Dorado** County are the names to watch for. Further south, off the map, geography plays the same trick, letting cool air inland to provide good grape country as far south as **Santa Barbara** – at 34 degrees north about as close to the Equator as fine wine gets.

Above: In the Mâconnais, southern Burgundy: here both Gamay and Pinot Noir grow alongside Chardonnay.

CARBONIC MACERATION

Martin Hudson MW explains a special technique used in the making of Beaujolais.

Many Beaujolais wines are made using a technique called carbonic maceration. Whole bunches of grapes are placed in a large fermentation vat that has first been filled with carbon dioxide – the gas that is produced by fermentation (it's usually piped from already-fermenting vats). The aim is to create some very fruity ester compounds, and to extract colour – but not tannins – from the skins.

It is important that the grapes are still attached to the stems, so that there is no break in the grape-skins. They then undergo a reaction driven by their natural enzymes – in effect fermenting the juice within the grape. This converts some of the sugar in their juice to alcohol (a level of around two per cent is reached), together with glycerol.

In practice, semi-carbonic maceration usually occurs, as the weight of the fruit crushes some of the grapes at the bottom of the vat, releasing juice which ferments normally due to the natural yeasts on their skins. Eventually the carbonic maceration process creates sufficient gas pressure inside the grapes to split the skins, allowing normal fermentation to take over.

Pinot Noir

KEY POINTS

- Red grape
- Crisp acidity
- Likes a cool climate
- Moderate alcohol
- Thin skins
- Pale colour
- Fine tannins
- Hard to grow
- Can age well

KEY REGIONS

Burgundy, Champagne, New Zealand, Oregon, Australia

Elegance before power is the key to Pinot Noir; it makes wines where subtlety tops strength. This is the grape of red Burgundy, the wine that can, at its pinnacle, be the costliest and rarest in the world.

Indeed, it is hard to find inexpensive or simple Pinot Noir: not just because it is fashionable, but because it is tricky – with its thin skins and low yields – to grow, and trickier still to make into wine. Despite the world's desire to emulate great Burgundy, this grape is choosy about travelling from its native land.

In consequence, Pinot Noir has a patchy success-rate around the world – in contrast to Cabernet Sauvignon or Syrah, the other two red grapes of similar status and renown. But where it is at home – and where winemakers have mastered it – Pinot Noir yields wines that reflect their terroir, respond well to oak-ageing, and mature to great elegance and complexity.

Burgundy apart, it is traditional in Alsace, the eastern Loire and parts of Germany (as Spätburgunder). It has migrated with success to New Zealand, Oregon and cooler corners in California. Australia works hard to find similarly cool places: Tasmania and Victoria have some.

Back in France, Pinot Noir is one of the three grapes of Champagne, and imitators/competitors use it to make sparkling wine in the Old World and the New.

But it is to Burgundy that every wine-lover returns in the sometimes frustrating search for Pinot perfection. The great names, the Grands Crus such as Chambertin, Musigny and Richebourg, are wines for millionaires; but dedicated and increasingly skilful producers conjure Pinot Noir magic from less-starry vineyards in the Côte d'Or heartland – and increasingly from other corners of Burgundy like the Côte Chalonnaise and the Auxerrois.

AROMA & FLAVOUR

With young Pinot Noir wines, look for bright, light-red colour, fine tannins and the scents and flavours of ripe summer fruits. Tasters hope to find a certain elegance, allied to acidity. As the wines mature, the characteristic earthy, mushroomy notes emerge. The finest Burgundies in their prime are silky, soft – yet with a backbone of fruit and discreet tannins.

When you try these wines, look out for:

- fine tannins
- crisp acidity
- elegance
- young wines: summer fruits and violets
- mature wines: savoury complexity

Would you agree that these wines are:

- perfumed and elegant, with fine tannins?

Maturity

Much Pinot Noir (such as simple generic Burgundy) is not made to age, and the jury is to an extent still out on all but the most ambitious New Zealand and Oregon wines, as they have yet to build a track-record. Serious Burgundy, though, has for centuries been famed for its long life. A Grand Cru can last four decades, a Premier Cru 10-15 years. For a vintage to age well, it must attain an elusive point of balance between fruit, acidity and tannin.

KEY AROMAS & FLAVOURS

- red fruits
- violets
- mushroom
- forest floor

Young
Mature

redcurrant
raspberry
strawberry
violets
plum
earthy
black cherry
mushroom
game
tobacco
oak
leather
truffle
forest floor
autumnal
farmyard

BLANC DE NOIR
(white from red) means just what it says: the colour of a red grape lies in its skin, so it's perfectly possible to use the clear juice to make a white wine. Champagne uses Pinot Noir in just this way.

BALANCE

THE CHARACTER OF
THE WINE
IN YOUR GLASS

Pinot Noir will only tolerate a narrow range of temperatures, so the 'warm' Otago district of New Zealand is cool by local standards, its short, hot summers tempered by colder winters. Here we contrast an Otago wine with a Premier Cru Burgundy.

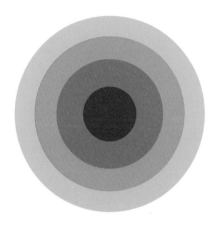

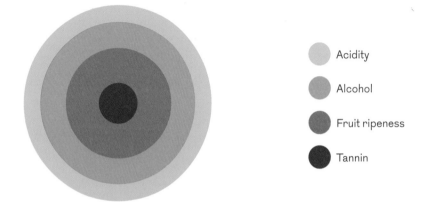

- Acidity
- Alcohol
- Fruit ripeness
- Tannin

CÔTE D'OR, BURGUNDY

In the Burgundy there is less obvious fruit ripeness and more acidity. The balance of fruit and acidity (unusually for a red grape) is all-important.

OTAGO, NEW ZEALAND

More alcohol and fruit, and less tannin, from grapes grown in a warmer — if still cool for New Zealand — region, give ripeness to the wine.

Food matches

It takes a mature red Burgundy to stand up to the rich flavours and sauces of classic Burgundian cuisine; crisper, more youthful reds partner today's lighter dishes and char-grilled meats. New World Pinots, with more up-front fruit, work well with stronger flavours, even oriental foods.

Some Pinot Noir-friendly foods:

Young wines:

- Pork, turkey, char-grilled meats
- Fish such as red mullet, tuna (particularly when wine is served cool)

Mature wines:

- Game, casseroles, sauced dishes
- Milder cheeses

KEY REGION:

Burgundy

Pinot Noir is the grape of red Burgundy, one of the best-known – and most expensive – wines in the world. Why is Burgundy so special, and why is it so costly?

Buy Burgundy and you pay the price of scarcity. There is not much Burgundy because there is not much land to grow it on. Take the heartland, the aptly-named Côte d'Or or 'golden slope': it's a mere ribbon of vineyards, covering the flanks of a sinuous ridge.

Each plot of vines here is ranked in a carefully-graded system that grants the best land the highest rank, and so on down a ladder of status.

So can we assume that every bottle with the same, ranked vineyard ('Cru') name on its label from the same year will be the same? No: this is only half the story. In Burgundy, these prized patches of vineyard each have a name – but rarely a single owner. And most wine-growers own land – often just a few rows of vines – in several vineyards.

Result: the 51-hectare (126-acre) Clos de Vougeot vineyard, once owned by the monks of Cîteaux Abbey, is nowadays split, thanks to inheritance or sales, between 80 owners. So you are looking, with a bottle of Burgundy, for both the name of the vineyard and that of the winemaker – who, typically, will have a patch of vines in this Grand Cru, a few rows in that, more in some Premier Cru vineyards....

Burgundy-lovers say that this skein of complexity, akin (to the novice) to chess in three dimensions, adds to the charm. It does mean that individuality will out: providing he or she can get their hands on some good land, a skilled vigneron can offer us wine that is truly the fruit of the mystic marriage between man and nature. But a clumsy one can disappoint. And even indifferent Burgundy can be expensive.

Bordeaux, organised by single-owner estates ('châteaux'), works quite differently: see right.

TOP TIP: BEYOND THE CÔTE

For red Burgundy value, look for wines labelled 'Bourgogne' (Burgundy) plus '-Hautes-Côtes de Nuits', from the back-country west of the main Côte. To the south, value can be found in the wine villages of the Côte Chalonnaise: Givry and Mercurey are two to note. Look, too, for Irancy, a village up near Chablis.

BURGUNDY	BORDEAUX
200 million litres of wine per year	**556** million litres of wine per year
28,000 hectares of vineyard	**120,000** hectares of vineyard
CLOS DE VOUGEOT Size of the medieval walled vineyard: **51 hectares**	CHATEAU LATOUR Size of the 'Enclos', sole source of the main wine: **47 hectares**
80 owners	**1** owner
...of which the largest owns 5.5 hectares	...which also owns a further 31 hectares
Bottles of Grand Cru Burgundy in a typical year: **1.4 million**	Bottles of classed-growth Bordeaux* in a typical year: **45 million**

*from the 61 Médoc & Graves 1855 châteaux

Burgundy family tree

The Côte d'Or is split into the northern, Nuits and southern, Beaune sections.
The names you'll find on the labels are those of the villages: they are listed below.
Names in red make mostly red wine; those in blue, mostly white.
Purple indicates both red and white.

Côte d'Or

Côte de Nuits

- Marsannay
- Fixin
- Gevrey-Chambertin
- Morey-St-Denis
- Chambolle-Musigny
- Vougeot
- Flagey-Echézeaux
- Vosne-Romanée
- Nuits-St-Georges

Côte de Beaune

- Aloxe-Corton
- Ladoix-Serrigny
- Pernand-Vergelesses
- Beaune
- Savigny-lès-Beaune
- Chorey-lès-Beaune
- Pommard
- Volnay
- Auxey-Duresses
- Monthélie
- St-Romain
- Meursault
- Blagny
- Puligny-Montrachet
- Chassagne-Montrachet
- St-Aubin
- Santenay
- Maranges

- Red
- White
- Both

DOUBLE-BARRELLED NAMES

Several villages have hyphenated names: Puligny-Montrachet, Vosne-Romanée, Nuits-St-Georges. They were once plain Puligny or Vosne — until the locals annexed the name of their most famous vineyard. These double-barrelled names can confuse. La Romanée, the Grand Cru that makes a small amount of very expensive Burgundy, is a tiny part (about a third of one per cent) of the village of Vosne. There will be more than 100 bottles of ordinary village wine — labelled Appellation Vosne-Romanée — for every one of La Romanée Grand Cru.

Slope and soil

The Côte d'Or hierarchy is, at its simplest, about slope. Vines grow on this long sweep of hillside, tilted largely south-east towards the morning and midday sun. There are few vines on the plain it overlooks, nor on the rocky hills above that are clothed with forest.

Just being on the hillside is not enough: there are good bits and better bits. Simply put, the Grands Crus are where everything comes right. Not too high up, for there the cool air and shade from the forest at the top of the hill delays ripening. Not too low down: there the soil is too deep, too damp, too fertile, and winter freezes are more of a risk. Nor too flat – a slope increases drainage as well as tilting the vines towards the sun.

So far, so explicable. However keen or expert the wine-grower, he or she will struggle to make top-rated wine from ill-drained, lower ground – though skill can mitigate geography. But why are some bits of slope Grands Crus, whereas the next field is mere 'village' land? To answer, a Burgundian will tell you, you must delve into geology, explore the mesoclimate (the climate of a specific place), check the map for the height, and for the steepness and direction of the slope....

The Burgundians will add, as a crowning argument, that many of the Grands Crus were spotted and planted by monks eight or nine centuries ago. With the choice of the entire hill, they saw where the snow melted first, the grapes ripened best. Often they built a wall round such a patch, called it a 'Clos' and kept that wine separate. You can still buy wine from these Clos today.

Outsiders may turn a sceptical eye on what they see as a tradition-based, hierarchical system. To some it hints at undeserved privilege and discrimination. Why, asks an Australian or a Californian, cannot a winegrower rise above the hierarchy by skill and hard work? The Burgundians reply that this is to confuse people with place. Place is what the hierarchy reflects; what people do with it is another dimension, though a grower with both skill and hard work will find that his or her wines follow the hierarchy of place.

Right: Looking up the slope of Clos St-Marc, a Burgundy Premier Cru in Nuits-St-Georges.

Burgundy: status on the label

CHAMBERTIN	BEAUNE	MEURSAULT
GRAND CRU	Premier Cru Les Grèves	Meursault Le Tesson
Appellation Chambertin Contrôlée	Appellation Beaune Premier Cru Contrôlée	Appellation Meursault Contrôlée
1999	1999	1999
Mis en Bouteille par Domaine Berry, Beaune, France 21200	*Mis en Bouteille par Domaine Berry, Beaune, France 21200*	*Mis en Bouteille par Domaine Berry, Beaune, France 21200*
13.5% vol. Product of France 75cl	13% vol. Product of France 75cl	12.5% vol. Product of France 75cl

Note that the name of the village is not given: the Grands Crus have an official status of their own.

The words Premier Cru and the name of the vineyard must be in the same-size type.

The vineyard name (Le Tesson in this example) must follow that of the village.

The top-ranking vineyards are the **Grands Crus**. A 'cru' is a vineyard: there are just 33 with this rank. Their names – Corton, Montrachet, Chambertin, Echézeaux – reverberate through history. Popes and emperors have squabbled over them, abbeys and dukes grown rich from them. Today, billionaires hoard their wines. Perhaps one and a half million bottles a year emerge from the Grands Crus, red and white – and that's not a lot.

Next come the **Premiers Crus**: over 600 of these. A typical Côte d'Or village will have a couple of dozen such vineyards, maybe more. The label will have the words 'Premier Cru' and will tell you which village it comes from plus the name of the cru, or vineyard – in this case Les Grèves.

All villages also make wines in the third division: these will carry the village name, occasionally a vineyard name too. These are the **commune** or **village** vineyards, where the Appellation Contrôlée is 'Meursault', 'Nuits-St-Georges' and so on. This wine can come from a specific vineyard, as in the example above from Le Tesson, or (more likely) it will be a blend from several plots. As always in Burgundy, the name of the grower is your guarantee.

NOTE: the name on the simplest, and usually least expensive, red Burgundies is **Bourgogne**. These are wines from the wider area, outside the Côte d'Or. Only these wines will have the word 'Bourgogne' on the label.

GROWERS AND NEGOCIANTS

Growers, in Burgundy parlance, own and cultivate vines, make the wine and bottle it under their name. Négociants, or merchants, buy wine (and/or grapes), age the wine and bottle it.

Right: A fine crop of Pinot Noir.

Pinot Noir worldwide

Looking around the world, the choosy Pinot Noir grape is far from being a big player in quantity terms, but such is its wine's charisma and quality that a network of aficionados has grown up.

Burgundy, sited as it is in the heart of France, is hardly a backwater, but in viticultural terms it used to be pretty self-absorbed. Not any more: its wine professionals are getting used to their output sharing shelf space, contests and media coverage with Pinot Noirs from around the world.

All the classic French grapes have spread worldwide, of course, but Pinot Noir is both hard to grow and highly rewarding if it works. From this challenge stems the fascination – and not a little glamour. A line-up of the top wines from the grape will range from Italy to Oregon, from Austria to Chile. In contests, New Zealand and German wines have on occasions trounced Burgundians.

The list of quality Pinot Noirs is, however, far shorter than that for other quality grapes such as Cabernet Sauvignon, which has done well in most countries to which it has been exported. With Pinot Noir there have been as many failures as successes. Many early attempts failed to find the subtlety and balance of Burgundy.

What does it take to produce good Pinot Noir wines? A narrow range of temperatures is the first requirement. If the conditions are too warm, the thin skins can get sunburn and the wines will tend to be jammy and flabby. If it is too cool and/or wet, rot in the ripening grapes becomes a problem – the grape's thin skins do not help here either. Even in Burgundy itself, the southern zones such as the Côte Chalonnaise can be too warm in some years for true finesse.

Then, too, Pinot Noir has a distinct affinity with well-drained limestone/chalk soils, as the Côte d'Or and Champagne show. The vine's impressive ability to reflect terroir means that a range of wine styles is emerging: even in small areas such as New Zealand's

Otago, growers are identifying quite narrow climate/soil zones as making differing styles of Pinot wine.

This vine has traditional strongholds in **Alsace**, the **Loire**, **Jura**, **Switzerland** (Blauburgunder is the name used), **Austria** and **Germany** (here the name is Spätburgunder: 'late Burgundian'). Elsewhere in Europe, it can be found in northern **Italy** – and increasingly in **England**, where it goes into sparkling wines alongside Chardonnay.

The worldwide quest for Pinot-friendly places with cool climates – and preferably limestone – has been unremitting for the last half-century. The New World shortlist has settled down to:

- The **Willamette Valley** and **Dundee Hills** of Oregon in the USA's Pacific North-West
- **Carneros** and **Sonoma** and the **Central Coast** in California, USA
- **British Columbia** and **Ontario** in Canada
- The **Central Otago**, **Marlborough**, **Nelson** and **Waipara** districts of New Zealand's South Island and **Martinborough/ Wairarapa** in the North Island
- **Tasmania**, **Yarra Valley** and the **Mornington Peninsula** in Australia.

More mass-market Pinot Noirs come from Chile, Romania, Moldova, even Brazil.... But these, whatever their virtues, are unlikely to remind you of Burgundy.

Right: Netting protects precious grapes in New Zealand.

Syrah/Shiraz

KEY POINTS

- Red grape
- Needs warmth
- Thick skins
- Deep colour
- High tannins
- Ages well
- Responds well to new oak
- Easy to grow

KEY REGIONS

Northern Rhône, Australia

One of the three great world travellers among red grapes, Syrah is often known in warmer climates as Shiraz.

Its heartland is the steep, stony landscape of the Northern Rhône Valley of France, where it is the sole grape of Cornas, and virtually so of Côte-Rôtie and Hermitage. Further down the valley, it is among the Châteauneuf-du-Pape varieties. And now it is increasingly grown, and blended with Grenache and other varieties, in the Côtes du Rhône districts: wines such as Gigondas and Rasteau often contain Syrah. Look for it too in the Languedoc (Southern France).

In Australia it is the heart of the long-lived and highly-priced (and -praised) Penfold's Grange (which used to add the name 'Hermitage' as a nod to the grape's origins). Other Australian Shiraz wines range in style from the heartily robust to the elegant: it is a grape that displays its terroir. At the everyday wine level, it is often blended with Cabernet Sauvignon.

South Africa, Chile and California have all taken to Shiraz. In California it is increasingly fashionable – perhaps as as a reaction to the ubiquity of Cabernet Sauvignon and Pinot Noir. Back in Europe, it is equally modish in Spain.

This is a dark, thick-skinned grape: this means high levels of tannin and lots of pigmentation – and thus a characteristic dark colour in the finished wine. It is easy to grow, but to ripen well demands a warm site, or a warm overall climate, if it is to show its true character.

Syrah/Shiraz wine can also be dilute and lacking interest if the vines are allowed to produce too much fruit: many of the benchmark sites are stony, almost soil-free, hillsides.

AROMA & FLAVOUR

The depth of colour of a typical Syrah is matched by powerful flavours of black fruits, black pepper, tar and (in its Shiraz guise) chocolate and herbs. Aromas can be more reticent, especially in young wines.

When you try these wines, look out for:

- dark berry fruits and black-pepper notes
- full body and high acidity
- high tannins in youth
- in mature wines, complex savoury aromas

Would you agree that these wines are:

- deeper in colour, richer and more tannic than the Pinot Noirs?

Maturity

Even the top Syrah wines of Côte-Rôtie and neighbours are enjoyable at five years old, but be patient: there is far more to come, and in good vintages they can last decades. Australian Shiraz, too, has demonstrated its ability to age superbly, with top examples in their prime at age 40-plus. More everyday Syrah/Shiraz wines – Crozes-Hermitage, St-Joseph, Australians above the basic brands – will be good to drink young but can improve for up to 3-6 years.

KEY AROMAS & FLAVOURS

- black pepper
- violets
- black & red fruits
- tar

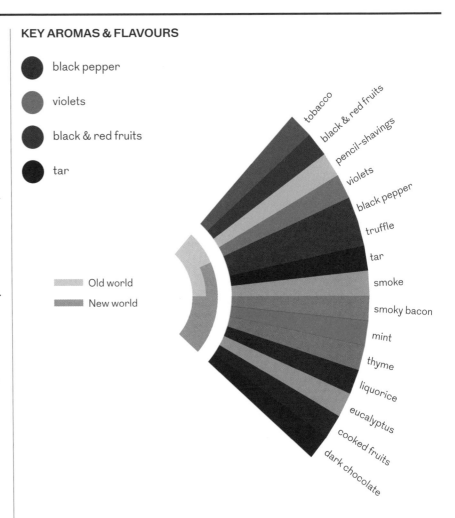

Old world
New world

tobacco
black & red fruits
pencil-shavings
violets
black pepper
truffle
tar
smoke
smoky bacon
mint
thyme
liquorice
eucalyptus
cooked fruits
dark chocolate

BALANCE

THE CHARACTER
OF THE WINE
IN YOUR GLASS

Compare a Côte-Rôtie from France's Rhône Valley with an equivalent-quality Australian Shiraz from Barossa, both at three years old. The French wine is high in tannin; fruit is masked. (Some producers do use new oak, though it is not traditional, and its influence is easily spotted.) The Barossa wine is softer, riper and higher in alcohol.

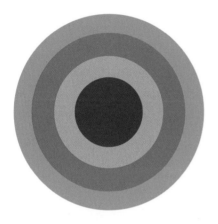

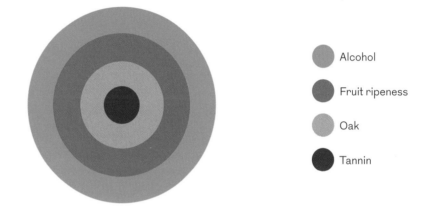

Alcohol

Fruit ripeness

Oak

Tannin

OLD WORLD
Côte-Rôtie

Fruit at this stage masked by tannin:
the wine will gain balance with maturity

NEW WORLD
Barossa, Australia

More in balance at three years old than the
French example, with the accent much more
on the fruit

Food matches

Syrah wines partner strong-flavoured meats and game, and work well with Mediterranean foods and strong cheeses. They have an affinity with smoked foods such as rustic hams, with robust charcuterie – and with barbecues.

Some Syrah/Shiraz-friendly foods:

- Goose
- Duck
- Pork
- Venison
- Wild boar
- Pheasant
- Sausages

KEY REGION:

Rhône

Syrah's heartland is the Northern Rhône Valley, south of Lyon and north of Valence. Wines like Côte-Rôtie, Hermitage and St-Joseph are dominated by, and are sometimes entirely made from, Syrah.

Further south, the variety is blended with Grenache and others to make many of the best Côtes du Rhône wines.

As the Latitude Ladder on page 140 shows, this part of France is quite a bit warmer than Burgundy to the north. Syrah needs warmth; indeed the most-prized vineyard land lies on steep, sun-trap hillsides where the sun is most intense. The **Hermitage** hill – a giant granite outcrop – faces due south. Its wine is prized, but there is not much of it.

Crozes-Hermitage is the name for wines made in a much wider zone. These, and the wines of the **St-Joseph** and **Cornas** appellations along the valley, offer good value and increasing quality.

A few miles north, the **Côte-Rôtie** hillsides loom above the river. Once again there is not much land, and thus not much wine: prices can be as steep as the hills. Côte-Rôtie growers can if they wish add modest amounts of the white grape Viognier to the Syrah.

The unifying style of Northern Rhône reds is spice, firm tannins and black-pepper aromas. At their best, they should not be heavy and dense: finesse must balance the ripeness. Côte-Rôtie wines are known for their elegance; Hermitage and Cornas tend towards weight. Vintages vary quite a lot, and producers adopt widely differing styles: choose with care.

SOUTHERN RHONE

Syrah is increasingly grown in the hot, wide southern vineyards of the Rhône Valley. Here, Syrah is blended with other grapes to make **Côtes du Rhône** wines (see Grenache in Session 6). Occasionally, growers use Syrah as the dominant partner, but it is normally subordinate to Grenache.

... AND IN THE LANGUEDOC

Leaving the Rhône and heading further south – and hotter – still, the fast-improving wine region of the Languedoc has taken to Syrah for both single-variety wines and as a blending partner. The best Syrahs come from the cooler, hilly **St-Chinian** and **Minervois** la Livinière AOC vineyards, though you will also find Syrah IGPs – 'country wines.'

Right: Steep terraced slopes in the Côte Blonde, part of the Côte-Rôtie district of the Northern Rhône Valley.

KEY REGION:

Australia

Syrah – Shiraz – is Australia's most widely-planted red grape. It's also long established there: it travelled across the globe nearly two centuries ago, so by now Shiraz wine is a truly indigenous style.

Typically, Australian growing conditions are both warmer and more predictable than those of France's Northern Rhône vineyards. Most antipodean Shiraz is easy-drinking, warm and full-bodied, though the most expensive wine in Australia – the serious, concentrated and long-lived Penfold's Grange – is also predominantly Shiraz. Relatively cooler zones, such as the **Margaret River** in Western Australia, yield Shiraz wines that are more akin to their Rhône counterparts.

The heartland of traditional-styled Shiraz is the **Barossa Valley** in South Australia, where many plantings of the grape go back over 100 years. Barossa Shiraz should be rich, spicy and suave, with hints of leather and pepper. The **Hunter Valley** in New South Wales and **Heathcote** in Victoria are also Shiraz strongholds.

Shiraz is frequently blended with Cabernet Sauvignon for everyday wines – a practice rare in France (though not unknown a century or so back, when Clarets were 'hermitaged' to make them darker and more muscular). Another Australian blend is 'GSM' – Grenache/Shiraz/Mourvèdre – used to make wines in the Southern Rhône style.

... AND ELSEWHERE

Rhône grapes, headed by Syrah/Shiraz, are the passion of a small but influential group of growers in **California** nicknamed the 'Rhône Rangers'. They have their counterparts in **South Africa** and in cooler-climate parts of **New Zealand** and **Chile**, too.

Syrah or Shiraz? It used to be that Shiraz was most common in the New World, but now you will find either – or both – names. Syrah is increasingly used by winemakers to signal that they are making Rhône-style wines.

SCIENCE SOUNDBITE: BLACK PEPPER

The black-pepper notes found in Syrah wines come from a compound called rotundone which is indeed also found in black pepper itself. Try it with a pepper mill in one hand and a glass of Syrah/Shiraz in the other....

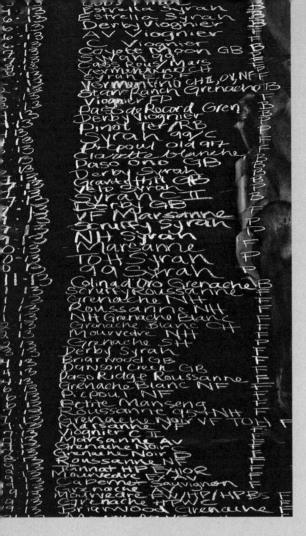

SOUTHERN GRAPES

Syrah shares the Rhône Valley with Grenache – see next Session – and a list of other characterful grapes. Simon Field MW revels in their quirky qualities.

As one descends from the mono-varietal rigour of the Northern Rhône, where the geographical near-coincidence of terraced vineyard, road, railway and river crowd the imagination with activity, there is an almost palpable sense of relief. Provence beckons, with intimations of 'luxe calme et volupté'; the countryside opens up and the climate shakes off continental briskness in favour of a Mediterranean balm.

The further south we go, the more Syrah becomes marginalised, its aristocratic purity now used to temper the generosity of heady blends of Grenache, Mourvèdre, Counoise and a legion of other indigenous varieties. Southern belles are not, in this context at least, prima donnas.

As with so much of the wine world, especially where the artisan holds sway over the industrial, a rediscovery of traditional values is well advanced. This applies as much to grapes as to methodologies, and it's fascinating to witness, for example, the reappraisal of the long-shunned **Carignan**, until recently a prime target for being grubbed up under the influence of EU subsidy. Nowadays, however, few styles capture as neatly the power and generosity of Mediterranean vineyards as old-vine Carignan. Centurian vines, gnarled and photogenic, yield parsimonious volumes and produce wines of great character and power.

In a similar vein, **Mourvèdre**, the great grape of Bandol, is becoming more and more popular. Mourvèdre, apparently, needs to have 'its feet in water and its head in the sunshine'. Patois personification does not always translate very well, but where these somewhat rigorous meteorological conditions can be met, we are likely to encounter superb wines, Beaucastel's Hommage à Jacques Perrin being probably the most outstanding example.

In the same vein, **Cinsault** is now re-emerging, not only for excellent rosés but also for charming reds, laced with herbs and the exuding warm aromatics of Baron Le Roy's 'laurel and thyme'.

It's fascinating to see these grapes also coming into their own further afield; indeed Californian Carignan and Australian Mourvèdre self-evidently make the grapes more visible in these and other New World countries where varietal labelling is actually permitted.

Left: The chalk-board 'menu' at Tablas Creek, California, spells out the winery's obsession: southern grapes.

The same applies to the whites; **Marsanne** from Tahbilk in Australia or **Viognier** from Californian 'Rhône Rangers' such as Randall Grahm at Bonny Doon are perhaps now as well-known as their distinguished European cousins.

Viognier and Marsanne have as their homestead the Northern Rhône appellations of Condrieu and Hermitage, the first a seductive fruit-basket of honeysuckled indulgence, the second one of the longest-lived and most enigmatic white wines in the vinous canon. **Roussanne**, better suited a little further south, has more natural acidity than Viognier, and perhaps more obvious and generous fruit flavours.

All three share rich texture, nuanced flavours and a capacity to age. It is no accident that white Hermitage, a century ago, was the most valued of all whites. The wheel has nearly completed another cycle....

Left: Condrieu, on the banks of the Rhône, is the heartland of Viognier.

ALSO TRY…

Zinfandel

California's own red grape, Zinfandel, comes in a range of styles from early-drinking and uncomplicated to more serious and age-worthy. It can be found in red, rosé/blush and fortified versions. There are even pale blush wines labelled 'white Zinfandel'.

The firm structure of red Zinfandels gives an impression of ageing potential, though most are not that age-worthy. Most 'Zin' is at the everyday end of the style range, stressing its hearty, fruity character: in a word, it is a hedonistic wine.

Tasters find black cherry and raspberry notes to complement the mixed spice. Other key aromas and flavours are raisins, mint, pepper, mushrooms…. Zinfandel-friendly foods include spicy meat dishes, barbecues and other hearty food.

The most prized Zinfandels are those from California's old-vine (often pre-Prohibition) plantings – these offer exotic, spicy notes and are usually high in alcohol.

• **Primitivo** Zinfandel is genetically identical to the Primitivo vine of Puglia, southern Italy: the wines can be similar in their dense, dark spiciness.

Right: Preparing the barrels at a California Zinfandel producer.

TASTING NOTES

Record your own impressions

Prompts: you are looking out for

Gamay: Bright purple colour, fresh summer fruits, high acidity

Pinot Noir: Fine tannins, red or black fruit depending on climate

Syrah: Dark berry fruits, black pepper and high tannins

GAMAY

1

2

PINOT NOIR

3

4

SYRAH/SHIRAZ

5

6

BLIND TASTING

7

8

9

10

QUESTIONS

In Session 5 we have looked at three grape varieties – Gamay, Pinot Noir and Syrah/Shiraz:

1. Which variety makes Côte-Rôtie and where does this wine come from?

2. Which of these varieties makes Gevrey-Chambertin and where does this wine come from?

3. Which of these varieties makes Fleurie and where does this wine come from?

4. Which is the trickiest to grow?

5. Which is often made into sparkling wine?

6. Which needs the most warmth and sunshine to ripen?

7. Which most often makes wines which are best enjoyed young?

Which might have aromas often described as:

8. — summer fruits and bubblegum?

9. — black pepper and blackberry?

10. — red fruits, violets and forest floor?

Name the grape variety for each description:

11. — full-bodied with high tannins and good warmth at the back of the throat; aromas and flavours of ripe dark fruits with hints of black pepper and spice?

12. — high acidity, low tannins, moderate alcohol and very fruity, with juicy strawberry and raspberry notes?

13. — autumnal, forest floor and mushroom aromas/flavours alongside raspberry and strawberry; fine tannins, high acidity, elegance and a silky texture?

Answers on page 221

6

Four grapes from southern Europe that make distinctive red wines

GRENACHE
TEMPRANILLO
SANGIOVESE
NEBBIOLO

GRENACHE
heady warmth

Ranging from rich reds to summer rosés, these are wines of the warm South, from France and Spain. Savoury aromas, ample alcohol, full-bodied and food-loving.

TEMPRANILLO
strawberries & cream

The Spanish aristocrat, heart of styles such as traditional Rioja, and modern wines too. Blended in Rioja; typically 100 per cent elsewhere.

SANGIOVESE
tea & cherries

The grape of Tuscany: Chianti and Montalcino. Aromas of tea, cherries; earthy, savoury. High acidity and grippy tannins: food wines.

NEBBIOLO
tar & roses

Northern Italy's counterpoint to Burgundy's Pinot Noir: perfumed, long-lived, subtle wines; pale colour contrasting with high tannins and high acidity.

Where the grapes grow

The four grapes in this Session have their origins in the Mediterranean lands of southern France, Italy and Spain. Each has spread to other parts of the world, but – more than most grapes – their identity is bound up with the specific places mapped here. The lists below note other winelands where they are found.

GRENACHE

● **Heartlands**
Southern Rhône Valley
Languedoc
Spain: Navarra & Priorat

Others
North Africa
California
Australia
South Africa

TEMPRANILLO

● **Heartlands**
Spain: Rioja & Ribera del Duero
Portugal: Douro

Others
California
Texas
Australia
Argentina

SANGIOVESE

● **Heartlands**
Italy: Tuscany, Umbria , Emilia-
Romagna, Le Marche

Others
Sardinia
Corsica
Argentina

NEBBIOLO

● **Heartlands**
Italy: Piedmont

Others
Lombardy
Australia
California
Argentina

Grenache/Garnacha

KEY POINTS

- Red grape
- Likes a hot climate
- Full-bodied wines
- High alcohol
- Thin skins
- Soft tannins

KEY REGIONS

Rhône Valley, Spain

Grenache is at the heart of many red wines from the warm South. It is the mainstay of the Southern Rhône, where it appears in famous wines such as Châteauneuf-du-Pape and also in more everyday ones like Côtes du Rhône. In Spain, too, under the name Garnacha, it is the most common grape and its wine spans the price and quality levels.

Much rosé (rosado in Spanish) wine is made from Grenache/Garnacha. In its varying guises, red and rosé, the wine always shows a soft, food-friendly character.

Grenache vines need sun: their produce is essentially a warm-climate wine: high – sometimes too high – in alcohol, low in tannins.

In Grenache's key regions, winemakers traditionally use large old-oak casks for ageing. Grenache is frequently blended with other varieties: in the New World the 'GSM' blends mingle Grenache with Syrah and Mourvèdre. Grenache gives warmth and generosity; the others confer structure and tannin.

Syrah is a favourite blending partner with Grenache in many good-value, interesting Southern Rhône wines from Gigondas, Cairanne, Vacqueyras and like places. Other partners are Mourvèdre and Carignan. Blending is taken to extremes in Châteauneuf-du-Pape, where 13 grape varieties are allowed – but some of the most august wines from this very varied area are 100 per cent Grenache.

Right round the southern shores of France, through the Languedoc into Roussillon, Grenache dominates. It is not as fashionable as, say, Syrah or the Cabernets, because of its use in some pretty everyday wine.

In Spain, Navarra is known for Garnacha, while winemakers in the ancient, but newly-fashionable, vineyards of Priorat blend the grape with other Spanish and French varieties to make deep, dark, rich wines.

Wine suggestions for this session, page 216

AROMA & FLAVOUR

Much depends on the winemaker: a Grenache wine can be a soft rosé or a chunky, deep-coloured Châteauneuf. The more interesting wines offer smoky, herby, even leathery notes: tasters say these wine convey hints of the garrigue (the Mediterranean undergrowth) of their sun-baked, stony homelands.

When you try these wines, look out for:

- scents of strawberry in young wines
- the warmth of high alcohol
- low tannins in unblended wines
- smoke, spice and savoury notes in mature ones

Would you agree that these wines:

- have a heady, warming character with ripe red fruit or smoky flavours?

Maturity

Much Grenache is made to be drunk young, but wines from old, low-yielding vines at places like Châteauneuf-du-Pape can age for 30 years, gaining deep, gamey notes. Some Côtes du Rhône estates offer two or more cuvées – blends or selections – under different names: one to drink young, another to age in bottle.

TOP TIP: OLD VINES – OR NOT?

Look out for 'Old Vines' ('Vieilles Vignes' in French) on labels . The 'old' points to low yields and high flavour from long-established vineyards. But there's no formal definition of how old 'old' is — and the term can be abused.

KEY AROMAS & FLAVOURS

- smoke
- pepper
- raspberry
- strawberry

Everyday
Serious

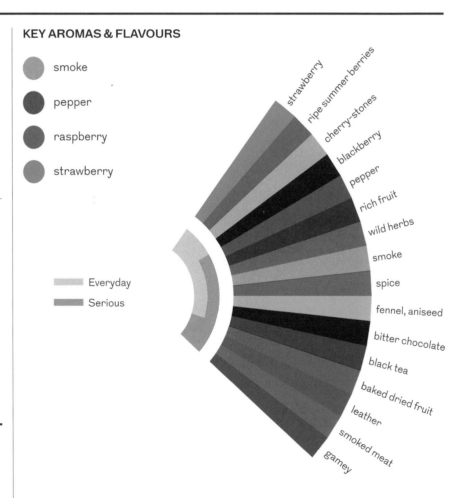

strawberry, ripe summer berries, cherry-stones, blackberry, pepper, rich fruit, wild herbs, smoke, spice, fennel, aniseed, bitter chocolate, black tea, baked dried fruit, leather, smoked meat, gamey

BALANCE

THE CHARACTER
OF THE WINE
IN YOUR GLASS

Here we compare a 'straight' unblended Garnacha/Grenache – a young, un-oaked, fruit-forward style from Navarra in northern Spain – with a mature French Châteauneuf-du-Pape.

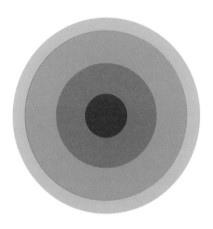

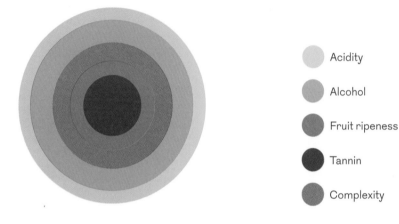

Acidity

Alcohol

Fruit ripeness

Tannin

Complexity

SPANISH GARNACHA

Soft, rich and savoury: high alcohol
behind the ripe fruit

CHATEAUNEUF-DU-PAPE

Higher in tannin, high in alcohol,
maturity brings complexity and fruit
is more muted

Food matches

Partner this hot-summer wine with hot-summer foods: the everyday bottles
will be great with the barbecue. More august ones will be a match for casssoulet,
duck paté and other flavoursome fare.

Some Grenache-friendly foods:

- Duck
- Game: wild boar, venison
- Spare ribs
- Barbecue food
- Smoked meats
- Chorizo etc

KEY REGION:

Southern Rhône

Much of the wine we drink from the southern part of the Rhône Valley (the largest, most productive part and source of 95 per cent of its wine) is based on Grenache – whether as a single variety or dominating a blend.

Grenache needs a hot climate; here in the south it gets it: as the Latitude Ladder on page 146 shows, the mean July temperature is hotter than, say, Burgundy's Côte d'Or. This is signalled to the south-bound traveller by the switch from chestnuts and fruit trees in the Northern Rhône to olives and Mediterranean pines in the south.

The local topography and soil accentuate the heat: much of the vineyard country is stony, and the stones store and reflect the fierce sun. Most famous are the large, disc-shaped pebbles found in parts of Châteauneuf-du-Pape: locals call them 'galets'.

TOP TIP

Some of the most prestigious estates and merchants make a Côtes du Rhône alongside their grander wines. These can be from younger vines, or outlying vineyards, and can be good value.

The terroir and climate shape the way the vineyards are cultivated and the vines pruned. Here, Grenache vines are typically grown as low bushes – without support from wires and trellises – and are well spread out. This is a response to the fierce Mistral winds that can damage the vines, and to the risk of summer drought: low, well-spaced vines can cope better with both.

CÔTES DU RHÔNE

One of the biggest wine zones in France, and one of the most variable, this is the name on some fascinating, good-value wines – and some boring, mediocre ones. Being so broad, the appellation is no guarantee of quality or even much of a pointer to style: the name of the producer, be they négociant (merchant) or grower, is essential information.

Côtes du Rhône wines have to be a minimum 40 per cent Grenache, and most have a higher proportion. Other grapes grown include Syrah (increasing), and Cinsault and Mourvèdre (minority vines): see page 158.

Most Côtes du Rhône falls into the 'drink young and fresh' category, though some Côtes du Rhône-Villages wines – see opposite – can age.

CHÂTEAUNEUF-DU-PAPE

The senior Southern Rhône appellation, both in status and age: this was the first AOC in France, and the rules devised here set the template for the rest.

Though Grenache makes up 70 per cent of the production, it is joined in the official grapes list here by a dozen other varieties; this gives the winemakers plenty of scope. Some domaines make purely Grenache wines; most blend in other grapes from the list (favourites rise and fall with fashion and changing climate).

Châteauneuf pressed for its appellation a century ago, to fight off imitators: its easy-to-say name, and its papal status (medieval popes had a palace hereabouts) made it a sitting target. Today, most wine carrying the label is well worthy of it – but there are still some sad concoctions that trade on the name. As ever, the maker's name counts: among the best are both single-family estates and wide-ranging négociants.

THE PROMOTION PYRAMID

The French wine laws provide a promotion pyramid for Côtes du Rhône wine producers and villages. It is open to change, and so an ambitious commune or village can (like a football team) aspire to elevation to a higher level.

- **Côtes du Rhône** is the basic product from 171 communes across the region.
- **Côtes du Rhône-Villages** Wines from around 100 communes judged better than their neighbours can add the word '-Villages'. Explore these and you open up a source of more individual, concentrated and longer-lived wines.

- **Village names added** The top 20 per cent of communes get to use their own name as well — thus Côtes du Rhône-Villages Cairanne, for example.
- **Village names alone** The top communes and areas can drop the 'Côtes du Rhône' and are labelled with their own name: Gigondas and Vacqueyras are the best-known: at their finest these can compete with the better-known Châteauneuf.

Above: Vines amid 'galet' pebbles at Châteauneuf.

Spain

In Spain they call the grape Garnacha. It is grown in several wine zones across the northern half of the country, and plays a supporting rôle in red **Rioja** (see page 176). Garnacha stars solo in red and rosé (rosado) wines from Navarra, and also in Priorat where it is blended with Cariñena and others.

NAVARRA

North-east of the more-famous Rioja zone lies Navarra, where Garnacha is prized for its deep, dark, fruity character – especially from old vines. The resulting wines can be high in alcohol, with powerful tannins, though ripe and fruit-laden; the best come from the central and eastern parts: here the hotter climate suits this vine.

In contrast, Navarra also makes pink (rosado) wines from Garnacha (see next page for how rosé is made). These are juicy, fresh and an attractive strawberry-pink.

PRIORAT

A wine-growing renaissance in this rugged corner of Catalonia has seen Priorat – usually a blend of Garnacha and Cariñena (Carignan) – attain cult status (and prices). Montsant is a surrounding zone with similar wines at more accessible prices.

POPULAR IN PINK

Interesting wines, still and sparkling, have led to a resurgence of rosé on wine lists. Anne McHale MW looks at how rosé is made.

Pink wine has become much more popular in recent years. Gone are the days when the sole association with the word 'rosé' was a certain mass-market semi-sweet, gently fizzy pink drink. These days, high-quality rosé is made all over the world and in a range of styles. So how exactly is it produced? There are two key methods.

The most obvious way – though this is generally not permitted in Europe – is to add a very small amount of red wine to a white wine. The exception to the ban is traditional-method sparkling wines (most notably Champagne). There was a proposal to make this method legal for still wines too, but it was hotly contested by producers in rosé's spiritual home, southern France; they felt that this would undermine their own traditional method – the second way of making rosé.

SKIN CONTACT

This can be described most simply as a shortened version of red winemaking: the 'skin contact' method. In red wine production, the skins and juice are left in contact with each other throughout the

Above: Rosé starts from red grapes: here being pumped over as they begin their fermentation.

fermentation process: this extracts colour and tannin. Grape juice, even from red grapes, is colourless – hence the ability to use red grapes in Champagne.

In rosé production red grapes are also used, but there will only be one or two days' skin contact, to give a small amount of colour and virtually no tannin (this tends to be extracted later on in the red-wine process). After this short period of contact, skins and juice are separated and fermentation continues as for a white wine.

A sub-type of the skin-contact method is known as 'saignée' (the French 'saigner' means 'to bleed'). Rosé produced in this way could be described as a by-product of red winemaking. Sometimes winemakers wish to increase the skin:juice ratio in their red wine fermentations to augment the colour and tannin levels, so they remove a small amount of juice in the initial stages of the

fermentation. This, having had only a short period of skin contact, is pink and so will be fermented separately to make a rosé. A classic example is pink Sancerre, typically a by-product of red Sancerre production where winemakers want to bump up the colour and tannin levels of wine from the thin-skinned Pinot Noir grape.

SOME ROSÉS TO TRY ON A SUMMER'S AFTERNOON:

Provence: the long-standing home of dry, pale rosés to match seafood

Sancerre Rosé: crisp, light, mineral

Navarra Rosado: Spanish pink made from Garnacha (Grenache)

New World pink wine: from many different grapes; look out for Shiraz ones from Australia or Malbecs from Argentina

Tempranillo

KEY POINTS

- Red grape
- Medium acidity
- Fine tannins
- Range of styles: light to robust
- Works well with oak
- Can age well

KEY REGIONS

Spain: Rioja, Ribera del Duero

The local hero of Northern Spain, Tempranillo is the backbone of the country's starriest red wines. In Rioja, it is blended with Garnacha and other grapes, but may be unblended in Ribera del Duero. It also makes a wide range of other wines across Spain, at quality levels from simple to sophisticated, and is grown in Portugal.

The grapes are small, thick-skinned and early to ripen, giving Tempranillo attributes akin to Cabernet Sauvignon and making it ideal for the higher, cooler, quality Spanish vineyards such as those of Rioja Alavesa.

It is prized for its firm, but not overpowering, acidity and its moderate to high tannins and alcohol; the aromatic wines it produces tend to age to a pale, fine colour.

Tempranillo matures well in oak, and its wine has good ageing potential in bottle, as venerable vintages of Vega Sicilia, the unofficial 'First Growth' of Ribera del Duero, and great Riojas prove.

Across the border, the Portuguese know Tempranillo by a variety of names – Aragonez in the south, Tinta Roriz in the north, where it goes into Port and the Douro and Dão wines. It is prized for the same reasons as in Spain: wine with fruit and firm tannins, but yields must be kept low if quality is the aim.

In the Rioja vineyards eight red vines in ten are Tempranillo, but the winemakers prize the minority vines – Garnacha, Graciano, Mazuelo – as part of the ideal Rioja blend.

Around the world, Tempranillo has had limited impact – as yet. Australia approves of its qualities, but so far grows little; Argentina uses it for everyday wines.

AROMA & FLAVOUR

Fruit, vanilla – perhaps from oak – cream, spice: these are classic notes on Riojas. However Tempranillo is less assertive than, say, Cabernet Sauvignon and, like Chardonnay, the taste of its wine owes more to the winemaker than the variety. See below for how modern and traditional Riojas vary across the flavour spectrum – with a big overlap, of course.

When you try these wines, look out for:

- fresh berry fruit and bright colour in young wines
- red fading to garnet, with cigar-box/dried fruit aromas, in mature wines
- creamy vanilla notes from ageing in oak

Would you agree that these wines are:

- elegant and smooth, and have a good affinity for oak, with creamy vanilla notes?

Maturity

Spain's subtle system of grading, ageing and naming Riojas and other wines is described on page 180. Maturity adds an extra dimension to the modern/traditional dichotomy. Classic-style wines, if high status, are aged before release. Modern ones gain by bottle-age.

TOP TIP: RIOJA VALUE

Rioja Reservas and Gran Reservas — unlike most other fine red wines — are aged to maturity by the producers and only released when ready to drink.

KEY AROMAS & FLAVOURS

- strawberry
- raspberry
- black fruits
- vanilla
- tobacco

Modern
Traditional

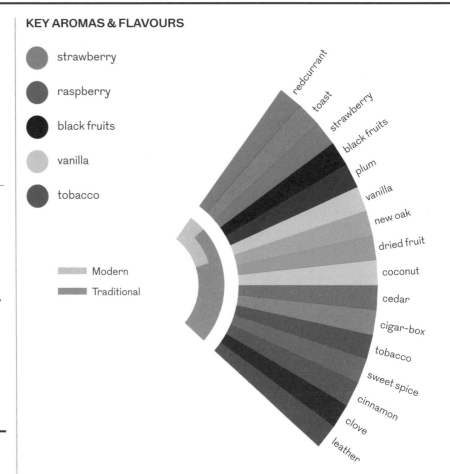

redcurrant
toast
strawberry
black fruits
plum
vanilla
new oak
dried fruit
coconut
cedar
cigar-box
tobacco
sweet spice
cinnamon
clove
leather

BALANCE

THE CHARACTER
OF THE WINE
IN YOUR GLASS

Cool-vineyard Tempranillo, such as the Spanish classics, has moderate acidity balanced by berry fruit, but the prevailing character comes from the way it is made and matured. Here we compare modern and traditional styles.

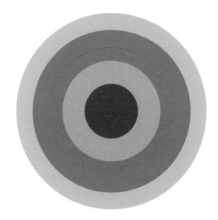

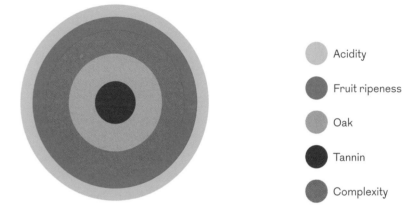

- Acidity
- Fruit ripeness
- Oak
- Tannin
- Complexity

MODERN
at 2 years old

The aim is fruit, balanced by tannins
and vanilla from the higher proportion
of new French oak used.

TRADITIONAL GRAN RESERVA
at 10 years old

American oak casks convey spicy aromas
and flavours from oxidative ageing,
which moderates fruit and tannins.

Food matches

Rioja usually gets high marks in food and wine matching events. In its traditional style it has the acidity to balance rich foods; in Spain slow-baked lamb is a classic partner, as is game. Modern-style Tempranillos work with strong Spanish flavours like chorizo and riñones (sherried kidneys).

Some Tempranillo-friendly foods:

- Suckling lamb
- Kid (young goat)
- Pork
- Slow-baked leg of lamb
- Chorizo
- Game
- Stews

KEY REGION:

Northern Spain

The two senior red wines of Spain – Rioja and Ribera del Duero – are built on backbones of Tempranillo. Both wine zones are sited in broad, high-altitude river valleys and plateaux in the north of Spain, where summer nights are cool and the winters cold, sunshine is plentiful and rainfall scant. Tempranillo also appears in **Toro**, and in the **Penedès**, **Navarra**, **Cigales**, **La Mancha** and **Valdepeñas** regions as part of their palette of grapes.

RIOJA

It is not that long since – in Spain and abroad – fine Spanish wine was Rioja, and Rioja was Spanish fine wine. Burgeoning quality elsewhere across this broad country means other stars have risen, and Rioja is no longer alone; but for interest, quality and value it still takes some beating.

The Rioja country follows the valley of the Ebro river, with the Pyrenees on the distant northern horizon (and France just beyond). There are three official zones – **Rioja Baja** in the east, **Rioja Alta** in the west and midway between them **Rioja Alavesa**: a pair of enclaves tucked up against the sheltering mountains of the Sierra Cantabria.

Most wines here are made by companies, as opposed to the 'small growers' of other regions. These concerns, the oldest of which date from the 19th century, traditionally bought rather than grew grapes, and the source of their fruit was lost in a series of brand-name-labelled blends (see following pages for the hows and whys of Rioja's quality levels). Recently, though, wines sourced from specific vineyards or districts have come to prominence. These may be labelled 'Viña X' (Viña is vineyard) and are offered as alternatives to the classic 'company' wines.

This trend parallels the emergence of Rioja's 'new wave' bodegas – concerns that stress terroir above tradition in their winemaking.

Tempranillo dominates the top Riojas, both classic and modern. The senior wines may be 100 per cent, or they may include modest doses of Graciano, Garnacha (Grenache) or Mazuelo. Lesser wines – those made to be drunk young, and/or from lesser districts – have less Tempranillo.

RIBERA DEL DUERO

From a landscape if anything even higher, wider and bigger-skied than Rioja comes Spain's other world-class Tempranillo red. When, a century ago, Rioja had its constellation of Marquis-titled concerns, Ribera del Duero had but one star – the blazing star of Vega Sicilia. Its stunningly long-lived, hand-crafted and costly wine has been joined by a widening clutch of other producers, all avid for world recognition.

All have the rich, creamy yet balanced character of Tempranillo (known sometimes as Tinta del País or Tinta Fino) in common. Traditionally, Ribera del Duero is 100 per cent from the grape, though Vega Sicilia holds to its 19th-century practice of blending with Merlot and Cabernet Sauvignon, and its neighbours increasingly add a small percentage of French varieties.

These wines are more international in character than the traditional Riojas: French oak in youth, maturity that benefits from bottle-age. Ribera del Duero was granted its DO (Denominación de Origen, equivalent to France's AOC) in 1982, at a time when only nine bodegas were operating there – today it has over 170. The wines range from the enjoyable everyday to the very seriously age-worthy. It was their rocketing rise to fame that turned the wine world's spotlight onto the grape (see opposite).

Right: The sun-baked, wide-skied landscape of Rioja.

Tempranillo worldwide

Portugal Spain's River Duero is perhaps better known after it flows on west across the Portuguese border and alters its name to become the Douro – the river of the Port country. The vertiginous, rugged, terraced Douro valley is very different to the high, wide Duero plateau and is hotter, but the underlying rock is similar.

Tempranillo grows in Port country under the name Tinta Roriz, and is one of the prime grapes allowed for blending in Port and in Douro table wines.

USA In California, Tempranillo spent many decades in obscurity before the rediscovery prompted by Ribera del Duero's new-found fame. It is doing well in Texas, and there have been experiments in Oregon and Washington.

Australia finds the vine promising – conditions that suit it in Spain can be reproduced – and there are now around 50 producers growing the variety.

Argentina is having success with Tempranillo in Mendoza, though most Argentinian Tempranillos are aimed at the mass market.

AGEING AND STATUS IN SPANISH WINE

Wine style: classic or modern? Oak: American or French, new or old? Simon Field MW explores the choices behind Spain's senior red wines.

Vinous paradise, for those who love what has become known as traditional Rioja, lies in a rather unlikely place: the Barrio Estación ('station yard') just outside Haro. This is where a number of now-famous bodegas were created in the second half of the 19th century, their location demonstrating not only the burgeoning primacy of the youthful railway network, but also the influence of French winemakers and viticulturists. These had settled in Rioja to escape the blight of the phylloxera disease that was ravaging vineyards in Bordeaux and other parts of south-west France. (Rioja, after all, is a mere 100km from the frontier.)

It is ironical, therefore, that these wineries, developed with French savoir-faire and thus initially using mainly French oak, are now most famous for ageing their wines in oak from America. Quite soon, those who advised entrepreneurial landowners such as the Marquises of Riscal, Murrieta and Vargas decided that Tempranillo was best suited, in terms of ageing, to American oak. This wood, with its relatively loose grain, was deemed to allow this early-ripening variety elegant self-expression, most often associated with 'strawberries and cream' descriptors.

Recently, however, a 'new wave' of bodegas has emerged in Rioja – and they stress their use of French oak. So you might conclude that, with the re-emergence of French oak for ageing, the modernists are in fact more traditional than those who have been using American oak for over a century.

Some attempt to argue this case, but generally to no avail: there is no way that one can describe López de Heredia as modern or Remírez de Ganuza as traditionalist, after all. The former make Tondonia, one of the most sublime and gloriously old-fashioned wines in the world; the latter the powerful, focused and thoroughly modern Trasnacho.

The marriage between American oak and Tempranillo has been a happy and enduring one in Rioja, the vows perennially renewed despite sub-plots such as the rise of other varieties, most particularly Graciano, Garnacha and Mazuelo – grapes that may or may not be deemed to suit the traditional wood.

Further sub-plots focus on the actual age of the wood – that is to say, the question of whether or not the oak should be new, and the not-unrelated issue of length of ageing. Even some of the most traditional names, such as CVNE's Imperial, are now ageing the wines for less time.

continued...

Right: Getting the oak question into perspective....

This reduction in time nevertheless still allows them, where they wish to, to fit into the traditional classification system of Crianza, Reserva and Gran Reserva (see below). Some of the new wave, on the other hand – bodegas such as the celebrated Artadí and Finca Allende – gave up using these descriptors long ago. Finally there are many producers who, heaven forfend, are now combining both types of wood. Can a traditionalist also be a pragmatist?

In other parts of Spain there seems to be a fairly reliable correlation between quality, or at least perceived quality, and selection of type of oak. Many smaller wine zones grow grapes that just so happen to be synonymous with Tempranillo: Cencibel, Tinto de Toro and Tinto Fino being just three examples. In the less-well-known communes, such as Cigales, American oak still dominates; but where there are realised or partially-realised aspirations towards quality, there tends to be more and more French oak. Tighter-grained wood equates to a firmer structure, which is seen to presage greater ageing capacity and therefore better quality. This certainly seems to be the case with the most famous bodega of them all, Vega Sicilia, which has never eschewed French wood and which, to bring the argument pirouetting to a standstill, makes the most traditional wines in Spain.

TERMS ON THE LABEL IN RIOJA

The traditional terms are not always used — see above — but where found, this is what they mean:

Crianza wines are aged for a year in oak followed by a year in bottle before being released for sale.

Reservas must have a minimum of three years' ageing before release, at least one of which should be in oak casks.

Gran Reservas, only produced in the finest vintages, must spend at least five years maturing, of which at least two must be in oak.

ALSO TRY...
Other Spanish grapes

Spain is a fairly recent convert to the idea that grape names belong on wine labels: you will look for them in vain in Rioja, for instance. However, Spain shelters a wide range of fascinating native varieties, and their names are increasingly used in less-traditional areas. Some to watch out for are:

WHITE

Albariño Dry yet fruity wines with spicy hints that brilliantly partner Atlantic seafood. From north-western zones, including Rías Baixas and Ribeira Sacra.

Godello Rescued from obscurity, now rising into fashion, Godello yields crisp white wines with underlying fruit in areas like Bierzo and Valdeorras, again in Spain's cool north-west.

Verdejo This has always been the grape of Rueda, the primarily white-wine zone along the River Duero, but the name is now common on labels. Verdejo wine is typically solid with fruit, yet with notes of acidic freshness.

RED

Bobal From Valencia, on the east coast, the source of rich, smoky, floral wines from a few quality-concious producers.

Cariñena Carignan to the French, and an ingredient, alongside Garnacha, in many Priorats. One or two pure Cariñenas can be found: deep, dark and long-lived wines that respond well to oak-ageing.

Mencía A speciality of the north-west's Bierzo and Valdeorras areas, making — typically — long-lived and sturdy wines that in skilled hands can be elegant and fine.

Monastrell The thick-skinned, robust Mourvèdre of southern France, grown in Spain's central and eastern vineyards, and yielding especially interesting wines — dark, tarry and long-lived — in Yecla, Jumilla and Alicante. Sometimes blended with Syrah and/or Cabernet Sauvignon.

Sangiovese

KEY POINTS

- Red grape
- Prominent acidity
- Chunky tannins
- Light- to medium-bodied

KEY REGION

Tuscany in central Italy

This is Italy's most widely-planted red grape, finding its best expression in Tuscany, where it is at the heart of all variants of Chianti and is the sole grape of Brunello di Montalcino.

Riserva wines from the Chianti Classico sub-zone can match serious Bordeaux in longevity and, to an extent, character.

The first clue to Sangiovese is in the colour: moderate brick-red, tending to light, when young; orange at the rim when old. It has plenty of tannin and acidity, creating the appetising 'cut' so typical of central Italian reds, so appropriate with food.

Chianti varies in style from soft, early-drinking and easy, to dark, brooding and long-lived. All of them will be at least 80 per cent Sangiovese – but much else, from vineyard site and clone through yield to winemaking technique, will differ markedly. Whatever the variations, all – whether simple Chianti or a top Classico – should partner food.

Sangiovese is back in favour after several decades when go-ahead Italian winemakers reckoned French classic varieties were a better bet. To plant them, they needed to escape from the bounds of the Italian wine laws (DOC and the like, see page 187), so these pioneers initially labelled their wines as simple 'Vini da Tavola' – table wines (now IGT).

The resulting 'Super-Tuscans', some entirely from Cabernet Sauvignon and other non-Tuscan vines, gained great acclaim and shook up the Italian wine scene. Today, Sangiovese has made a come-back and appears in many Super-Tuscans alongside Cabernet.

A century or so ago, Italian emigrants took the vine to the New World: it thrives in Argentina and California. It has little fame and less image as a 'varietal' wine though, and the grape name may not be prominent.

AROMA & FLAVOUR

Sangiovese is the quintessential Italian red: its assertive acidity and tannins are a delight with food, unbalanced alone. The exceptions are mature wines from grand estates that can emerge, after ageing for a decade or so, elegant, subtle and aromatic.

When you try these wines, look out for:

- high acidity and chewy tannins
- pale colour intensity and fresh, sour-cherry flavours in simple wines
- earth, tea and leather notes in more serious wines

Would you agree that these wines are:

- tough and austere to taste on their own because of the high acidity and tannin, but taste smoother with food?

Maturity

Simple Chianti is designed to be drunk young. Classico from good estates, and Montalcino and Montepulciano wines, can mature in bottle for a decade or longer. Brunello di Montalcino must be aged for at least two years in wood before bottling, and a further four months minimum in bottle (six for Riserva) before release.

KEY AROMAS & FLAVOURS

- herbs
- raspberry
- leather
- earthy

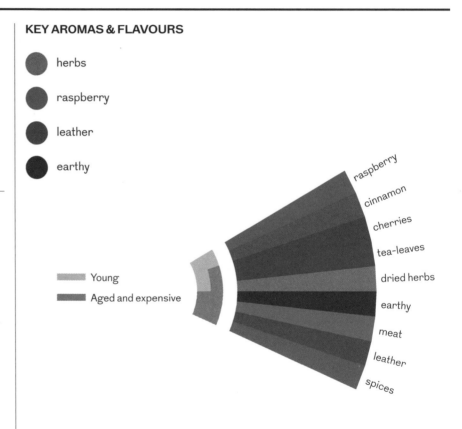

Young

Aged and expensive

raspberry
cinnamon
cherries
tea-leaves
dried herbs
earthy
meat
leather
spices

BALANCE

THE CHARACTER
OF THE WINE
IN YOUR GLASS

Chianti, the best-known wine made from Sangiovese, comes in a wide range of styles from simple to seriously complex (and expensive). Here we compare a simple Chianti at 18 months old with a Brunello di Montalcino – another Tuscan wine, from the neighbouring Montalcino district, at six years old.

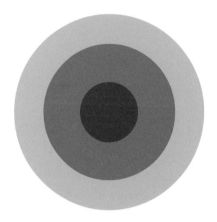

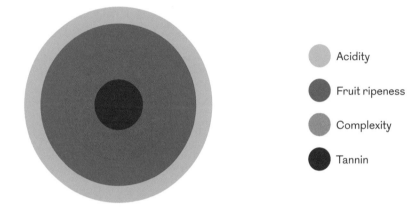

- Acidity
- Fruit ripeness
- Complexity
- Tannin

SIMPLE CHIANTI

No oak is involved in this example, so the grape's natural acidity and tannins balance the youthful fruit.

BRUNELLO DI MONTALCINO

Oak-ageing, and time in bottle, soften the acidity and tannins. Complex aromas and flavours develop.

Food matches

Traditionally, Italian reds are food wines; their high acidity will stand up, naturally, to tomato-based sauces. Traditional Tuscan cuisine stresses grilled or roasted meats, particularly with herbs.

Some Sangiovese-friendly foods:

- Beef: steak, roasts
- Game: hare, partridge
- Rustic dishes such as soups and beans
- Duck
- Pasta with meat-based sauces

KEY REGION:

Tuscany

The wines of Tuscany – Toscana – are predominantly red, and mostly Sangiovese (but don't expect the labels to tell you so). Sangiovese can vary widely: there are different sub-strains of the variety, with different names – and different clones (see page 34). Some Sangiovese clones, formerly in vogue, yielded large crops of pale, thin wine; but today most vineyards in the first-division zones grow the superior, deeper-coloured sorts. Indeed, the Classico rules limit growers to seven approved clones.

It is this change – allied to improved winemaking, and to a growing realisation that the vine is particular about choice of site – that has brought the great red wines of Tuscany back to the forefront of world esteem. The top names are:

Chianti Classico Made in the heart of the broad Chianti region on rocky, limestone soil, and at least 80 per cent Sangiovese;

Brunello di Montalcino 100 per cent Sangiovese – its local name is Brunello – and traditionally darker and stronger than Chianti;

Vino Nobile di Montepulciano From around the town of that name, this is at least 70 per cent Sangiovese and can age as well as a serious Chianti Classico.

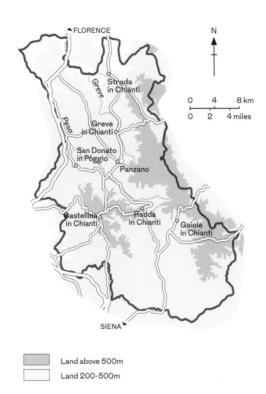

Left: The heartland of Chianti is the Classico zone, first delineated in the 18th century, and making one bottle for every four of straight Chianti. The best wine villages are those marked.

These are the peaks: great amounts of wine of lesser status are made from Sangiovese. Straight Chianti, with no local name, is made right across Tuscany and is nearly always an early-drinking, refreshing red.

Chianti sub-zones abound: apart from Classico, the best wines are likely to be those (in Italy the definite is to be avoided) from **Chianti Rufina**, east of Florence, and **Chianti Colli Senesi**, around Siena.

Both the Montalcino and Montepulciano districts have junior, early-drinking grades

of Sangiovese reds to enjoy while you wait for the main wines to age: look for the district name prefixed with 'Rosso di'.

The senior Tuscan reds tend to come from long-established estates, where the name of the property took precedence over the 'terreno' (terroir). There is a recent trend towards using comune (village) and even vigna (vineyard) names to distinguish individual wines.

Vintages vary quite a bit in this hilly, varied landscape: growers are experimenting with higher, cooler vineyards, though these can be more vulnerable in cool years.

RISERVA

The term is used for estates' senior wines, sometimes aged at least in part in small oak barrels rather than the traditional large casks. Chianti Classico wines labelled Riserva must undergo at least 24 months' ageing before sale; a Riserva Vino Nobile di Montepulciano has 36 months, while Brunello di Montalcino Riserva must be aged for five years.

Elsewhere in Italy – and the world

Any list of Sangiovese wines is always going to be dominated by Tuscany, but the variety does crop up elsewhere.

Beyond its heartland, discussed left, Sangiovese is grown in the coastal strip of Tuscany – the Maremma – and yields wines such as Montecucco. Here, there is yet another local name for the grape: Morellino, which appears on the labels of some Sangiovese wines. Sangiovese is also grown in **Umbria**, south of Tuscany, where it is responsible for Torgiano, and for some wines from the Montefalco zone. In **Le Marche**, Sangiovese plays a minor role in Rosso Conero and a major one in Rosso Piceno, both with the Montelpulciano grape. It is common, though usually undistinguished, in the **Emilia-Romagna** region, where it makes everyday reds. On the island of **Sardinia** (and in **Corsica**) they call the vine Nielluccio.

In the New World, **California, USA** has experimented with Sangiovese, and a recent census found several dozen wineries offering the variety.

Argentina grows Sangiovese on quite a large scale, and it is also found in **Australia**. In neither southern-hemisphere country has the grape had much impact.

Above: Sangiovese's warm Italian heartland.

THE RISE OF THE SUPER-TUSCANS – AND THE RESPONSE

The arrival of French grapes in Tuscany produced a clutch of new wines – and helped to spark a revival in the region's own classic varieties, as Chris Pollington reports.

Sangiovese, the great indigenous grape of Tuscany, is heralded today as one of the world's top varieties – but this hasn't always been the case. Forty years ago the use of poor clones, and of vineyard and cellar techniques designed to put quantity before quality, had caused many Tuscans to lose faith in their local variety.

The first response to this was the creation of wines made using French varieties, either on their own or blended with Sangiovese. These wines were either made outside the traditional production zones, or fell outside the legal requirements of the DOCs – or both.

The heartland of these experiments was (and is) a coastal tract well away from the main Tuscan vineyards. It so happened that a major landowner there hankered after Claret, and planted Cabernet Sauvignon. One experiment led to others, more French vines were planted, and the world began to take notice: the 'Super-Tuscans' had arrived.

Their success was startling: they became the height of vinous fashion, both inside Italy and in the opinion-forming markets of London and New York.

Perhaps buoyed by the success of these international-influenced wines, the mainstream winemakers of Tuscany then started experimenting with their indigenous varieties – led by Sangiovese. They created a second wave of Super-Tuscans made entirely with Sangiovese – but with much better-quality fruit than ever before, due to today's improved techniques in both the vineyards and the winery.

This new emphasis on control and technique also began to raise the quality of the classic DOC and DOCG wines of the region.

So the great wines of Tuscany today come from both French varieties and from indigenous ones – with blends of the two also making an important contribution. The countryside around Bolgheri, on the coast, is still home to the 'Bordeaux Blend' wines of Sassicaia, Ornellaia and Guado al Tasso, which contrast completely with the 100 per cent Sangiovese wines of Brunello di Montalcino away to the south.

Chianti Classico is much more complicated, with excellent wines made from pure Sangiovese as well as ones made of Sangiovese blended with other indigenous and/or French varieties. The rules insist on a minimum 80 per cent Sangiovese; Cabernet Sauvignon and Merlot feature in the remaining 20 per cent of many Chianti Classico wines.

Observers reckon that the challenge of the Super-Tuscans – allied to improved winemaking and better clones – has sparked an impressive revival in the quality of Chianti Classico.

Left: This lovely estate in the Montalcino district makes the traditional, and now thriving, Brunello di Montalcino — and other wines including a Merlot-Cabernet Toscana IGT.

ITALY'S WINE RULES: LETTERS ON THE LABEL

DOCG The top grade: like DOC, but the G stands for 'guaranteed'

DOC (or European DOP) Like French AOC (AOP): wine from a defined zone, made to set rules

IGT (or IGP) Junior grade: wine from a specific zone; also used by makers for wines from non-traditional grapes

Vino Wine made according to the basic EU rules

ALSO TRY...

Other Italian grapes: centre and south

Italian grape varieties are numbered in the hundreds: recently, some of the traditional but more local ones have made comebacks as growers and wine-drinkers rediscover their virtues. A few names to watch for from the centre and south of the country are:

RED

Aglianico Dramatic dark reds from Campania and Basilicata in the south that conjure up liquorice-and-violets notes. Key areas include Taurasi and Aglianico del Vulture.

Montepulciano d'Abruzzo Robust everyday reds from the high country east of the Apennines.

Nero d'Avola Widely grown across Sicily: some wines are dark and tarry; the best, however, are subtle and precise. As ever in Italy, the grower matters more than the grape.

Nerello Mascalese Another Sicilian, scarcer but perhaps finer than Nero d'Avola.

Sagrantino Age-worthy wines from Umbria, especially the Montefalco zone.

Primitivo From Puglia in Italy's south-east corner: source of velvety, plummy wines that show that this vine is California's Zinfandel under another name.

WHITE

Fiano Whites with good acidity and solid fruit that can age to interesting complexity; from Campania and elsewhere in the south.

Greco More everyday than Fiano, but offers interesting, earthy wines from Puglia and Campania.

Verdicchio A speciality of the Marche region: crisp, pale, herbal whites that in good years, and from serious producers, can age well.

Trebbiano d'Abruzzo A few growers make complex, interesting, age-worthy wines from this otherwise uninspired workhorse grape: worth seeking these out.

Nebbiolo

KEY POINTS

- Red grape
- High acidity
- High tannins
- High alcohol
- Good ageing potential

KEY REGION

Piedmont in north-western Italy

If Sangiovese can be found along the length of Italy, Nebbiolo is stubbornly local. It rarely strays beyond the north-western region of Piedmont – Piemonte – and is most at home in the misty tangle of the hill-and-valley country of the Langhe. Here, it makes the classic Barolo and Barbaresco wines, long the delight of the gourmets of Turin and Milan – and, more recently, international stars.

Advocates of Nebbiolo compare it to Burgundy's Pinot Noir, and its wine has similarities in its pale colour, its fussiness in vineyard and cellar, its ability to age and its subtle complexity when mature. Like Pinot Noir, it is nearly always unblended – and it is nearly always expensive, high-status wine. It differs from its French counterpart in being high in alcohol and very tannic when young.

Nebbiolo is not the sole red grape of Piedmont. This late-ripening variety is only planted in the best sites: south-facing and well-drained hillsides, where it can yield the ripe, intense fruit that makes long-lived wines. Other sites are planted with Barbera and Dolcetto for less massive, earlier-drinking red wines.

Barolo and Barbaresco come from small areas, and the world wants them: they (again, like Burgundy) will never be cheap.

Nebbiolo d'Alba is all from the named grape and the wider area, and is a useful alternative to the grand wines. It has only a year of age on release – unlike Barolo and Barbaresco, where the law demands two years for Barbaresco and three for Barolo.

Nebbiolo is grown as far away as California, Argentina and Australia – but nowhere as widely as in its homeland.

AROMA & FLAVOUR

Nebbiolo has a 'love or hate' style. The tannins are prominent when young, and time in bottle – at least four years – is generally needed to tame them. High in acidity and alcohol, pale in colour with an autumnal feel, it is unlike any other red wine. The Aroma & Flavour spectrum below takes us from a lighter young Barbaresco to a rich, fully-mature Barolo.

When you try these wines, look out for:

- pale, reddish-brown colour
- high tannins balancing fruit
- high alcohol
- fragrance on the nose — aromas of roses and tar

Would you agree that these wines are:

- fragrant but also have grip and depth, with noticeably high tannins, cleansing acidity and alcohol?

Maturity

Traditional Barolo from a good vintage (vintages vary a lot here) needs a decade in bottle, and that is after the minimum two years it spends in wood. Well-made examples can be delicious at four years old – but better still after ten. However, some producers have modified their style to bring us wines that need less time. The name on the label matters here. Barbaresco is normally quicker to emerge from its shell – but again, winemakers vary widely in their styles.

KEY AROMAS & FLAVOURS

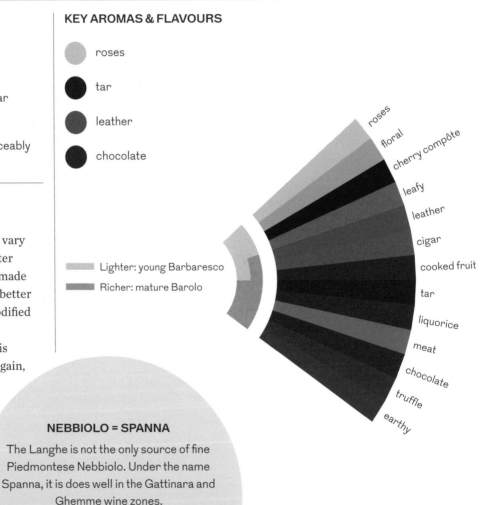

roses

tar

leather

chocolate

Lighter: young Barbaresco

Richer: mature Barolo

roses
floral
cherry compôte
leafy
leather
cigar
cooked fruit
tar
liquorice
meat
chocolate
truffle
earthy

NEBBIOLO = SPANNA

The Langhe is not the only source of fine Piedmontese Nebbiolo. Under the name Spanna, it is does well in the Gattinara and Ghemme wine zones.

BALANCE

THE CHARACTER OF
THE WINE
IN YOUR GLASS

In Piedmont's Langhe hills, tradition and modernity battle for the favour of the critics (and, rather in the rear, the consumers). The classic style means long periods in massive oak casks, perhaps a decade in bottle; the new stresses riper fruit, shorter fermentations, small oak barriques and quicker maturity. Here are a contrasting pair at six years old.

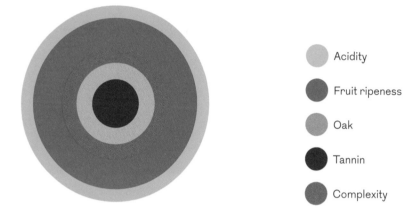

- Acidity
- Fruit ripeness
- Oak
- Tannin
- Complexity

TRADITIONAL BAROLO

The traditional style aims at a perfect balance between fresh ripe fruit, acidity and tannin. It needs time to soften the acidity and tannins.

MODERN BAROLO

Less time in wood, but more oak apparent on the taste from new French oak casks. The maker stresses fruit and approachability: ready sooner.

Food matches

The classic cuisine of its homeland is northern, meat-based, rich; the wines match it well. Outside Italy try game, beef, the richer risottos: serious dishes that belong in lengthy meals. Not wines for a casual lunch, these.

Some Nebbiolo-friendly foods:

- Mushrooms, truffles – all funghi
- Rich stews
- Game
- Liver and kidney
- Duck pâté

KEY REGION:

Piedmont

Nebbiolo is not only the most stubbornly local of the grapes profiled in this Course, it is the most finicky. It only thrives in a narrow range of conditions: plentiful sunshine, well-drained soil and freedom from frost. Its picky character is due in most part to its long growing season: being early to bud and flower, then late to ripen, it demands a carefully-chosen site.

The Langhe hills of Piedmont, in north-western Italy, provide these sites – but even there, growers have to choose carefully. Nebbiolo is only satisfied with south- or southwest-facing slopes – plenty of sun there, especially in the autumn when the sun angle is lower. It thrives best on well-drained, preferably limestone, soil – though the two classic zones offer a range of terroirs.

It follows that variations between vintages can be important here, with much of the character of a wine stemming from the conditions in the ripening period of late summer/autumn.

The capital of Nebbiolo in Piedmont (Piemonte in Italian) is the town of Alba, at the foot of the Langhe hills. To the south-east is Barbaresco, to the south-west is Barolo. Both these wine zones are of DOCG status (Italy's highest rank) and both specialise in Nebbiolo, though other grapes are grown in places that Nebbiolo will not countenance.

VINEYARDS ON THE LABEL

There is no formal, Burgundy-like, classification of vineyards or crus, but many site names are in traditional use, and there is growing recognition that the best wines are born in the vineyard, not the marketplace. Increasingly, growers make and market their wines under the name of the vigna – the vineyard, or cru (this French term has become used in the Langhe). Look too for more local terms for vigna such as sorì, bric and bricco. New to the two zones is a law that allows wine to be labelled as from specific vineyards. The term to look

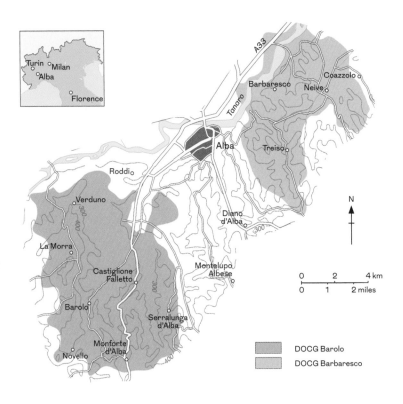

Above: The key villages in the Barolo and Barbaresco zones.

THE BAROLO DEBATE

While the arguments around modern and traditional Barolo are well rehearsed, they are being ambushed by the next generation of producers, who are technically better trained and often more worldly in outlook. Their wines are marked by a greater understanding of the region's vineyard complexity and a more intuitive feeling for the expression of the unique Nebbiolo. They are profound wines, still marked by the grape's trademark tannins and acidity, but finding a purer, more vital expression without recourse to intrusive winemaking methods, be they ancient or modern.

Above: View from the Barbaresco vineyards: the Tanaro river in the foreground, the Alps away to the north. This is the landscape of the map opposite.

for is 'Menzione Geografiche Aggiuntive' ('additional geographical definitions' is the rather clumsy official translation).

Behind the advent of the law is a wonderfully convoluted row about whether it's allowed to blend wine from more than one cru: officially it is not, but....

BARBARESCO

Arguably the junior of the two zones in status as well as age, and smaller. Any attempt to generalise about the wines falls before the individuality of the producers and their vineyards, but if forced one might say that Barbaresco is a lighter, earlier-maturing wine than Barolo. Elegance is more to the fore than power, in part due to the shorter ageing (officially at least 26 months, nine in wood) that most wines undergo.

BAROLO

Bigger, older, higher (thus cooler) and longer-lived, Barolo guards and retains its status as Italy's greatest red wine. The 11 hilly communes within the DOCG zone treasure a bewildering list of sites and microclimates, and vineyard names are even more in evidence (and dispute) than in Barbaresco. Barolo is aged for longer and can – from a traditionalist estate – last and improve for decades.

Right: Lovers of Langhe red wines sometimes assert that these are the Burgundies of Italy. How do Barolo and Barbaresco compare with the Côte de Nuits, home of the greatest red Burgundies?

BURGUNDY	LANGHE
Côte de Nuits	Barolo & Barbaresco
PINOT NOIR sole variety allowed for red wines	**NEBBIOLO** sole variety allowed for red wines
9 communes or villages	**15** communes or villages
9 million litres of wine per year	**13.2** million litres of wine per year
1,815 hectares of vineyard	**2,661** hectares of vineyard
157 Grands & Premiers Crus	**247** Crus (Menzioni Geografiche Aggiuntive)
564 wine producers (merchants & domaines)	**171** wine producers (merchants & domaines)
CLOS DE VOUGEOT size of the medieval walled vineyard: **51 hectares**	ROCCHE DELL'ANNUNZIATA (in La Morra, Barolo) size of the defined cru: **49 hectares**
80 owners	**15** owners
35 hectolitres per hectare Maximum permitted Grand Cru yield	**56** hectolitres per hectare Maximum permitted Barolo yield

ITALIAN WINE, ANCIENT & MODERN

David Berry Green reflects on how Italian wine got from the Etruscans to here, and celebrates today's rediscovery of the best of the traditional.

After decades – centuries even – in the shadow of its neighbour France, Italy is finally getting the attention, the limelight, it deserves for its ancient and classic fine wines.

It has always held the cards to play at the 'top table' of fine wine – lofty sedimentary, calcareous and volcanic soils; noble, indigenous grapes (bringing their terroir to life); a peerless gastronomic culture; a rich viticultural heritage. But for centuries history has dealt it a tough hand.

It started well enough, via the propagators of modern viticulture, the Etruscans and then the Romans who colonised their Empire with the help of the vine. With its breakup, and until Italy was reunited in 1861, the peninsula was divided by occupying forces: Bourbons, the Vatican, Austrians, French. It had become the place where other European countries duelled to sort out their differences.

The legacy of these centuries of occupation scarred the nation, and in wine terms ensured that the common sharecropping system, mezzadria, which prized quantity over quality for a local market, remained in place until the 1970s. A polycultural way of life enforced by phylloxera, Fascists and a general state of poverty in the countryside was epitomised by the infamous straw-covered Chianti fiasco bottle.

Fast-forward to the emergence of export markets from the 1970s onwards, stimulated by the recently-created DOC(G) – Denominazione di Origine Controllata (e Garantita) – which motivated former grape-growers to bottle for quality.

The north and centre of Italy initially benefited from the proximity of the Swiss and German markets, while a new American market took a shine to the so-called 'Super-Tuscan' wines that exploded out into the world during the mid-'70s.

The south has suffered from the stigma of being a bulk producer, being slow adopters of the bottle.

Come the advent of serious wine journalism in the 1980s, of Robert Parker and the Wine Spectator in the USA, a channel was effectively created to feed a rapidly-growing demand for fine wine that accompanied unprecedented wealth.

The results were potent: revolutionary winemakers and their equally famous consultants took centre-stage; each one vying to be more extreme so as to catch

the eye of the now-influential journalists. In Piedmont, one of these so-called 'Barolo Boys' took a chainsaw to his father's (traditional) 'botti grandi' (big barrels), replacing them with barriques; provocatively planting French varieties instead of the native Nebbiolo. This ignited a mainly American thirst for sensationalist wines, leading one magazine to announce in the mid-'90s that 'Napa Valley had finally arrived in the Langhe'.

But with the bursting of the economic bubble in 2008 (and, coincidentally, the end of the Berlusconi reign), now it seems that even the most radical producer has turned full circle, returning to the traditional, conservative style of fine winemaking.

Global warming appears to have had its say in Italy since 1995, delivering good to very good or excellent vintages in all but a handful of years: another factor building confidence. The flip-side to the climate change, though, being unruly levels of sugar/alcohol. Indigenous grapes are back in fashion as international (read French) grapes wither on the vine.

Fruit is therefore increasingly cleaner, healthier and better-balanced, allowing for a wider drinking window starting a few years after the harvest and lasting for up to 20 years. This is a most welcome development; a far cry from the dirty, tough wines of the immediate post-war years – and from the alcoholic fruit-bombs that characterised the 'bunga-bunga' Berlusconi era.

ALSO TRY...

Other Italian grapes: the north

Northern Italy's wide range of wines stem from international varieties, such as Merlot and Chardonnay, and its own local classics. The most important of these, Nebbiolo apart, are:

RED

Barbera Piedmont's key Nebbiolo districts, Barolo and Barbaresco, are surrounded and underlaid by zones where Barbera can be grown. It takes the name of its area, thus Barbera d'Asti, d'Alba, etc. These wines are deep red while Nebbiolo is pale, hearty where it is subtle — and increasingly respected.

Dolcetto From much the same country as Barbera, but tolerates higher, cooler sites. Its wines are balanced, refreshingly sweet-and-sour: ideal partners to rich local food. Drink young.

Corvina The key quality grape of the Veneto reds — Valpolicella and Bardolino. Corvina comes into its own when partially dried before pressing to yield the Amarone (rich but dry) and Recioto (rich and sweet) sub-species of Valpolicella.

WHITE

Arneis Widely grown in Piedmont; the best ones come from the Roero district, where top wines offer peach-stone and lime-flower fragrance, and great elegance.

Cortese From Gavi, in Piedmont: soft, precise, delicate whites.

Friulano From Friuli; restrained wines with delicate apricot, honeyed aromatics and a light- to medium-bodied, minerally almond palate.

Garganega The best grape in Soave, where serious producers are showing the vine's potential when carefully grown and handled.

Moscato Source of lots of fizzy and still wine, all gently to intensely sweet, from Piedmont (mildly frothy, sweet Moscato d'Asti is a favourite) and right down the peninsula.

Pinot Grigio Workhorse grape of eastern Friuli, and — again, if in good hands — capable of being better than its insipid reputation.

TASTING NOTES
Record your own impressions

Prompts: you are looking out for

Grenache: Warm alcohol and baked strawberries
Tempranillo: Red fruit and vanilla/tobacco
Sangiovese: High acidity and tannins, cherry, tea and earth
Nebbiolo: Very high tannins, liquorice, rose petals and tar

GRENACHE

1 _____

_____

2 _____

_____

TEMPRANILLO

3 _____

_____

4 _____

_____

SANGIOVESE

5 _____

_____

6 _____

_____

NEBBIOLO

7 _____

_____

8 _____

_____

BLIND TASTING

9 _____

_____

10 _____

_____

11 _____

_____

12 _____

_____

13 _____

_____

14 _____

_____

QUESTIONS

In Session 6 we have looked at four grape varieties, Grenache, Tempranillo, Sangiovese and Nebbiolo:

1. Which variety makes Chianti and where does this wine come from?

2. Which variety makes Rioja and where does this wine come from?

3. Which is the main variety in Châteauneuf-du-Pape and where does this wine come from?

4. Which has high levels of tannin yet pale colour?

5. Which two of these varieties are sometimes blended together?

6. What is the Spanish name for Grenache?

7. Which Italian variety is sometimes blended with Bordeaux grape varieties?

Which might have aromas often described as:

8. – strawberries, vanilla, tobacco?

9. – herbs, leather, earth?

10. – cherries, roses, tar, chocolate?

Name the grape variety for each description:

11. – full-bodied with very high tannins and good warmth at the back of the throat, aromas and flavours of roses, liquorice, tar, leather and chocolate?

12. – high acidity and tannins with aromas and flavours of herbs, raspberry, leather, earth?

13. – soft tannins, full-bodied with high alcohol, aromas and flavours of smoke, pepper and baked strawberry?

Answers on page 221

Right: Repairing barrels in Rioja.

Overleaf: Vineyards amid woods in Catalonia, north-eastern Spain.

GT 2011

X.6   04.12

GEWURZTRAMINER
2011
V.T.

CHOOSING & ENJOYING WINE

WINE & FOOD MATCHING: REASONS, NOT RULES
CORKSCREWS AND CLOSURES | OPENING CHAMPAGNE
SERVING WINE | DECANTING: THE HOW, WHY & IF
CHOOSING GLASSES | STORING YOUR WINE | TASTING AT HOME
WHICH WINE AM I? A TASTING CRIB-SHEET

EU WINE LAWS | ANSWERS | GLOSSARY | INDEX | CREDITS

WHICH WINE? WHAT FOOD?

Rebecca Lamont, head of the Wine School, offers an approach to matching wine with food

As we all have different tastes in food, it follows that we also have different preferences when it comes to the wine we want to pair with our food. Nor will our choices necessarily stay the same: you may be guided by mood at one point, or peer pressure at another.

At other times it might be a significant memory that inspires choice – or avoidance – of a particular wine. We could also mention habit and ritual: that, too, can be important when it comes to choosing wine. Some of us will always go for classics, or what we know; others enjoy seeking out the less well-known.

Think, too, what you want the wine to achieve: some of us are looking for the palate to be refreshed by the wine between each mouthful of food; it is the acidity in wine that helps with this, and will also aid digestion.

HOW IS IT COOKED?

Finally, don't forget that how, as well as what, you cook can affect your choice of wine. Gauge the intensity of flavour produced by the cooking method: as a broad-brush example, think of chicken crisply fried or poached. The first is able to take a wine fairly high in acidity to cut through the frying; poached foods tend to have more gentle flavours, so try more subtle wines.

The choice of wine may be less important.

Others will be highly engaged in the search for sensory utopia: the wine enhancing, contrasting with or matching the flavours of what we are eating.

Many instinctively match weight – choosing a full-bodied wine with a full-bodied food. Or you can match the intensity of flavour, so light foods with lots of flavour go with wines with the same characteristics. The food and wine matching recommendations in this book tend to follow this approach. Treat them as ideas to help you develop your own....

There is also a school of thought that holds that the taste elements should be stronger in the wine than the food, so that the food doesn't dominate. So if you have an acidic food the wine should have even higher acidity (that is why tomatoes are considered tricky: few wines have higher acidity).

Many prefer their wine to be sweeter than the food. For a pudding this is fairly easy to comprehend, but as awareness of sugar content in savoury food grows, there is a growing trend to make sure the wine (although technically dry) has an element of sweetness. An example may be partnering a rich, ripe Chardonnay from a warmer climate with a creamy sauce in the dish.

Sometimes you may choose to have fun contrasting elements in both food and wine.

Sweetness in wine with salty foods appeals to many (Sauternes and Roquefort is considered a classic), or acidic wines with oiliness in food (Sancerre with smoked salmon).

The realistic view is to pick what brings you pleasure, and to have a reason for your choice. No one can dictate what you like and don't like. But novel cuisines, and new wines, are emerging all the time, so don't be afraid to try new experiences and food/wine combinations: experiment!

If you'd like others to suggest matches, just go ahead and ask. Any self-respecting sommelier or wine merchant will be delighted, and should aim to please. Many in the wine trade do this all the time.

Altogether, it is a wine-win situation.

Reasons, not rules

Anne McHale MW

As we have tried to emphasise, we each have a unique sense of smell and taste, so a prescriptive list of 'this dish = that wine' will not work. The food notes on the Balance pages are to give you a quick idea of what generally works; but here we give you the reasons, not the rules, to guide your choices.

ACIDITY & FOOD

WHAT WORKS

After a mouthful of food, acidity in wine cleanses the palate so that you can taste the next mouthful better

Try a bite of cheese, a mouthful of wine, then another bite of cheese

WHAT DOESN'T WORK

In general avoid a low-acidity wine with a dish high in acidity (e.g. a salad which has a vinaigrette dressing)

The acidity in the food will make a low-acidity wine appear flat or 'flabby'

Experiment with smoked salmon and lemon

TANNIN & FOOD

WHAT WORKS

Animal and milk protein in foods like red meat and cheese, and vegetable protein e.g. pulses, bind with tannins, reducing the effect of bitterness and astringency and making tannic red wines seem rounder and smoother

WHAT DOESN'T WORK

Avoid tannic red wines with foods which are not high in protein, e.g. plain white fish or salad

But don't rule out red wine and fish completely — the way the fish is served (e.g. cooked in butter, or with a creamy sauce) can make this a good match

SWEETNESS & FOOD

WHAT WORKS

Sweet wines are versatile and a lot comes down to personal taste

A sweet wine with chocolate or dessert can be wonderful

Many enjoy the contrast of 'sweet and salty', e.g. a sweet wine with blue cheese (Port & Stilton)

Wines with some sweetness are frequently suggested as a match for spicy foods — sweetness and spice balance each other

WHAT DOESN'T WORK

Avoid matching a dry wine with a sweet food

The wine must always be sweeter than, or the same sweetness as, the food! Otherwise the wine will appear astringent, thin and acidic

If you cannot avoid this, at least choose a ripe, soft, higher-alcohol style of dry wine which will appear 'sweeter' than one from a cool climate

UMAMI

THE FIFTH TASTE

Japanese for 'pleasant savoury taste'

The human tongue has receptors for L-glutamate, which is the main source of umami flavour

It's thus distinct from saltiness: known as 'the fifth taste'

UMAMI AND WINE

High levels of L-glutamate are found in many foods, for example fish, mushrooms and tomatoes

Umami also forms particularly in foods and wines which are aged

A dish high in umami can therefore match really well with an aged, savoury wine

TEXTURE IN FOOD & WINE MATCHING

Personal! E.g. with a creamy sauce, try the complementary smooth texture of Chardonnay — or the leanness of Sauvignon Blanc to cut through the creaminess. With reds, a lot is to do with tannins, as before

WEIGHT IN FOOD & WINE MATCHING

Matching the weight of your food and wine is important, as otherwise one will dominate

Roast meat in a rich gravy needs a full-bodied wine

Plain white fish requires a light-bodied wine

Watch out for the sauce — its weight can be the dominant factor in the dish

FLAVOUR IN FOOD & WINE MATCHING

Very personal!

You can choose to match the flavours in the food and wine — e.g. Sauvignon Blanc with asparagus, oaky Chardonnay with smoked salmon

OR… you can let the food's flavours shine through by pairing it with a neutral wine — e.g. a vegetable risotto with a neutral, crisp Italian white

NOTE weight vs. flavour in food:

A food can be intense in flavour but not weighty/rich — e.g. cucumber, red peppers

A food can be weighty but low in flavour — e.g. potatoes

SUMMARY

FOOD & WINE MATCHES TO AVOID

- A dry wine with a sweet food
- A low-acidity wine with a high-acidity food
- A tannic red wine with a food low in protein
- A full-bodied wine with a lightweight food
- A light-bodied wine with a full, rich dish

MATCHES WHICH WORK

- Full-bodied wines with rich foods
- Light-bodied wines with delicate foods
- Tannic red wines with food high in protein
- Aged wines with savoury foods (umami)
- Matching flavours in the food and wine

CORKS AND CAPS AND CLOSURES

The wine trade has been sealing bottles with the compressed bark of the Portuguese cork oak for over 200 years. Natural and environmental, cork gives a near-perfect seal – very important when its compressibility helped to overcome the irregularities of early glass bottles. However, cork can be infected by a mould that creates off-flavours and aromas, known as cork-taint. 'Corked' bottles are in single-figure percentages, but this has spurred producers to seek alternatives. The most widely accepted is the screwcap, which can give a perfect seal and needs no special tool to remove it, but lacks the tradition or cachet of a cork. There are fears over the ability of the screwcap to enable wine to age gracefully, although long-term tests in Bordeaux, New Zealand and Australia suggest these are groundless. Plastic corks allow more oxygen in, so are only suitable for wines drunk within a couple of years of bottling. They still need a corkscrew, and can be quite difficult to remove. Innovative (and expensive) closures include so-called technical cork, and Vinolok, a finely-ground glass stopper that would not look out of place in a chemistry laboratory. Ultimately, cork is still the most important closure in the world of wine, for practicality and tradition, but an increasing proportion of bottles are now being sealed under screwcap, to eliminate cork-taint.

GETTING AT IT

A good corkscrew needs two things: an open spiral to grip the cork and some form of leverage. Plenty on sale have neither.

The open spiral is best spotted by looking up the shaft of the screw from the tip. You should see a hollow spiral, not a solid shaft with a screw thread around it. The latter is good for drilling holes, but much less use for gripping a cork.

A corkscrew can be a simple T-shape, but these are hard work to use. Leverage rather than a straight pull is the most efficient way to extract a cork steadily and slowly.

Corkscrews gain leverage either by having a counter-acting thread – the screw pushes against the body of the corkscrew, which is in turn pushing, via a sleeve, on the bottle neck – or by using an arm to provide a fulcrum.

The 'Waiters' Friend' shown here uses the fold-out arms to grip the rim, one after the other to allow a change in position. By placing these arms on the bottle neck, the corkscrew handle becomes an efficient lever.

This corkscrew also has a small knife for cutting away the foil on the bottle. This is good practice as the foil may conceal dirt or dust, and can cause drips when pouring. Always remove the entire foil when decanting, so you can see into the bottle neck. Otherwise, you can just cut away the top of the foil, then wipe the bottle rim with a cloth. Beware sharp edges to foil.

If a cork breaks in half while still in the neck, or starts to crumble, remove the corkscrew and try again with the screw at an angle. This improves the worm's grip on the remaining cork.

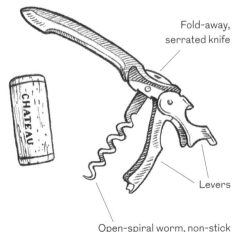

The 'Waiters' Friend' type can be used with one hand

Fold-away, serrated knife

Levers

Open-spiral worm, non-stick coated for ease of insertion

CHATEAU

Opening sparkling wine

Standing on the Winner's Podium, the triumphant athlete shakes the Champagne bottle and releases a fountain of fizz....

This image of celebration (or shocking waste, if you are a winemaker or Champagne lover) is nevertheless one worth keeping in mind when any bottle of sparkling wine needs opening: it demonstrates the power of the gas behind the cork.

This is one instance where the packaging has a point. The instantly-recognisable mushroom cork with its wire cage and the thick glass bottle are not there for effect. Be aware that a badly-handled bottle can send its cork flying for 50 metres – and at up to 30mph. Broken windows, shattered mirrors – worse, broken noses, can ensue....

So, when you pick up that bottle it will, ideally, have been resting gently in fridge or ice-bucket: take extra care if it has been at all shaken – and warmth, too, makes the gas dissolved in the wine more volatile and your fizz less pleasant to drink.

Then three more things are needed:

- **your aim**: point it away from your face, your friends and your furnishings
- **a glass**: to catch the first of it should it turn out to be a gassy bottle after all
- **your thumb**

Follow the steps below and, with care, the cork should release with a gentle pop and a wisp of gas: be ready to pour. And having undertaken such a dangerous operation, you now deserve to enjoy the results....

TOP TIP
Hold the glass at an angle and gently slide the fizz in to avoid too much frothing

1. Remove any foil covering to reveal the cork with its wire 'cage'. Keeping your thumb over the top, untwist the wire loop.

2. Point bottle away from you. Remove cage. Replace thumb.

3. The trick is to twist the bottle — not the cork: more leverage, less chance of breaking the cork. Keep thumb there. Gently ease the cork from the neck: the gas will help.

SERVING WINE

TEMPERATURE

Most people do not use a temperature gauge for their wine service at home because they learn to match their preference with their fridge temperature.

Chilling wine emphasises acidity and/or tannin, but can dull aroma and flavour. For this reason, most prefer to:

Gently chill (one hour in the fridge/outside on a cold evening):

- Complex subtle whites (such as white Burgundies) so as not to obliterate their delicacy
- Vintage Champagnes and other sparkling wines
- Sweet wines

Well chill (two hours in the fridge/outside on a cold evening):

- Whites that have high acidity and not much aroma, such as easy-drinking wines (e.g. house whites in restaurants)
- Intensely aromatic whites such as Sauvignon Blanc
- Non-vintage sparkling wines
- Light reds such as Beaujolais

Serve at room temperature (cool is better than too warm)

- Reds that have medium to high tannin

KEEPING IT COOL/WARMING IT UP

The quickest way to lower the temperature of a bottle is to immerse it in a bucket of ice and water. Note — not just ice: the water carries the chill. Don't use a freezer: pressure will build and the bottle can explode.

Also resist the temptation to heat wine in a microwave or put it on a radiator if you feel it needs heating up. It cooks the wine and spoils its delicacy. Warm wine gently by cupping the wine in the glass with your palm.

BOTTLE SIZES

A standard bottle is 75cl: three-quarters of a litre, or six small glasses. A half-bottle is just that. A magnum – a double bottle, or 150cl – is a useful size for dinner parties; also, wine matures more slowly in a magnum, and some wine-lovers lay down a few for special occasions. Some wines, including some fortified and dessert wines, are bottled in the half-litre (50cl) size. Some mass-market wines are sold in litre bottles. Other sizes are multiples of a standard bottle. Names and capacities vary: a Jereboam, for instance, is four bottles in Champagne and Burgundy – but six in Bordeaux.

HOW MUCH ALCOHOL: WINE AND HEALTH

Wines vary widely in the amount of alcohol they contain – generally from around 7 to 17 per cent ABV (alcohol by volume). This affects the taste – see Session 1 – and, of course, it affects you.

Health authorities in several countries have guidelines on the amount of alcohol to consume. The UK has devised 'units': defined as 10ml of pure alcohol per unit. So you can work out the units if you know the alcoholic strength and the size of your drink:

Take a 250ml glass of a 12% wine: 250x12 = 3,000. Divide this by 100 = 30ml of alcohol, therefore 3 units.

The 'lower-risk guidelines' currently state that you shouldn't regularly drink more than 14 units a week – best spread evenly across the week. See drinkaware.co.uk.

A 750ml bottle of wine at 14% would contain (750x14) ÷100 =105ml of alcohol, therefore 10.5 units.

A wine does not need to be fortified to top 15 per cent: a glance down the list shows some Rhône and Spanish reds, South Africans, Australians, Italians. There are even non-fortified wines at 16.5 per cent: handle with care. Some wines are naturally and delightfully lower in alcohol: German Riesling whites, especially Mosel Kabinetts, can be as low as 7 per cent ABV.

And then there are all the calories in any alcohol....

DECANTING

Some wines – young ones as well as old – gain when moved from their original bottle into a jug or decanter

There is no mystique to decanting. To begin with, the term simply means opening a bottle and pouring the contents into another container. You might do this for a number of reasons: for one thing, a glass jug or a carafe is a more stable thing to have on a crowded supper-table than a bottle. Also, it's a quick way of letting the air get at a young, robust red (far more effective than just removing the cork to let it 'breathe'). This will also allow any bottle-stink to dispel. If you have guests, you may just want to show off your lovely decanter.

You do not, by the way, need to buy any gadget that claims to aerate the wine for you.

But a fine red wine of some considerable maturity is likely to have developed ('thrown') a deposit in the bottle, which would make for an unpleasant final mouthful. So those wines, and even more so vintage port, need to be decanted.

To do so, gently remove the bottle from the wine-rack and leave it standing upright for at least a couple of hours (a few days is even better) so that the deposit settles down to the bottom of the bottle.

The only equipment you need is a funnel if the container you're pouring into has a narrow neck (a funnel with a strainer or filter will deal with the heavier deposit of vintage port), plus a light-source – a torch or a small candle will do – and a steady hand.

Position the light so that when you pour the wine into the container, it will shine through the neck of the bottle.

Start to pour slowly and steadily, in a single stream…. The only trick is not to let the wine 'glug' back into the bottle: you are trying to avoid stirring up the deposit and mixing it back into the wine.

When you get close to the end, keep looking down through the neck: the light shining up through it should show you the moment when the dark, opaque deposit begins to appear under the clear wine. Stop pouring – and save the stuff left for the gravy.

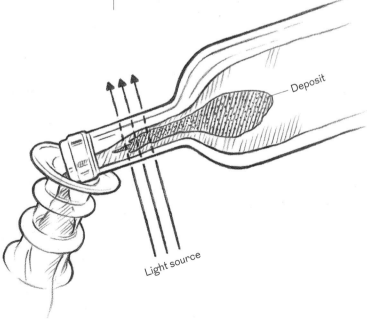

Deposit

Light source

THE GREAT DECANTING DEBATE

Anne McHale MW reflects on decanting, and reports on her Wine School experiments tasting the same wines, but decanted for differing periods

Welcome to one of the big questions in the world of wine service: to decant or not to decant. As you will have discovered throughout the course of this book, there is no simple answer to many wine-related questions. Whether or not to decant is no different.

Why might we decant a wine? There are two main reasons. The first is that where the wine has thrown a deposit, usually due to a significant period of bottle-ageing. It should be separated from the wine before service. This sediment is harmless but can taste unpleasantly bitter, so you don't want it to end up in your glass.

The second reason, generally accepted among wine experts, is that since decanting a wine saturates it with air, decanting at least two hours in advance can improve the experience of drinking certain wine styles – particularly young, tannic reds. The thinking behind this is that aeration mimics the effects of ageing by softening tannins and speeding up the wine's development.

Aeration can also improve the taste of young wines which show a 'reductive' character: in wine-geek language this means aromas of volatile sulphur compounds, and in ordinary language means the smell of struck match, flint, rubber or smoke.

These are characteristics you may often find in wines sealed with a screw-cap.

Respected Bordeaux oenologist Emile Peynaud, however, was famous for his opinion that decanting wine should be avoided where possible. According to Peynaud, one should only decant in cases where the wine has thrown a sediment, and even then only at the last possible moment before service, since the effects of dissolved oxygen are detrimental to the wine's taste and aromas.

Among the wider world of wine experts this is a controversial stance. At the Berry Bros. & Rudd Wine School, we have several times attempted to answer this crucial question through experimentation rather than theory alone.

We have conducted sessions with our Wine School students where we have tasted four different wine styles, but three bottles of each one. The first is decanted 24 hours in advance, the second two hours in advance and the third served straight from the bottle. The wines were served blind and in no particular order.

While our number of participants has never been large enough to yield statistically significant results, we have nevertheless observed a few trends – as well as results which prove only that wine-tasting is a subjective activity and depends on our own personal palates and preferences!

Our observations are summarised below:

REDUCTIVE WHITES
These have most definitely been shown to benefit from decanting two hours in advance. The air gets rid of the unattractive 'struck match' aromas. No need to decant a day in advance, however: this caused some of the attractive aromatic qualities of the wine to be lost.

RED WINES AGED FOR A LONG TIME IN BARREL
The best-known wine in this style (known as 'oxidatively-aged' wines) is probably Gran Reserva Rioja, top examples of which can spend at least five or six years in oak before being bottled.

One might expect that, since a wine like this has already been exposed to so much oxygen during its maturation, it wouldn't necessarily benefit from more exposure, but in fact in our experiments the examples decanted the day before tended to be the most aromatically complex and the silkiest in texture. These wines are obviously well-used to air and want more of it.

YOUNG CLARET

Results for young claret have been the most surprising, since throughout our experiments there has always been a clear preference for the just-opened bottle, despite received wisdom.

Why is this? I feel that it is to do with the aromatic qualities of the wine. The just-opened examples tend to have pure and crisp aromas of cassis and a lovely freshness, whereas those which have been decanted seem to have lost that immediacy; the flavours of the wine tend to have evolved more towards the dried-fruit end of the spectrum.

What is more, even bottles decanted 24 hours earlier did not show any signs of softer tannins.

Indeed this fits with the comments of some wine scientists that decanting in advance would not mimic ageing because there simply would not be enough time for the oxygen to change the chemical structure of the tannins; many years in bottle are needed for this to happen. This point remains a controversial one, but perhaps Emile Peynaud's opinion has more validity than we give it credit for....

VINTAGE PORT

Experiments with mature vintage port, which is usually decanted at some stage, even if just before service, to remove it from its heavy crust of sediment, have proved very interesting. In our trials the majority of tasters have found it nearly impossible to distinguish any nuances between the three samples.

One conclusion could be that, even at 20-30 years of age, a vintage port is so firmly structured that the antioxidant properties of its very robust tannins render its defences against the onslaught of oxygen very strong indeed.

So although you should stand your vintage port up at least a couple of hours (better still, a few days) before serving in order to allow the sediment to sink to the bottom, and you should decant it at some point, there is no rush to do so well in advance.

IN SUMMARY

To decant or not to decant? Our advice is this – experiment. If you have a case of a particular wine, each time you open a bottle try a different option for decanting it. Soon your own personal preferences will emerge. There may be no straightforward answer.... But let's face it, the process of learning will be a pleasurable one – and at the end of the day, we want wine that is good to drink.

TAKING WINE TO DINNER PARTIES

- Should a guest's wine always be served?

  Not necessarily. If a meal has been planned to precision to match special wines then no. If the hosts have gone to such trouble, it's bound to be a talking-point over dinner

- On occasion, it may upset a guest if wine is unopened when they have gone to a lot of trouble over their wine choice — use your intuition

DOUBLE-DECANTING

This somewhat mysterious term simply means returning a wine to its own, rinsed, bottle for serving after carefully decanting it off its sediment. This has the added advantage of getting even more air into the wine.

GLASSWARE

'Twenty per cent of the enjoyment of wine comes from the glass it is drunk from' – *Francis Berry, 1931*

In any shop you'll find a range of glasses for wine: larger, smaller, taller, narrower.... There are good reasons for this diversity of shapes; but whether or not you want to invest in a complete range, here are the things to look out for in any glass, whether everyday or expensive.

First, look for clear glass: avoid colours, patterns or heavy engraving. As we saw in Session One, you'll want to be able to look at, and enjoy, the colour and density of your wine.

Next, look for a 'tulip' shape, with the top curving inwards to the rim: this will help concentrate the aromas for you to inhale. Shape is important, too, for sparkling wines: the tall, narrow 'flute' stops the bubbles escaping too fast. The old-fashioned saucer-shaped glass may be fun, but your fizz will go flat faster.

Another good tip when buying inexpensive glasses for everyday use is to look for a fairly thin rim: for some reason, this makes the wine taste better. (Hence, too, glass: wine doesn't taste the same out of china, or pottery, or plastic – nor, indeed, out of silver or gold!)

Sadly, even the best dishwasher will eventually dull and scratch glassware. Good glasses should never be machine-washed. Ever. And if you do succumb to dishwashing the more everyday glasses (on the lowest temperature), please rinse them in fresh hot water to ensure your precious wine is not tainted by any rinse-aid residue.

Rinsing is an important tool, whatever the glass. Even hand-washed and -dried ones can pick up smells if stored in a cardboard box, or upside-down in a cupboard (don't). So rinse, dry quickly with a lint-free cloth – or at least air and polish them – before a meal or a tasting with good wines.

Decanters present a particular problem: rinsing out quickly after use will stop them staining (people have been known to resort to denture-cleaning tablets, then lots and lots of rinsing, when this has been overlooked...). But drying requires care: they are difficult to stand upside-down. You can buy special decanter-drying racks; or 'decanter socks' full of water-absorbing crystals are helpful. Wedging them neck-down between the slats of a clothes-drying cupboard if you have one also works. Wide-necked carafes or glass jugs are more practical day to day. Note: store decanters without the stopper in. As with glasses stored upside down, stale air can leave a taint.

SIZE

A glass ought to be large enough to take a sensible amount of wine – perhaps a sixth or an eighth of a bottle – without being more than a quarter or a third full.

To summarise, better a pool of wine in a big glass than brimful in a small one.

The reasons: to allow you to swirl the wine around, releasing its aromas and flavours, and to let you sniff the wine with the glass around it, funnelling the aromas up to your nose.

Size aside, many different shapes exist. The only essential is a slightly in-turned rim. Scholars (some call them fanatics) and glass manufacturers believe that there is a 'correct' shape for every last style of wine. This leads to glasses for young red Burgundy, and different ones for mature red Burgundy, a third type for Tuscan reds.... And so on. For most of us, a range like the one opposite provides ample scope.

In practice, most people begin with three basic shapes:

- A tall 'flute' for sparkling wine, designed to show off the bubbles to best effect.
- A larger glass, with a more pronounced bowl, for red wines. This gives room for the wine to emit its aromas, and as temperature-change is less of a concern than with whites, the red-wine glass can be bigger.
- A moderate-sized glass for white wines, which can be smaller than its red partner because we tend to serve smaller servings of whites to avoid the wine warming up in the glass. Also we are less in search of mature aromas, and thus less inclined to swirl, than with reds.

The examples shown here are glasses designed by Berry Bros & Rudd, reflecting three centuries of experience of what gives most pleasure. The current range has evolved from that designed by Francis Berry in 1931.

The glasses are named for benchmark styles of wine. Wines made from the same grapes, and/or in the same styles, as the benchmark wines, will work well in them. Thus a Cabernet Sauvignon will taste good from the red Bordeaux glass, as will Rhône reds. For a Pinot Noir or, say, Italian reds, the red Burgundy glass is designed to accentuate aromas.

Young white wines and aromatic styles suit the white Bordeaux glass, which is shaped to stress fruit, aromas and elegance. The wider bowl of the white Burgundy glass works well with all Chardonnay-based wines and with other rich white styles, such as those from the Rhône or Rioja.

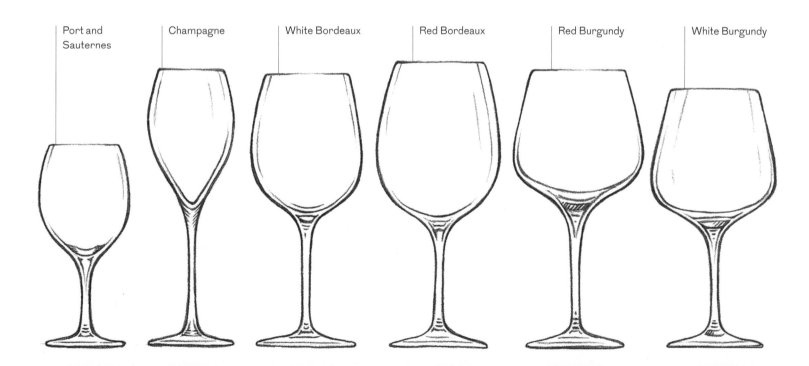

Port and Sauternes   Champagne   White Bordeaux   Red Bordeaux   Red Burgundy   White Burgundy

KEEPING WINE

A store of wine brings a number of benefits

WHY START A CELLAR AT ALL?

There are few wine merchants that allow their stocks of wine to develop fully (this would tie up capital for lengthy periods), and so starting a cellar is often the only way people can afford to drink mature wine. When you do stumble across a supply of mature wine it will be costly, so by investing in younger wines and storing them yourself you will drink better wines in the future for less money.

WHICH WINES ARE SUITABLE FOR CELLARING?

The majority of wines produced today are made to be drunk immediately and are not capable of maturing. Good-quality wine made to mature in bottle is suitable for cellaring, where its tannins soften, fruit develops and balance changes over time. The period of time depends on the wine in question, and can be anything from several months to many years. In each case it is a finite period, after which a wine no longer improves but reaches a plateau of maturity. Eventually it will slowly decline in quality.

IS WINE A GOOD INVESTMENT?

Well, you'll certainly be investing in future pleasure at today's prices. That said, with careful, informed buying it is also possible to make money by investing in wine.

CHOOSING WINES FOR YOUR CELLAR

First of all you should buy what you like to drink. There's no point in nurturing a vintage Port for decades if you don't like Port! Then you need to consider a number of factors before taking the plunge:

- **Vintages** It's best not to stick to one vintage, otherwise you might find your cellar lacks the variety afforded by different years. Also, different vintages age at different rates, which will safeguard against the entire contents of your cellar becoming ready to drink at the same time.

- **Grape Varieties** The classic red grapes that age best are Cabernet Sauvignon, Merlot, Pinot Noir, Syrah and Nebbiolo. Whites include Chardonnay, Riesling and Sémillon.

- **Regions** Top French regions like Bordeaux, Burgundy, Rhône, Alsace, Champagne and Loire. Apart from Port, the best areas in the rest of Europe include Ribero del Duero and Rioja in Spain, and Piedmont and Tuscany in Italy, not forgetting the best German Rieslings. From the New World, the Californian and Australian greats also age gracefully.

KEEPING TRACK OF YOUR CELLAR

To ensure that you don't forget what's in your cellar, and run the risk of not drinking up wines before they deteriorate, it is essential to keep track of your purchases. A spreadsheet on your home computer would suffice, but an old-fashioned cellar book would also allow you to save wine labels too. By recording where, and for how much, you bought your wines – in case you want to buy more in the future – and by also keeping tasting notes, you will build up a library of information that will help you to identify which wines you like best. Some share notes with others online, thus widening everyone's knowledge of how particular wines are faring.

You can, if you wish, join a wine merchant's regular purchase scheme. The merchant should not only provide you with lists of your stock-holding, but also with advice on what to buy and when to drink your wine.

Sometimes this sort of scheme includes an online facility to give you the most up-to-date information about your wine collection whenever you need it.

CELLAR CONDITIONS

Few homes boast the ideal wine-storage conditions offered by a deep underground cellar. Such a gem will have equable temperature, moderate humidity and freedom from vibration. Wines 'laid down' here (as the traditional term has it) will mature slowly to the best attainable peak.

Lacking such a cellar, some wine-lovers use commercial storage facilities, calling in wine when they need it. Others invest in sophisticated home 'wine rooms' or storage cabinets.

What does wine need? The basics are:

- Keep it dark
- Keep the bottles lying down
- Keep it still
- Keep it at a cool, even temperature (and if possible, slightly humid)

Damp or humid cellars can cause labels to peel off: elastic bands (or clingfilm) can help with this

Any wine will benefit from these conditions; fragile old wines really need them.

Much can be done with negatives: **don't** –

- Store bottles upright: the corks will dry out and the wine will spoil
- Store wine in the kitchen, where it will get too warm
- Store wine in any space, be it cellar or no, that has hot pipes
- Subject wine to vibration, for instance beside a busy staircase
- Store wine somewhere too humid or damp with no ventilation

Once you have avoided the 'don'ts', it is possible in most homes to achieve the basic needs. A dark cupboard can be insulated to keep it cool, as can an out-building, to stop it getting too hot or too cold.

TEMPERATURE

Wine is tolerant of most things – except sudden change. Ideally, the temperature should stay even over the year at around 10-12°C (50-54°F). In practice, nearly every cellar will be a little warmer in summer and cooler in winter. This seasonal change is fine: what wine hates is sudden swings.

BINS, BOXES AND RACKS

Most cellars today have single-bottle storage spaces – at their simplest, holes in a rack. It can be useful to have spaces that will store six or 12 bottles of the same wine together. The traditional cellar's brick 'bins' were designed for the bottles from a whole cask – a less common purchase today....

Wine that you buy in wooden cases can be stored in them until ready. Keep them off the floor with a wooden batten or two to allow air to circulate. This avoids rot or mould.

WHICH WINE IS WHERE?

The organised wine-lover will combine his or her cellar book (see Keeping Track above) with a record of which bottles are where. The less efficient will revel in the serendipitous discoveries a cluttered cellar provides – but will regret those overlooked wines that go past their peak, unopened and unloved.

TASTING AT HOME
The bottles to help you follow this Course

TASTING WITH FRIENDS

Hold your own tastings at home as you study the sessions. Get a group of friends together, share the cost and learn from each other. You can have a lot of fun exchanging your impressions – preferably without having seen the label on the bottle.

SOME PRACTICAL SUGGESTIONS

Ideally, you'll need a glass for each wine you're tasting. Mark them in some way to prevent them from becoming mixed as you compare one wine with another. The simplest is to draw up a sheet of paper with numbered circles so you can put the glasses back in the right order; or use tags, sticky dots or elastic bands to identify them.

Have some covers to disguise the bottles, or three (ideally identical) decanters or jugs for the recognition game at the end of each tasting.

SHOPPING LIST...

Go to **www.bbr.com/coursewines** to download this list to take into your local wine merchant. You can also see Berry Bros. & Rudd's current suggestions.

WINES TO CHOOSE:

At the Wine School, we taste wines like those listed below. For home use, adapt your list to what's available to you.

SESSION 1

To discover and think about ripeness, acidity, oak/no oak:

Wine 1: Chablis

Wine 2: New World Chardonnay

To discover and think about alcohol, how you perceive it:

Wine 3: German Riesling

Wine 4: Amarone

To discover and think about tannin:

Wine 5: Beaujolais

Wine 6: Barolo

To discover and think about age and maturity:

Wine 7: Young Spanish red wine

Wine 8: Old Rioja

For Sessions 2 to 6, pour the wines into the numbered glasses. You can do this 'blind', from covered bottles, without saying which is which – or you can be open about the identities of the wines.

SESSION 2

Sauvignon Blanc

Wine 1: Sauvignon Blanc, Marlborough, New Zealand

Wine 2: Pouilly-Fumé, Loire, France

Chardonnay

Wine 3: Pouilly-Fuissé, Burgundy, France

Wine 4: Chardonnay, California

Sémillon

Wine 5: Graves Blanc, Bordeaux, France

Wine 6: Sauternes, Bordeaux, France

Now try mixing them up and guessing which is which (you may need to pour more samples — ask someone else to do this for you to get the best chance of not cheating....)

SESSION 3

Cabernet Franc

Wine 1: Bourgueil, Loire, France

Wine 2: Chinon, Loire, France

Merlot

Wine 3: Merlot, South of France

Wine 4: Merlot, Chile

Cabernet Sauvignon

Wine 5: Cabernet Sauvignon, South Australia

Wine 6: Cabernet Sauvignon, Maipo, Chile

Wine 7: Bordeaux, France

As before, then try mixing them up and guessing which is which....

SESSION 4

Riesling

Wine 1: Riesling, Germany/Austria

Wine 2: Riesling, Eden Valley, Australia

Gewurztraminer

Wine 3: Gewurztraminer, Chile

Wine 4: Gewurztraminer, Alsace, France

Chenin Blanc

Wine 5: Chenin Blanc, South Africa

Wine 6: Vouvray, Loire, France

As before, then try mixing them up and guessing which is which….

SESSION 5

Gamay

Wine 1: Beaujolais, France

Wine 2: Morgon, France

Pinot Noir

Wine 3: Red Burgundy, France

Wine 4: Pinot Noir, New Zealand

Syrah/Shiraz

Wine 5: Crozes-Hermitage, Northern Rhône, France

Wine 6: Shiraz, South Australia

As before, then try mixing them up and guessing which is which….

SESSION 6

Grenache

Wine 1: Tavel Rosé, Southern Rhône, France

Wine 2: Châteauneuf-du-Pape, Southern Rhône, France

Tempranillo

Wine 3: Joven Rioja

Wine 4: Gran Reserva Rioja

Sangiovese

Wine 5: Chianti Classico, Tuscany, Italy

Wine 6: Brunello di Montalcino, Italy

Nebbiolo

Wine 7: Barolo, Piedmont, Italy

Wine 8: Barbaresco, Piedmont, Italy

As before, then try mixing them up and guessing which is which….

...And don't forget:

Bread or dry plain crackers and water, to refresh your palate (and use a drop of water to rinse glasses between wines). See also The Practicalities of Tasting, Session One.

CHOOSING WINE IN A RESTAURANT

When you look at a restaurant wine list, it will help you to choose wines if you almost conduct a 'virtual tasting' of the wines in your imagination! Consider the following:

- The grape variety/ies of the wine. This will affect the style of the wine — aromas, flavours, acidity, body.

- The origin of the wine. Is it from a cool or hot climate? As you have learnt throughout this book, this will affect the style of the wine, in terms of acidity, alcohol, body and ripeness of flavours.

- Which wine you might enjoy with each course (see page 204–5 on Food & Wine Matching for more details). With smoked salmon, for instance, a high acidity, zesty Sauvignon Blanc will cut through the richness of the fish; alternatively the smoothness of a Chardonnay can be an equally good match because it complements the richness (and the hint of oak matches the smoked flavour). It's very personal; you must find what you enjoy.

Ask the sommelier. If the restaurant you're in has a good sommelier, do take advantage of him or her – wine professionals do as well. Now that you know how to describe wines, ask questions that will help guide you to the style you enjoy – for example 'how oaked is your Chardonnay from Carneros?'

SPOT THE WINE: A BLIND TASTING CRIB

Someone hands you a glass of wine and asks 'what is this?' Rebecca Lamont has tips on how to bring out your inner Sherlock by being receptive to clues that help you work out the climate, winemaking, maturation and age of your wine

AGE ON WHITES	
Is it more pale lemon than gold?	Likely to be young
Is it more gold than pale lemon?	Likely to be older, or has been in an oak barrel

AGE ON REDS	
Is it more purple than red?	Likely to be very young
Is it more red than brick-coloured?	Likely to be younger
Is it more brick-coloured than red?	Likely to be older

CLIMATE AROMAS	
Are they more fruity, richer, riper, leaping from the glass?	More likely to be warmer climate/New World
Are they more gentle aromas, less fruity, more mineral?	More likely to be cooler climate/Old World

WINEMAKING	
Aromas of butter in a white wine?	Malolactic fermentation in whites, most likely Chardonnay
No aromas of butter in a white wine?	No malolactic
Aromas and textures of cream?	Lees-stirring or lees-contact in white or red
Aromas and flavours that are rich, rounded vanilla on a white?	Likely to be fermented in new oak and aged in new oak, most likely French oak species
Aromas and flavours of rich, rounded coconut on a white?	Likely to be fermented in new oak and aged in new oak, most likely American oak species
No aromas of vanilla, spice, toast, coconut?	Likely to have had no new oak contact
No aromas of vanilla, spice, toast, coconut and not vibrantly fruity and soft?	Likely no new oak contact but possibly old oak contact
Vibrantly fruity with no vanilla, spice, toast, coconut?	Likely produced in stainless steel

ALCOHOL	
Lots of legs on the glass, richness at the back of the throat?	Likely to be higher in alcohol
Fewer legs and not as warm at the back of throat?	Likely to be lower in alcohol
In between the above two?	Likely to be medium alcohol around 13%
Very delicate, with some initial sweetness, richness from the sweetness but no warmth at the back of the throat?	Likely to be lower than 11% ABV

WHICH GRAPE AM I? AROMAS/FLAVOURS/CHARACTERISTICS OF:	
WHITES	
'Cat's pee'; light- to medium-bodied, with high acidity	Sauvignon Blanc, likely from Loire
Kiwi-fruit, passion-fruit and grapefruit	Sauvignon Blanc, likely from New Zealand
Wax and marmalade; very sweet, with high acidity	Sweet Sémillon made from Botrytis-affected grapes, as made in Sauternes
Wax and lime	Dry Semillon, typical of Hunter Valley
Petrol, white blossom and slate; light-bodied, touch of sweetness	Riesling, likely from Germany
Lime and stone; very dry	Riesling, likely from Germany
Butter, cream, touch of vanilla, nuts; subtle mix of apple and stone fruits	Cool-climate Chardonnay with malolactic fermentation, lees-stirring, small proportion of oak
Butter, cream, nuts and subtle mix of more tropical fruits	Warmer-climate Chardonnay with malolactic fermentation, lees-stirring and small proportion of oak contact
Spice, ginger, Turkish delight, lychees; low acidity, viscous	Gewurztraminer
Apple, honey, wet wool; high acidity, no vanilla	Chenin Blanc, likely from Loire, likely with old-oak contact or stainless steel
Apple, honey, some floral notes; high acidity	Chenin Blanc, more likely from South Africa
Apricots, peaches and their kernels; fairly viscous on the palate	Viognier
REDS/ROSÉS	
Bubblegum, strawberries; high acidity, light- to medium-bodied, low tannin, bit of warmth at the back of the throat	Gamay, likely Beaujolais or Beaujolais-Villages
Tobacco, earth and strawberry, tiniest hint of bubblegum; high acidity, medium-bodied, medium tannin	Gamay, likely Cru Beaujolais
Red summer fruits; pale colour, high acidity, fine tannin, medium-bodied, more silky texture	Young Pinot Noir, likely from Burgundy
Red summer fruits; pale colour, some black fruits; intense, velvety texture with balancing acidity	Pinot Noir, likely from New Zealand
Black fruits, pencil-shavings, earthy, rich fruit on palate camouflaging high tannin; inky dark colour	Syrah, likely from Northern Rhône
Black fruits, eucalyptus, mint, touch of vanilla and spice; rich on the palate, warmth at back of palate; inky dark colour	Syrah, likely from the New World, possibly South Australia; likely new oak
Raisin, charred cassis; low acidity, low tannin, warmth at back of the throat	Zinfandel
Strawberries; low tannin, warmth at back of the throat; rosé colour	Grenache rosé from Spain
Strawberries, earth, meat, leather; full-bodied, medium tannin, warmth at back of the throat	Grenache from Southern Rhône
Strawberry tart, tobacco, spice; integrated tannin, long finish; brick-tinged red	Tempranillo, likely aged (Reserva or Gran Reserva)
Tar and roses; high acidity, high tannin and lots of warmth at the back of the throat	Nebbiolo

EUROPEAN UNION WINE LAWS

Official EU legal categories and terms found on labels

PDO (Protected Designation of Origin)

The top of the hierarchy, with the strictest rules regarding (for example) which grape varieties to use, vineyard techniques, ageing requirements and the delimited area of production.

PGI (Protected Geographical Indication)

Grapes can come from a wider geographical area; regulations are less strict e.g. more flexibility in terms of grape varieties. Occasionally these can command prices higher than PDO wines (for example Italy's 'Super-Tuscans', page 187).

Wine without a Geographical Indication

Replaces the former 'table wine' category and refers to wines blended from across a much larger area, e.g. regions all across France (Vin de France). Tends to be used for inexpensive wines.

The table right shows the terms that you are most likely to encounter on wine labels and how they correspond to the top two categories of EU wine law. You may see either the EU terminology or the country's traditional terminology on the label.

Note: in certain countries, PDO covers two traditional sub-categories.

FRENCH WINE

EU TERMINOLOGY	FRENCH TRANSLATION OF EU TERMINOLOGY	TRADITIONAL FRENCH TERMINOLOGY
PDO	Appellation d'Origine Protégée (AOP)	Appellation d'Origine Contrôlée (AOC or AC)
PGI	Indication Géographique Protégée (IGP)	Vin de Pays

ITALIAN WINE

EU TERMINOLOGY	ITALIAN TRANSLATION OF EU TERMINOLOGY	TRADITIONAL ITALIAN TERMINOLOGY
PDO	Denominazione di Origine Protetta (DOP)	Denominazione di Origine Controllata (DOC) and Denominazione di Origine Controllata e Garanitita (DOCG)
PGI	Indicazione Geografica Protetta (IGP)	Indicazione Geografica Tipica (IGT)

SPANISH WINE

EU TERMINOLOGY	SPANISH TRANSLATION OF EU TERMINOLOGY	TRADITIONAL SPANISH TERMINOLOGY
PDO	Denominación de Origen Protegida (DOP)	Denominación de Origen (DO) and Denominación de Origen Calificada (DOCa)
PGI	Indicación Geográfica Protegida	Vino de la Tierra

GERMAN WINE

EU TERMINOLOGY	GERMAN TRANSLATION OF EU TERMINOLOGY	TRADITIONAL GERMAN TERMINOLOGY
PDO	Geschützte Ursprungsbezeichnung (trips right off the tongue)	Quälitatswein bestimmter Anbaugebiete (Qba) and Prädikatswein
PGI	Geschützte Geografische Angabe	Landwein

ANSWERS

SESSION 1

1. Acidity, alcohol, tannin, fruit ripeness, oak, complexity
2. A mouthwatering effect/a tingling sharpness on the tongue
3. A cooler climate
4. A hotter climate
5. It warms the back of the throat and adds weight and body to wine. A high-alcohol wine can also taste slightly sweet, even if there is no sugar in the wine.
6. Aromas/flavours of toast and vanilla
7. The amount of time the flavours linger in your mouth. In general, the better the wine, the longer its taste will linger.

SESSION 2

1. Chardonnay, Burgundy
2. Sauvignon Blanc, the Upper Loire
3. Noble rot/botrytis
4. Sauvignon Blanc
5. Chardonnay
6. Sémillon
7. Sauvignon Blanc
8. Sauvignon Blanc
9. Sémillon
10. Sauvignon Blanc and Sémillon
11. Sauvignon Blanc from, for example, Pouilly-Fumé in the Loire
12. Sauvignon Blanc from, for example, Marlborough in New Zealand
13. Chardonnay from the warmer climates of the New World
14. Chardonnay from Chablis in Burgundy
15. Sémillon from Hunter Valley in Australia
16. Sémillon from Sauternes in Bordeaux

SESSION 3

1. Cabernet Franc; Central Loire
2. Merlot; Bordeaux
3. Cabernet Sauvignon
4. Merlot
5. Cabernet Sauvignon
6. Merlot
7. Cabernet Franc
8. Bordeaux
9. Merlot
10. Cabernet Franc
11. Cabernet Sauvignon
12. St-Julien, Pauillac, Margaux, St-Estèphe, Pessac-Léognan
13. St-Emilion, Pomerol

SESSION 4

1. Chenin Blanc; Loire Valley
2. Gewurztraminer, Riesling
3. South Africa
4. Australia (e.g. Clare Valley), Canada, California, New Zealand, Chile
5. New Zealand, Chile, West Coast USA
6. Chenin Blanc
7. Gewurztraminer
8. Chenin Blanc
9. Riesling
10. Gewurztraminer
11. Gewurztraminer
12. Chenin Blanc
13. Riesling

SESSION 5

1. Syrah; Northern Rhône
2. Pinot Noir; Burgundy
3. Gamay; Beaujolais
4. Pinot Noir
5. Pinot Noir
6. Syrah
7. Gamay
8. Gamay
9. Syrah
10. Pinot Noir
11. Syrah/Shiraz
12. Gamay
13. Pinot Noir

SESSION 6

1. Sangiovese; Tuscany
2. Tempranillo; Spain
3. Grenache; Rhône
4. Nebbiolo
5. Tempranillo and Grenache
6. Garnacha
7. Sangiovese
8. Tempranillo
9. Sangiovese
10. Nebbiolo
11. Nebbiolo
12. Sangiovese
13. Grenache

GLOSSARY of wine terms

ABV alcohol by volume, shown on the bottle as a percentage or degree

Acidity see page 20

Additives substances used in winemaking to control processes: sulphur dioxide (SO2: appears on some labels as 'sulphites' or 'sulfites') is the most common: a preservative, it controls microbes and slows oxidation. Among other additives, enzymes may be used to manage fermentation and clarify wine.

Anaerobic winemaking keeping out as much oxygen as possible during winemaking to enhance fruitiness

AOC, Appellation French official wine zone; pages 78, 220

AVA American viticultural area

Barrel, barrique oak cask for fermenting and/or maturing; affects taste and development of the wine

Biodynamic vine-growing and wine-making philosophy and techniques; page 120

Bordeaux blend wine made from the classic trio of Cabernet Sauvignon, Cabernet Franc and Merlot

Blanc de blancs white wine made only from white grapes

Blanc de noirs white wine made only from black grapes (as in Champagne)

Botrytis cinerea fungus known as 'noble rot'; can help create great sweet wines; page 62

Bouquet the aroma of a wine

Brett, Brettanomyces a yeast which in wine gives an aroma of 'sweaty saddle' and a drying at back of palate – differing views on its appeal

Brut dry style of Champagne and other sparkling wines

Brut nature very dry Champagne/sparkling wine with no dosage

Carbonic maceration red winemaking technique; page 142

Cask see barrel

Cépage grape variety

Château wine estate, especially in Bordeaux, with or without an actual house/castle

Claret red Bordeaux wine; page 75

Classed growth page 98

Clos single, often walled, vineyard in Burgundy and elsewhere

Corked wine tainted by mould in the cork; page 16

Courtier wine broker; page 86

Cru literally 'growth' but has many meanings in winespeak: the two most frequent are 1) an area granted special recognition for its superior terroir (a whole commune as in Beaujolais or the Rhône, or a single vineyard as in Burgundy) and 2) an estate granted special recognition for its prestige and wine quality (as in Bordeaux)

Cru Classé page 98; **Grand Cru, Premier Cru** pages 98, 150; **Cru Bourgeois** mid-rank red Bordeaux

Cuvée, tête de cuvée selection or batch of wine; tête (head) signals 'best'

Deposit see sediment

DOC (Spain/Italy/Portugal) quality wine grade; page 220

DOCG (Italy) top wine grade page 220

Domaine as château; implies wine made and bottled by the landowner

Dosage small amount of wine and sugar added to Champagne before its second fermentation

Doux sweet

Dry the astringency of tannins on the palate. Also used when no sweetness can be detected on the palate.

Eiswein, Ice Wine wine made from grapes frozen at time of picking: concentrated, rich and sweet

Elevage all the processes employed to nurture wine between fermentation and bottling

En primeur wine sold before bottling, usually in the spring after the harvest

Fermentation conversion of grape sugars by yeast into alcohol; page 29

Fortified wine, e.g. port, sherry, to which grape spirit is added to halt fermentation

GSM shorthand for Grenache-Syrah-Mourvèdre, a blending of Rhône grapes

Grand Cru top-quality wine: used in different senses in several regions; page 98

Grand vin main wine of a château; sometimes used for an estate's only wine

Growth: classed, first, etc; page 98

Halbtrocken (Germany/Austria) medium-dry; page 110

Lees sediment left in tank/cask after fermentation; page 57

Legs page 16

Magnum bottle holding 1.5 litres, double a normal bottle

Malolactic fermentation turns malic into lactic acid: softens a wine; page 57

Maturation after making, all wine is matured; times vary from 3 months to 10 years plus

Meso-climate, micro-climate: *meso-*: the climate of an area of land, such as a hillside; *micro-*: the climate influenced by very local factors, actually within the rows of vines, such as shade, shelter, aspect.

Minerality appetising, stony, flinty character in some whites; page 53

Must-weight sugar content of the grapes at picking

MW Master of Wine: top wine qualification, gained by examination and experience

Négociant buyer of wine and/or grapes, making and/or maturing wine to sell to wholesalers, exporters

New World/Old World page 46

Noble rot see botrytis cinerea

Oaked contact with oak in fermentation and/or maturation page 35

Organic wine page 120

Oxidised wine spoiled by too much oxygen contact. Stale, flat taste; dull appearance.

Phylloxera vine disorder caused by aphid that attacks roots; cause of major devastation in France in the 19th century, and in California in the late 20th

Premox premature oxidation of wine, considered a fault

Redox term linking reduction and oxidation, two chemical reactions that occur as wine matures and that can affect quality and stability

Reductive (fault) eggy aroma; sometimes results from anaerobic winemaking

Reserva, Gran Reserva (Spain) page 180

INDEX of grapes and places

This edition published in the United Kingdom in 2016 by
Pavilion
43 Great Ormond Street London WC1N 3HZ

Copyright © Berry Bros. & Rudd Press 2015, 2016
Text, maps & images Copyright © Berry Bros. & Rudd Press 2015, 2016
Balance targets Copyright © Lizzie B Design 2015, 2016

First published in 2015 by Berry Bros. & Rudd Press
3 St James's Street, London SW1A 1EG

This book can be ordered direct from the publisher at www.pavilionbooks.com

wineschoolbook@bbr.com

ISBN: 978-1-910-90470-1

Created by Segrave Foulkes Publishers for Berry Bros. & Rudd Press. www.segravefoulkes.com

Design & Art Direction Lizzie Ballantyne, Lizzie B Design.
www.lizziebdesign.com

Text compiled by Segrave Foulkes based upon the Introduction to Wine course taught by the Berry Bros. & Rudd Wine School, No 3 St James's Street, London SW1

Editorial team
Chris Foulkes
Rebecca Lamont, Head, Berry Bros. & Rudd Wine School
Anne McHale MW, Berry Bros. & Rudd Wine School
Jasper Morris MW
Carrie Segrave

About Berry Bros. & Rudd

Berry Bros. & Rudd is Britain's oldest wine merchant, established in 1698 and still family-run. The firm is still trading from the same shop at No. 3 St James's Street, London; it has been serving the royal family since the time of George III and today holds two Royal Warrants.

Despite its age, the firm embraces the best of today: it was the first wine merchant to begin on-line sales, in 1994, and its award-winning Wine School courses, held in the historic Pickering Cellars below the shop, have been running since 2000. The conversation with customers which began over the shop counter in 1698 continues there today; at the Wine School classes; and now, via the internet, across the world.

Contributions by

David Berry Green
Barbara Drew
Catriona Felstead MW
Simon Field MW
Martin Hudson MW
Rebecca Lamont
Anne McHale MW
Jasper Morris MW
Mark Pardoe MW
Chris Pollington
Demetri Walters MW

Photographs Jason Lowe **Post production** Scott MacSween
Photograph page 4 Nick Haddow
Maps Eugene Fleury, Leanne Kelman
Illustrations Ilyanna Kerr

Set in Chronicle, Chronicle Display & Grot10

Colour reproduction Mission, Hong Kong
Printed by Toppan Leefung, China
10 9 8 7 6 5 4 3 2